August Sartorius von Waltershausen

The Workers' Movement in the United States, 1879–1885

August Sartorius von Waltershausen (1852–1938) was an eminent German economist who visited the United States at the beginning of the 1880s and wrote a series of articles on the U.S. labor movement, which were published in Germany. His training in the historical school of economics provided him with a different perspective from that of laissez-faire economists or socialists of his time. The articles are translated in this book, and presented with a biographical essay by Marcel van der Linden and Gregory Zieren and with an essay on his contribution to the writing of American labor history by David Montgomery. This book provides rich insights into the character of American workers' organizations as they recovered from the depression of the 1870s, before the establishment of strong national institutions.

David Montgomery is Farnam Professor of History at Yale University. He has also taught at Oxford, the Universidade Estadual de Campinas, and the University of Amsterdam. His previous work includes *Citizen Worker: The Experience of Workers in the United States with Democracy and the Free Market during the Nineteenth Century* (1993), *The Fall of the House of Labor* (1988), and *Workers' Control in America* (1980).

Marcel van der Linden is Senior Research Fellow at the International Institute of Social History, Amsterdam; Professor of Social Movement History at Amsterdam University; Executive Editor of the *International Review of Social History*. He has published widely on labor history and the history of ideas.

August Sartorius von Waltershausen, c. 1880

August Sartorius von Waltershausen

The Workers' Movement in the United States, 1879–1885

Edited by

David Montgomery   Marcel van der Linden

Translated by

Harry Drost

In Collaboration with

Jan Gielkens   Gregory Zieren

CAMBRIDGE UNIVERSITY PRESS

PUBLISHED BY THE PRESS SYNDICATE OF THE UNIVERSITY OF CAMBRIDGE
The Pitt Building, Trumpington Street, Cambridge CB2 1RP, United Kingdom

CAMBRIDGE UNIVERSITY PRESS
The Edinburgh Building, Cambridge CB2 2RU, UK   http: //www.cup.cam.ac.uk
40 West 20th Street, New York, NY 10011-4211, USA   http: //www.cup.org
10 Stamford Road, Oakleigh, Melbourne 3166, Australia

First published 1998

Printed in the United States of America

Typeset in Sabon 10.25/13 pt, in Quark XPress™ [BB]

A catalog record for this book is available from the British Library.

Library of Congress Cataloging-in-Publication Data
August Sartorius von Waltershausen : the workers' movement in the
United States, 1879–1885 / edited by David Montgomery, Marcel van der Linden.
p. cm.
Includes bibliographical references and index.
ISBN 0-521-63021-5
1. Labor movement – United States – History – 19th century. 2. Trade –
unions – United States – History – 19th century. 3. Sartorius von
Waltershausen, August, 1852–1938. 4. Economists – Germany –
Biography. I. Montgomery, David, 1927–   . II. Linden, Marcel
van der, 1952–   .
HD8072.A84   1998
330′.092 – dc21
[B]   97-47495
                                                 CIP
ISBN 0 521 63021 5 hardback

This book was published with the assistance of grants from the International Institute
of Social History, Amsterdam, and the Frederick W. Hilles Publication Fund of Yale.

Contents

Acknowledgments

The editors wish to acknowledge the assistance of individuals and institutions without whose efforts this book could not have been written. Harry Drost of London provided an excellent initial translation, which was subsequently revised at points by the editors. Gregory Zieren of Austin Peay University in Tennessee, coauthor of the biographical essay, contributed his rich knowledge of the nineteenth-century German academic world. Jan Gielkens of the International Institute of Social History, in a manner of which any great investigator would have been proud, ferreted out the diaries and memoirs of Sartorius von Waltershausen. Mark Weiner of Yale University, Hope Hague of the University of Wisconsin, and Ileen A. DeVault of the New York School of Industrial and Labor Relations at Cornell University provided valuable assistance in locating the original English-language texts of documents used by Sartorius von Waltershausen. Mary H. Blewett generously shared with us letters to British newspapers from immigrants in textile towns of the United States. Eric Jarosinski of the University of Wisconsin located references in the contemporary Milwaukee press to the visit of Sartorius von Waltershausen to that city in 1881. Markus Bürgi traced documents on Sartorius's Zurich years.

The International Institute of Social History in Amsterdam provided generous material assistance to both editors. Elizabeth Pauk of the Manuscripts and Archives Division of the Sterling Library, Yale University, and Andrew Lee of the Robert Wagner Archives of the Tamiment Institute at the Bobst Library of New York University helped locate important sources. Rob Kroes of the University of Amsterdam enabled David Montgomery to join the staff of the American Institute, thus facilitating collaboration between the editors. Hermann and

Lieselotte Wundt of Tübingen, and Petra Käßer of the Waltershausen Seminar in Munich, made archival materials accessible.

Gregory Zieren is especially grateful to those individuals in Germany and the United States who have provided him with invaluable assistance during his years of research related to this subject: Prof. Rolf Breuer and Cordula Breuer (University of Paderborn); Frau Tina Hindelang and Frau Gabriele Schäfer at the Internationale Begegnungszentrum at the University of Erlangen-Nuremberg; Prof. Reinhard Doerries, Dr. Michael Wala, and Frau Heidi Thiessen at the same university; Dr. Martin Meyer of the University of Kassel; Dr. Reinhard Flessner of the University of Freiburg; Carol Kimmel of the Woodward Library, Dr. D'Ann Campbell of the College of Arts and Sciences, and Dr. Richard Gildrie at Austin Peay State University; and, last but not least, Caroline Dieterle.

1

Introduction

DAVID MONTGOMERY

The writings of August Sartorius von Waltershausen provide a rich source for the study of the labor movement in the United States during the 1880s. The author's extensive reproduction of union statutes and his concern for ways in which workers' organizations imposed some order on the chaotic workings of industrial capitalism combine to make these articles both a treasure trove of documentary evidence, much of which is otherwise inaccessible, and a provocative assortment of insights and opinions, some of which differ significantly from the thrust of more recent historical interpretations.

Nevertheless, these articles have scarcely been tapped by historians for more than half a century. Their two most influential uses are to be found in Selig Perlman's account of the labor movement's resurgence after 1879, which was published in 1918, and in the discussion of trade unions on the New Orleans waterfront in Sterling D. Spero and Abram L. Harris, *The Black Worker*, which was published in 1931. More recently, Gregory R. Zieren and Eric Arnesen have returned to the information and insights offered by Sartorius. Zieren reminded readers of the German economist's pioneering research on American strikes, as well as his assessment of the assimilation of German immigrants.[1]

---

1. Selig Perlman, "Upheaval and Reorganization (Since 1876)," in John R. Commons et al., *History of Labour in the United States* (New York, 1918–35), II, 310–18; Sterling D. Spero and Abram L. Harris, *The Black Worker: The Negro and the Labor Movement* (New York, 1931), 184–90; Gregory R. Zieren, "The Incidence of Strikes in the U.S., 1879–1880," *Labor History*, 32 (Winter 1991), 136–42; Zieren, "Late Nineteenth-Century Industrialization and the Forces of Assimilation on German Immigrants: The Views of Economist August Sartorius von Waltershausen," *Yearbook of German-American Studies*, 21 (1986), 127–36; Eric Arnesen, *Waterfront Workers of New Orleans: Race, Class, and Politics, 1863–1923* (New York and Oxford, 1991), 64, 92–3, 106, 288. All of these authors referred not to the articles published in this volume, but to the book that

I

This neglect cannot be attributed to lack of scholarly interest in the period. On the contrary, the decade of what Perlman called "the Great Upheaval"[2] has attracted considerable attention from historians during the last quarter of a century and has provoked intense debates among them. A proliferation of studies of social conflict at the local level, inspired largely by the writings of Herbert G. Gutman, led to new interpretations of the role of the Knights of Labor in American social and political history and subsequently to innovative and insightful commentaries on the role of the law in shaping workers' movements, on the place of women in those movements, on the interconnections of race, class, and ethnicity during that period, and on the comparison of workers' movements in the United States and in Europe.[3]

Two aspects of what came to be called the New Labor History may explain the paucity of attention to Sartorius von Waltershausen's research on this epoch. The first is that scholars who read German with some ease tended to focus their attention on German Americans. Their writings have greatly enriched our knowledge of working-class life in the United States during the second half of the nineteenth century, when immigrants from Germany were more numerous than those from any other country in the world.[4] In his articles on trade unionism, however, Sartorius von Waltershausen devoted remarkably little attention specifically to workers or practices of German origin. In a manner that typified his approach to writing, he reserved his observations on Germans for a special article on German immigrants and for his later book on socialism in the United States.

Sartorius von Waltershausen had developed from them: *Die nordamerikanischen Gewerkschaften unter dem Einfluss der fortschreitenden Productionstechnik* (Berlin, 1886). Perlman classed Sartorius von Waltershausen "among the keenest observers of American industrial life." Commons, *History of Labour,* II, 576.

2. Commons, *History of Labour,* II, 356.
3. Herbert G. Gutman, *Work, Culture, and Society in Industrializing America* (New York, 1976); David Brody, "The Old Labor History and the New: In Search of an American Working Class," *Labor History,* 20 (Winter 1979), 110–26; David Montgomery, "Gutman's Nineteenth-Century America," *Labor History,* 19 (Summer 1978), 416–29; Christopher L. Tomlins and Andrew J. King, eds., *Labor Law in America: Historical and Critical Essays* (Baltimore and London, 1992).
4. Hartmut Keil and John B. Jentz, eds., *German Workers in Chicago: A Documentary History of Working-Class Culture from 1850 to World War I* (Urbana, Ill., 1988); Keil and Jentz, eds., *German Workers in Industrial Chicago, 1850–1910: A Comparative Perspective* (DeKalb, Ill., 1983); Dorothee Schneider, *Trade Unions and Community: The German Working Class in New York City, 1870–1900* (Urbana, Ill., 1994); Bruce Levine, *The Spirit of 1848: German Immigrants, Labor Conflict, and the Coming of the Civil War* (Urbana, Ill., 1992).

The language barrier does not, however, offer a full explanation of the declining use of this valuable research. At least as important has been the determination of the New Labor Historians to direct their own attention away from the trade unions and political parties that John R. Commons and his disciples had made the central topic of labor history, and toward an effort to re-create the everyday lives, thoughts, and struggles of working-class men and women during an epoch in which unions embraced only a small and often relatively privileged segment of the working class. The purpose of this generation of historians, whose publications began to appear around 1960, was to understand the nature and historical significance of working-class culture. Sartorius von Waltershausen had fixed his eyes squarely on the institutions created by workers – on the organized labor movement. He did so, however, in a manner that can shed light not only on working-class culture, as well as trade union history, but also on controversies that have more recently grown out of applications of critical legal studies and of the analysis of discourse to the study of working people.

The observations of Sartorius von Waltershausen and the documentary material that he reproduced at length deserve to be reintroduced into the historical debate. The articles selected for translation here represent but a small portion of his scholarly writings. Most of what is found here was published in 1886 as a book entitled *Die nordamerikanischen Gewerkschaften unter dem Einfluss der fortschreitenden Productionstechnik* (*North American Unions under the Influence of Technological Progress in Industry*).[5] The editors chose to translate the original articles in preference to that book for two reasons. First, the book adds to the articles some 84 pages devoted to the history of the labor movement in the United States prior to the 1880s. That historical section is based on secondary works that were available at the time and that have been rendered obsolete by more recent scholarship. Second, the only portion of the article on relief funds that appears in the book is that related directly to the activities of trade unions. Since the article itself demonstrates that trade union benefit funds played only a small role in providing financial aid and insurance to American workers, it seemed important to the editors to retain the information on the agencies to which workers ordinarily turned for the assistance they so often needed.

Once the articles had been selected, it was necessary to edit them carefully, providing complete citations for sources Sartorius used,

5. See note 1.

rechecking his sometimes dubious arithmetic, identifying individuals
and organizations where he had not done so, and searching for numerous English-language texts, which he had translated into German, so
that the reader could be provided with the actual words of the document quoted rather than wording that had been twice translated. By
no means was that quest always successful. In addition to the facts
that Sartorius had often found documents from American trade unions
in German-language newspapers and that some unions had written
their statutes in German, many of the English-language constitutions,
bylaws, and editorials that he translated into German for these articles
have disappeared without a trace. Indeed, an important contribution
of these articles is the glimpse they offer of documents from ephemeral
organizations or early versions of the statutes of more durable institutions that cannot now be found elsewhere. Footnotes will identify every
text that has been retranslated from the German. They and other editorial comments or additions are identified by square brackets ([. . .])
that surround them.

Much of the material Sartorius gathered about the United States
appeared not in these articles about the trade union movement but
in other articles and books that dealt with other specific aspects of
working-class life. Among those subjects were the socialist movement,
the German-American community, the movement for a shorter working
day and its economic implications, free and slave labor in the British
North American colonies, and Chinese immigration.[6] This introduction
will discuss some of the ideas and information found in those works
when doing so clarifies or amplifies important points.

It should also be noted that on the eve of Sartorius's visit to the
United States, the first scholarly study of the country's trade unions
by an American had appeared in print. It was written by the Yale University economist and future president of the American Economic Association, Henry W. Farnam, but, significantly, it was written in German
and published in Germany. That short but informative book was used

6. *Der moderne Socialismus in den Vereinigten Staaten von Amerika* (Berlin, 1890); *Die
Zukunft des Deutschthums in den Vereinigten Staaten von Amerika* (Berlin, 1885);
"Arbeitszeit und Normalarbeitstag in den Vereinigten Staaten von Amerika," *Jahr-
bücher für Nationalökonomie und Statistik*, 38 (1882), 461–73, 39 (1882), 107–46; *Die
Arbeits-Verfassung der englischen Kolonien in Nordamerika* (Strassburg, 1894); "Die
Chinesen in den Vereinigten Staaten von Amerika," *Zeitschrift für die gesammte
Staatswissenschaft*, 39 (1883), 320–431.

by Sartorius, possibly more than the credits in the latter's footnotes would suggest. It is useful to read Farnam's book in conjunction with these articles for two reasons. First, Farnam supplemented his readings of union statutes with extensive correspondence with trade union officers. Although unfortunately his book virtually never names the individuals who sent him information, Farnam had access to the personal reflections of a wider variety of American labor activists than did Sartorius. Second, Farnam conducted his research while the movement still lay in the grip of the depression of the seventies. His information reflects national organizations that had by then mostly been reduced to rather few active members, while that gathered by Sartorius features the local activity of a revived and exuberant movement.[7]

Much of the value of this series of articles derives from the timing of the German economist's visit to the United States. The brutal depression, which had begun with the bank crisis of 1873, had lifted (for some industries, like coal mining, shoe manufacturing, and textiles, it had only just lifted) when he set out to study the economic practices of North America firsthand. Heeding the most important lesson learned from his mentor, Georg Hanssen, "the need to rely on direct experience rather than on books and doctrines," Sartorius had ventured "into the open air, off to distant lands," to the United States, Cuba, Mexico, and Canada.[8]

A young man, but one with excellent family connections, who had recently been appointed a *Privatdozent* at the University of Göttingen, Sartorius was well aware of the intense interest in the burgeoning industrial economy of the United States that the Philadelphia Centennial Exhibition of 1876 had aroused in German academic, business, and political circles. The focal point of German curiosity was quite different from that of French "Opportunist" Republican leaders, who had facilitated a visit of their country's trade unionists to the Philadelphia

---

7. Henry W. Farnam, *Die Amerikanischen Gewerkvereine, Schriften des Vereins für Socialpolitik,* 18 (Leipzig, 1879; reprint Vaduz, 1988). The letters written by Farnam soliciting information from labor activists can be found in the Farnam Family Papers, Yale University Manuscript Collections, Group no. 203, series 11, box 202, letterbooks, 1879–89. Unfortunately, the replies to his letters were not preserved, and Benjamin Scully, longtime leader of the shoe workers' union, Knights of St. Crispin, is the only respondent referred to by name in Farnam's book. The German influence on American scholarship is discussed in Jürgen Herbst, *The German Historical School in American Scholarship: A Study in the Transfer of Culture* (Ithaca, N.Y., 1965).
8. August Sartorius von Waltershausen, *Memoirs* (typescript), 108–9.

Exhibition in the hope of cultivating workers' support for the fragile
Third Republic, which was beset by monarchists and socialists.[9] Nor
was it guided by the question of whether it would be wise to emigrate
to the New World, as was the steady stream of personal and journalis-
tic correspondence that then reached working people in the British
Isles, epitomized by the "News from America" reports in the Lan-
cashire *Cotton Factory Times*.[10] Scholarly attention in imperial Germany was drawn to the causes and future trajectory of America's
industrial growth and to the lessons German policy makers might draw
from the U.S. experience. Sartorius von Waltershausen's training in the
German historical school of economics had equipped him well to write
about just those matters.

The context of his visit makes the economist's use of his training and
of his inclinations toward the "open air" fortunate for subsequent historians of the American working class. After half a dozen years of slug-
gish economic activity, falling prices and wages, and chronic unemployment, the demand for labor had by 1880 again become vigorous.
Immigrants disembarked at U.S. ports in unprecedented numbers, an
especially large group of them from the author's own country. Both
skilled and unskilled workers engaged in numerous strikes, most of
them successful efforts to improve their incomes and working conditions, in contrast to the brutally protracted lost strikes against wage
cuts that had dominated the previous half dozen years. Sartorius was
among the first scholars to scrutinize the relationship between business
cycles and strikes systematically. His analysis of the strikes that had
taken place during the ten months beginning in November 1879 was
welcomed by the informative business journal *Bradstreet's,* which
lamented the absence of national strike statistics and remarked: "To our

9. Philip S. Foner, "The French Trade Union Delegation to the Philadelphia Centennial
    Exposition, 1876," *Science and Society,* 40 (1976), 257–87.
10. Rowland T. Berthoff, *British Immigrants in Industrial America, 1790–1850* (Cam-
    bridge, Mass., 1953); Charlotte Erickson, *Invisible Immigrants: The Adaptation of
    English and Scottish Immigrants in Nineteenth-Century America* (Coral Gables, Fla.,
    1972); J. T. Cumbler, "Transatlantic Working-Class Institutions," *Journal of Histori-
    cal Geography,* 6 (1980), 284; Allan Conway, *The Welsh in America: Letters from
    Immigrants* (Minneapolis, 1961); Wolfgang Helbich, Walter D. Kamphoefner, and
    Ulrike Sommer (eds.), *News from the Land of Freedom: German Immigrants Write
    Home,* translated by Susan Carter Vogel (Ithaca, N.Y., 1991); William I. Thomas and
    Florian Znaniecki, *The Polish Peasant in Europe and America* (2nd ed., 2 vols., New
    York, 1927). I am indebted to Mary Blewett for sharing her collection of letters from
    America to *The Burnley Gazette* and the *Preston Herald* with me.

knowledge it has remained for a German to make the most scientific inquiry on this point, even in our own country."[11]

Documenting the Revival of the Trade Unions

The quickening of economic activity and the frequent success of strikes stimulated a resurgence of labor organizing, which Sartorius observed firsthand. He assiduously gathered constitutions and bylaws of trade unions in every locality he visited, as well as those that were reprinted or described in the labor movement press. These statutes shed light on the ways workers tried to deal with immigration, strikes, and the insecurities of industrial life.

Neither trade unions nor labor parties were new to the American scene: they had played a significant role in national life since the 1830s. Local and national unions had flourished between the last years of the Civil War and the onset of the depression in 1873. At that time, representatives of different unions had coordinated their program and activities through national labor congresses, and they had created a short-lived national labor party.[12] Many of the labor reformers who helped launch new organizations or reinvigorate old ones at the end of the 1870s drew upon their personal experience with some of those earlier efforts, though many others had come of age only during the depression years.

At the time of Sartorius's visit, however, the resurgence of the labor movement was distinctly local in nature. Although the Knights of Labor had existed since 1869 and the order was already attracting coalminers and telegraphers in many parts of the land, its influence over labor organizing was still concentrated in Pennsylvania (Philadelphia, the anthracite coal fields, and Pittsburgh). The Federation of Organized Trades and Labor Unions did not hold its founding convention until three months after Sartorius had returned home, and in any event that precursor of the American Federation of Labor initially functioned primarily as a legislative committee of the trade unions, not as an agency that directed or coordinated their economic strategies.[13]

11. *Bradstreet's*, April 25, 1885.
12. David Montgomery, *Beyond Equality: Labor and the Radical Republicans, 1862–1872* (New York, 1967).
13. Norman J. Ware, *The Labor Movement in the United States, 1860–1895* (New York and London, 1929).

The documents Sartorius examined in a variety of local settings contribute greatly to our understanding of the ways in which workers' organizations tried to come to grips with immigration, strikes, the insecurity of industrial life, and the need for solidarity among unions. The steady influx of migrants from abroad had influenced union practice in three important ways. First, the same prosperity that encouraged trade union growth also stimulated the influx of newcomers, who could be used by employers to block union demands. In the sources Sartorius collected, workers who were immigrants themselves appear to have been as much concerned with the threat to their efforts posed by the urgent need of more recent arrivals for jobs as were those who had been born in the United States. Second, the variety of languages used by immigrants generated not only a multilingual press for the labor movement, but also a variety of union structures and rules designed to cope with the language problem. Third, immigrants often brought with them experience, practices, and beliefs from their homelands that informed their behavior as union members in the United States. For example, Sartorius draws the reader's attention to the pronounced imprint of British influence on the statutes of the Amalgamated Association of Iron and Steel Workers and to the interaction of German theoretical debates and American experience reflected in the editorials of the *Gewerkschafts-Zeitung*.[14]

The role of strikes in trade union development is evident not only in the author's analysis of their relationship to economic conditions and in his discussion of the role of public opinion in shaping the outcome of strikes. It is also apparent in the elaboration of union rules designed to regulate the conduct of strikes by union members. Just as trade unions gathered funds to help their adherents survive strikes, they also formulated a variety of procedures with which members had to comply before they were authorized to use those funds. Sartorius has reproduced many of these rules, providing historians with valuable evidence to help them interpret union rhetoric on the strike question in the context of the revival of the working-class struggle at the beginning of the 1880s. By themselves, however, these sources offer few clues regarding the actual interaction between leaders and strikers, which the statutes attempted to regulate.[15]

14. See Section I, Essay 3, this volume.
15. See Section II, Essay 3, this volume. For exemplary studies of the response to union strike rules by strikers and potential strikers in this epoch, see Shelton Stromquist, *A Generation of Boomers: The Pattern of Railroad Labor Conflict in Nineteenth-Century America* (Urbana, Ill., 1987); Mary H. Blewett, *Men, Women, and Work:*

Trade union benefit funds were of special interest to Sartorius. The research he had recently completed on assistance funds for invalids and the elderly in Germany had alerted him to the importance of this topic for working people. He examined closely discussions of the subject in the American labor press, to which we shall return, and he also catalogued carefully the efforts of unions to reduce the economic insecurity of working-class life. Sick benefits, life insurance, and accident insurance he found widespread, though undermined by the tendency of workers in the United States to change their occupations and domiciles. He subjected efforts to insure union members against unemployment to close scrutiny, but he reached pessimistic conclusions. Like many European observers, he was intrigued by American craftsmen's large boxes of tools, which they owned personally. Nevertheless, it was only a union of German immigrants, the Furniture Workers, that actually provided insurance against the destruction of tools by fire.[16]

Sartorius's interest in the response of trade unions to immigration, strike control, arbitration, and technological development led him to direct close attention to trades assemblies, which coordinated the activities of diverse unions on a citywide level. Although such bodies had frequently been formed and subsequently disintegrated since the 1820s, they reemerged with the return of prosperity at the end of the 1870s like mushrooms after a spring rain. He subjected their bylaws to careful scrutiny.

Like every other foreign investigator of the late nineteenth century, Sartorius also admired and extracted much information from reports of state bureaus of labor statistics, which were the first agencies of their kind in the industrial world.[17]

He read the labor movement's press voraciously, but he profited especially from his reading of *Die Gewerkschafts-Zeitung*, which appeared for only a few years in New York City. It was edited by a remarkable trio of German-born union activists and autodidacts, who reported and

    Class, Gender, and Protest in the New England Shoe Industry, 1780–1910 (Urbana, Ill., 1988); Augusta Emile Galster, *The Labor Movement in the Shoe Industry, With Special Reference to Philadelphia* (New York, 1924).

16. See Section II, Essay 5, this volume.
17. Discussions of precursors of trades assemblies can be found in many books, among them Bruce Laurie, *The Working People of Philadelphia, 1800–1850* (Philadelphia, 1980), 85–104; Sean Wilentz, *Chants Democratic: New York City and the Rise of the American Working Class, 1788–1850* (New York, 1984), 172–254; Montgomery, *Beyond Equality*, 160–70. For the history of labor statistics, see Michelle Perrot, *Les ouvriers en grève. France 1871–1890* (2 vols., Paris and the Hague, 1974), I, 18–31.

commented upon new developments in trade unionism throughout the land: Adolph Strasser, Carl Speyer, and Hugo Müller.[18] The information and insights their journal provided were exactly the stuff that Gustav von Schmoller and Lujo Brentano trained their students to seek out.

Wherever he traveled throughout the United States, the visiting German met with fellow countrymen who had become prominent citizens of their new homeland. Among them were socialist journalists, like Alexander Jonas and Alexander Schlesinger, and the emigre chemist Wilhelm Hasselmann, who had but recently been expelled from both the Reichstag and the German Social Democratic Party for his public advocacy of armed insurrection against the bourgeoisie. In Chicago his host was Anton Hesing, editor of the mass-circulation newspaper *Illinois Staats-Zeitung* and boss of a political machine that directed the votes of German Americans to one political party or another in such a way as to keep it a major power in municipal politics.[19]

Conspicuously absent from his sources, however, are the voices of working men and women other than Strasser, Speyer, and Müller. Although Sartorius visited many factories, docks, and warehouses, and met with socialist journalists, who were often well informed, he reported no conversations with workers or even observations of working conditions (with the important exception of his report on the organization of work on the New Orleans docks). By contrast, visiting French, German, and British workers often commented on the intense concentration on work and dearth of conversation in American factories.[20] The New York apartment of the German-born printer Jean

18. On Strasser and Speyer, often depicted as theoretical founders of "pure and simple unionism," see Stuart Bruce Kaufman, *Samuel Gompers and the Origins of the American Federation of Labor, 1848–1896* (Westport, Conn., 1973); Bernard Mandel, *Samuel Gompers: A Biography* (Yellow Springs, Ohio, 1963). Hugo Müller joined the German-American Typographia upon his arrival in the United States in 1873 and served as its national secretary between 1886 and 1894, by which time he had changed his name to Miller. He was also the German secretary of the Federation of Organized Trades and Labor Unions from 1882 to 1886. *Gompers Papers,* I, 372, 497.

19. See Essay 2, this volume. On Hasselmann's role in American revolutionary politics, see Paul Avrich, *The Haymarket Tragedy* (Princeton, N.J., 1984), 49–50, 160. On Hesing, see Bessie Louise Pierce, *A History of Chicago* (3 vols, Chicago, 1957), III, 343–56; Karen Sawislak, *Smoldering City: Chicagoans and the Great Fire, 1871–1874* (Chicago, 1995), 148–58, 247–55.

20. J. T., "Letters on America," *Burnley Gazette,* May 1, 1875, and May 15, 1875; [James D. Burn,] *Three Years among the Working-Classes of the United States during the War* (London, 1865), 186–7; Alfred Kolb, *Als Arbeiter in Amerika. Unter deutsch-amerikanischen Großstadt-Proletariern* (Berlin, 1904), 43–5, 55–6; E. Levasseur, *L'ouvrier américain* (2 vols., Paris, 1898), I, 233. The socialist journalists, like their counterparts in the United States, had all been practicing journalists in Germany before they

Weil was apparently the only worker's home Sartorius even entered. Moreover, he showed little interest in working or living conditions, or even in earnings, except as they were the cause of industrial conflict or related to relief funds (whose efforts to provide some modicum of income security in a market-driven economy attracted his close attention). Wages, company practices, living conditions, and legal regulation of hours of work, safety and health, and child labor were left to the investigations of such scholars as Arthur von Studnitz, who had toured the United States in 1876 on behalf of the Association for the Welfare of the Working Classes (*Central-Verein für das Wohl der arbeitenden Klassen* – a counterpart of New York's Association for Improving the Condition of the Poor and of the Charities Organization Society).[21]

Sartorius focused his attention on the institutions created by civil society to regulate economic life, especially the organizations devised for that purpose by workers themselves. Unlike most twentieth-century researchers, he did not relegate trade unions to the category of "industrial relations." On the contrary, he attributed their development to the human impulse to associate for the promotion of group welfare, and found in the theoretical writings of Henry C. Carey an explanation of why that impulse was particularly potent in conditions of recent settlement, in which people combined forces to master the natural environment. In Carey's view, the relatively light grip of government and tradition in a country with vast natural resources strengthened both private property and cooperation. Only through organized social effort, he believed, could harmonious relations be cultivated among the various strata of an industrializing country.[22]

emigrated. Hartmut Keil and John B. Jentz, *German Workers in Chicago: A Documentary History of Working-Class Culture from 1850 to World War I* (Urbana, Ill., 1988), 222.

21. Arthur von Studnitz, *Nordamerikanische Arbeiterverhältnisse* (Leipzig, 1879); "Amerikanische Arbeiterverhältnisse," *Der Arbeiterfreund. Zeitschrift des Centralvereins für das Wohl der arbeitenden Klassen*, 15 (1877), 113–27. Similar interests were shown by numerous European investigators of the 1890s. See, for example, Carl Kindermann, *Zur organischen Güterverteilung* (2 vols., Leipzig, 1894, 1896); Levasseur, *L'ouvrier américain*. On the Association for Improving the Condition of the Poor, see Iver Bernstein, *The New York City Draft Riots: Their Significance for American Society and Politics in the Age of the Civil War* (New York, 1990), 65–70, 183–90.

22. Carey, who died in 1879, was the favorite economist of the radical wing of the Republican Party. He repudiated the free trade doctrines of British classical economics and advocated protective tariffs; government aid to transportation, education, and scientific agriculture; and incorporation of enterprises as means for promoting national welfare and social harmony. His own business career is examined in Anthony F. C. Wal-

Although Carey himself harbored little sympathy for trade unions, his style of thinking about economy and society fit far better with the institutional emphasis of the German historical school than did the laissez-faire doctrines that were in vogue in American academic circles in 1880. The latter encouraged contempt for unions, like that expressed by the Liberal editor of *The Nation*, E. L. Godkin. The best that could be said for unions, Godkin argued, was that they represented a passing phase between ill-considered demands by workers for government interference in economic life and the ultimate achievement of modern society: such cooperation between employers and employees as did not interfere with "any well-settled economic law" or involve "a repudiation of the principles of competition." If unions sought a lasting and influential role, Godkin added:

we should regard their existence [. . .] as one of the most ingenious means of debasing the workingman's character ever invented. They unquestionably promote insubordination, want of punctuality, sluggishness, and indifference, and systematically repress excellence and ambition.[23]

Sartorius von Waltershausen agreed with Godkin that for an industrial economy to flourish, workers had to be subordinated to the authority of an employer, technological innovation had to be encouraged, and wages should (and ultimately would) be set by the law of supply and demand. Nevertheless, the German's training in institutional economics made him more appreciative than the American was of the economic and social role of workers' collective efforts. Sartorius repudiated the notion that the forces of competition would suffice to secure the general welfare through the conflicting strivings of individuals. "A national economy," he insisted, "has rightly been called an organic whole." And he added: "when a part of the social body is ill, the whole body feels the pain."[24] Thus his close attention to schemes for arbitrating wage disputes was informed by a quest for social peace. More

lace, *St. Clair: A Nineteenth-Century Coal Town's Experience with a Disaster-Prone Industry* (New York, 1987), 54–70. His theories were coming under intense criticism from such diverse rising American writers as Francis A. Walker, William Graham Sumner, and John Bates Clark at the very time German advocates of state aid to industrialization were attracted to them. Dorothy Ross, *The Origins of American Social Science* (Cambridge and New York, 1991), 42–140.

23. E. L. Godkin, "Co-operation," *North American Review,* 56 (January 1868), 169–70, 173.

24. See Section III, Essay 3, this volume.

remarkable from the vantage point of the dominant American economic thought of his time, he likened union labels approvingly to protective tariffs, and even described union boycotts as a legitimate use of market power to provide workers with self-protection on "occasions when the state's laws and judicial system cannot or will not protect one social class from another."[25]

The law of supply and demand, in this view, became not an omnipotent force working in defiance of human wishes, but rather a depiction of wage fixing that was in practice the result of social contestation. Arbitration became a means to measure the relative power of adversaries, so that their disputes could be resolved with a minimum of damage to themselves and to the rest of society. More important for historians, that conception of wage determination led Sartorius to the empirical study of particular labor markets, such as the Tuscarawas Valley coal fields, rather than to the elaboration of abstract principles of political economy. In this respect, his investigations anticipated the influential writings of Sidney and Beatrice Webb on British trade union practice and those of John R. Commons on American methods.[26]

Civil Society and the Regulation of Industrial Conflict

Late-nineteenth-century efforts to resolve industrial disputes by conciliation and arbitration have seldom been taken as seriously by recent historians as they were by Sartorius von Waltershausen.[27] In part this is because the historian's attention is most easily captured by great strikes, or waves of strikes, such as those of 1877 and 1886, which made a mockery of all talk of reconciling labor and capital. Another historiographical tendency has also encouraged this neglect. In the quest to "bring politics back" into the study of labor history, influential authors have turned away from the thick description of local conflicts, made famous by Herbert Gutman, toward ideological and legal controversies that surrounded national labor organizations. That ten-

25. See Essay 4, this volume.
26. Sidney Webb and Beatrice Webb, *Industrial Democracy* (London, 1897); John R. Commons, ed., *Trade Unionism and Labor Problems* (Boston, 1905); *Trade Unionism and Labor Problems. Second Series* (Boston, 1921).
27. A noteworthy exception to this generalization is Mary H. Blewett, *We Will Rise in Our Might: Workingwomen's Voices from Nineteenth-Century New England* (Ithaca, N.Y., and London, 1991). This collection of documents with commentary devotes careful attention to the use of arbitration by the Knights of Labor on pp. 162–74.

dency has favored rigorous analysis of movement discourse over close scrutiny of what workers did on their jobs and in their neighborhoods.

Focusing their attention on ideology and the power of the law, writers like Victoria Hattam and William E. Forbath have discerned in the Knights' public aversion to strikes a nostalgia for the harmony of the small workshop and an ideology of *producer republicanism,* which had been rendered obsolete by industrial development and judicial repression. They contrasted the Knights' *producerist* ideology with that of the trade unions, which accepted the wage system and fought for improved conditions within it. Their approach encouraged the treatment of arbitration as largely rhetorical, and associated it with the Knights' struggles for legislative reform rather than with trade union struggles over wages.[28]

The case studies provided by Sartorius make a valuable contribution to this discussion, first because they are numerous and, second, because they draw attention to practice rather than discourse. As the author stresses, the term *arbitration,* as then used in the United States, had a variety of meanings. As part of their effort to husband strike funds and make strikes better planned and more effective, the trade union rules he reproduced required that union members submit their grievances to the adjudication of fellow members, who were not directly involved in the dispute, as a precondition of official authorization to strike. In other instances, boards composed of equal numbers of employers and workers passed on disputes that arose in affiliated workshops. In both instances the workers designated their efforts as arbitration.

The board established for the Cincinnati shoe industry, and attributed by Sartorius to the owner of Stribley and Company, functioned effectively (as he fails to note) because the men and women who worked in the city's shoe factories were solidly enrolled in the Knights of Labor between 1882 and 1888. The order negotiated wages and conditions

---

28. Victoria Hattam, *Labor Visions and State Power: The Origins of Business Unionism in the United States* (Princeton, N.J., 1993); William E. Forbath, *Law and the Shaping of the American Labor Movement* (Cambridge, Mass., 1991). See also Karen Orren, *Belated Feudalism: Labor, the Law, and Liberal Development in the United States* (Cambridge and New York, 1991); Gerald N. Grob, *Workers and Utopia: A Study of Ideological Conflict in the American Labor Movement, 1865–1900* (Evanston, Ill., 1961). Knights efforts at arbitration are accorded a more serious, though critical, assessment in Blewett, *Rise with All Our Might;* Gregory S. Kealey and Bryan D. Palmer, *Dreaming of What Might Be: The Knights of Labor in Ontario, 1880–1900* (Cambridge, 1982); and Galster, *The Labor Movement in the Boot and Shoe Industry.*

through the arbitration board until its power was broken by an employers' lockout (spearheaded by Stribley himself) in 1888. As was the case in other shoe manufacturing and textile centers, the Knights' commitment to arbitration was put into practice. It is also noteworthy, however, that this and other arbitration plans in the city were promoted not only by the Knights, but also by the Cincinnati Trades and Labor Assembly, which affiliated in 1881 with the Federation of Organized Trades and Labor Unions.[29] While the Cincinnati case study reveals that both the Knights of Labor and local trade unions participated in arbitration plans, it also reminds us that the statutes governing such arbitration do not by themselves provide sufficient evidence of how and why the plans functioned.

Two major strongholds of trade unionism, coal mining and iron rolling mills, also loom large in Sartorius's evidence. Much of his information was drawn from the writings of Joseph D. Weeks, manager of the Pittsburgh office of *Iron Age* (the journal of the associated iron rolling mills and a vigorous advocate of tariff protection) and in 1892 secretary of the national committee of the Republican Party. Weeks coupled his enthusiasm for boards representing both manufacturers' associations and trade unions with faith in a sliding scale of wages, which pegged the piece rates earned by workers to the selling price received by the manufacturer for the product. Sliding scales were then also found in coal fields in Wales, Belgium, and northern England.[30] Sartorius's commentaries on these attempts at organized conciliation within a highly competitive economy underscore his anxious conviction that without such agencies "today's mode of produc-

---

29. Steven J. Ross, *Workers on the Edge: Work, Leisure, and Politics in Industrializing Cincinnati, 1788–1890*, 258–64; James M. Morris, "The Cincinnati Shoemakers' Lockout of 1888: A Case Study in the Demise of the Knights of Labor," *Labor History*, 13 (Fall 1972), 505–19. For a general discussion of Knights of Labor arbitration efforts involving factory operatives, see David Montgomery, *The Fall of the House of Labor: The Workplace, the State, and American Labor Activism, 1865–1925* (Cambridge and New York, 1987), 148–70.

30. On Weeks, see John N. Ingham, *Making Iron and Steel: Independent Mills in Pittsburgh, 1820–1920* (Columbus, Ohio, 1991), 115–27. The contrast between the attitude of the iron mills and the newer steel companies toward unions is explained in Paul Krause, *The Battle for Homestead, 1880–1892: Politics, Culture, and Steel* (Pittsburgh, Pa., 1992), 102–18, 155–76. A comparative analysis of sliding scales in Europe is offered by Joël Michel, "Politique syndicale et conjoncture économique: La limitation de la production de charbon chez les mineurs européens au XIXe siècle," *Le Mouvement Social*, 119 (April-June 1982), 63–90.

tion will neither achieve a reconciliation of capital and labor nor, assuming their continued opposition, be assured of a prosperous future."[31] They also highlight the fragility of both arbitration boards and sliding scales in practice. Perhaps the newer historical interpretations are not entirely wrong: class harmony was pursued more easily in word than in deed.

Sartorius von Waltershausen's discussion of boycotts is perceptive, but not as richly informative as that of arbitration. The boycotts article was written four years after he had returned from the United States, and it relied heavily on a single source: the weekly journal put out by New York's Typographical Union No. 6, *The Boycotter*. Nevertheless, in addition to exhibiting a positive evaluation of boycotts, which contrasted sharply with the vituperation heaped on the practice by most of the American press, and examining carefully the conditions that made for their success or failure, it stressed the importance of this weapon as a practical manifestation of solidarity among different groups of workers. The author was especially intrigued by the evolution of a typographers' boycott of the New York *Tribune* into an attempt to influence the outcome of the 1884 presidential election. His expectation that the Republican Party would repudiate the *Tribune* after that year's electoral defeat, however, did not come to pass.

In sharp contrast to recent discussions of boycotts by historians of American labor law, Sartorius virtually ignored the legal response to boycotts. As was the case with his American colleague Henry Farnam, his references to the law were few, focusing on registration and incorporation of unions and on the legal status of union funds rather than on conspiracy law and injunctions. Shortly after Sartorius published his article, the business journal *Bradstreet's* offered a systematic survey of labor boycotts, listing 237 that had taken place during the previous two years and counting three-quarters of them as successful. Most of them had been instituted by the Knights of Labor, which considered the boycott an "arbitration persuader."[32] The following year the Illinois Bureau of Labor Statistics counted 10,186 boycotts around the country, 4,259 conducted by trade unions and 5,927 by the Knights, with results vary-

31. See Section III, Essay 3, this volume.
32. *Bradstreet's*, December 19, 1885, 394–7. The term *arbitration persuader* is from T. Fulton Gantt's novel *Breaking the Chains: A Story of the Present Industrial Struggle,* which was originally published in serial form in the Salem, Oregon, newspaper *The Lance* in 1887 and is reprinted in Mary C. Grimes, *The Knights in Fiction: Two Labor Novels of the 1880s* (Urbana, Ill., and Chicago, 1986), 44.

ing substantially in accordance with public responses to the issues involved.[33]

Although the judicial attack on boycotts did not get underway until late 1885 and early 1886 (after the publication of this article), Sartorius did warn that any attempt to outlaw the practice would only augment workers' "antipathy towards capital" with "an antipathy towards the state order, and the banned weapon would be replaced with an even more dangerous one."[34] In fact, many of the 189 municipal labor party tickets fielded between 1885 and 1888 (among them the famous campaign of Henry George for mayor of New York) were inspired by judicial repression of boycotts.[35]

There is also evidence, however, that even as the practice of boycotting reached its historic peak, activists within the labor movement had qualms about some of its uses. The prominent Philadelphia cigarmakers' leader John Kirschner charged that boycotts "had been abused by designing persons connected with the labor movement."[36] In Decatur, Illinois, the trades assembly and Knights joined in a boycott of a local cigar manufacturer because his employees belonged to a socialist union. In Philadelphia, the socialist paper *Tageblatt* fired printers who refused to set type for an article criticizing their typographical union, provoking boycotts and counterboycotts that tore the city's labor movement asunder, until Samuel Gompers successfully mediated the dispute in 1887. Even the New York *Boycotter* changed its name after the 1886 elections to *Union Printer*, explaining that the practice of boycotting had been perverted.[37] Although historians can learn much

---

33. Illinois Bureau of Labor Statistics, *Fourth Annual Report, 1886* (Springfield, 1887), 446–7.
34. See Essay 4, this volume.
35. Peter A. Speek, *The Singletax and the Labor Movement* (Madison, Wis., 1917); David Scobey, "Boycotting the Politics Factory: Labor Radicalism and the New York City Mayoral Election of 1884 [sic]," *Radical History Review*, 28–30 (1984), 280–326; Peter J. Rachleff, *Black Labor in the South: Richmond, Virginia, 1865–1890* (Philadelphia, 1984), 124–56. On the labor reform parties of the 1880s, see Leon Fink, *Workingmen's Democracy: The Knights of Labor and American Politics* (Urbana, Ill., 1983). The calculation of 189 labor tickets is in Fink, 26, and the towns involved are listed by Fink on pp. 28–9.
36. *Bradstreet's*, December 12, 1885, p. 379.
37. [Decatur] *John Swinton's Paper*, August 23, 1885; [Philadelphia] Elliott Shore, Ken Fones-Wolf, and James P. Danky, eds., *The German-American Radical Press: The Shaping of a Left Political Culture, 1850–1940* (Urbana, Ill., 1992), 71–3; *Gompers Papers*, II, 25–6; [New York] *Union Printer*, November 13, 1886. Cf. the argument of Forbath that judicial repression ended citywide boycotts. Forbath, *Law and the Shaping of the American Labor Movement*, 79–90. A useful survey of this period is found

from this article by Sartorius, they will need other sources from later years to understand fully the role of boycotting in the nineteenth-century labor movement.

Finally, attention should be drawn to the author's many suggestions that the efforts of civil society to regulate a competitive industrial economy transformed the character of the people involved, as well as the operation of markets. Sartorius von Waltershausen portrays both unions and mutual insurance societies as agencies of working-class self-improvement. It was not simply the case that those most likely to organize came from the more skilled and better-paid ranks of workers, but also that the very act of organizing modified their behavior. Unionization, he wrote, gives workers "not only power, but also understanding." It converts a "mindless, clumsy mass" into "a disciplined, thinking community."[38]

Sartorius's image of collectively self-made workers bears upon the much-debated concept of the *labor aristocracy*.[39] He clearly considered most workers indolent and attributed their chronic insecurity to their own lack of foresight. Societies and trade unions that provided insurance against life's hazards served, in his view, as a form of forced savings because the member missing a payment lost all his or her investment. He also feared, however, that even this beneficial consequence of union membership was eroded by the propensity of workers in the United States to change their occupations and places of residence. That mobility made the appeal of trade union beneficial features far weaker in the United States than it was in England, and encouraged workers to regard their unions primarily as aggressive combinations to support strikes, raise wages, and uphold work rules.

in Harry W. Laidler, *Boycotts and the Labor Struggle: Economic and Legal Aspects* (New York, 1913), 70–97.

38. See Section III, Essay 3, this volume.
39. See Eric J. Hobsbawm, "The Labour Aristocracy in Nineteenth-Century Britain," in Hobsbawm, *Labouring Men: Studies in the History of Labour* (London, 1964), 272–315; Henry Pelling, "The Concept of the Labour Aristocracy," in Pelling, *Popular Politics and Society in Late Victorian Britain* (London and New York, 1968), 37–61; John Foster, *Class Struggle and the Industrial Revolution: Early Industrial Capitalism in Three English Towns* (New York, 1975); Robert Gray, *The Aristocracy of Labour in Nineteenth-Century Britain, c. 1850–1900* (London and New York, 1981); Neville Kirk, "Class and the 'Linguistic Turn' in Chartist and Post-Chartist Historiography," in Kirk, ed., *Social Class and Marxism: Defences and Challenges* (Aldershot, 1996), 87–134; David Montgomery, "Workers' Control of Machine Production in the Nineteenth Century," in *Workers' Control in America: Studies in the History of Work, Technology, and Labor Struggles* (Cambridge and New York, 1979), 9–31.

The editors of *Die Gewerkschafts-Zeitung,* for whom he had evident admiration, endorsed the view that trade union consciousness was the product of organized behavior, not simply a natural response to oppression. The relief funds of unions, they argued, not only shielded families against distress, but also provided

the only way to get through to the lax working masses. The funds impose a highly necessary discipline on the members. The notion of one for all and all for one engendered by participation in a support fund generates the feelings of solidarity and fraternity, which enables the human spirit and curbs selfishness.[40]

Moreover, the ability to rely on union funds for some support in times of need strengthened workers' ability to defy their employers and refuse to scab. Organization thus nurtured *manliness,* to use a favorite expression of the period. The editorial went on to offer a revealing glimpse of the authors' view of the relationship of women to the trade unions:

The support funds [. . .] generate interest for the organization concerned, even among our women, who because they are less idealistic and more egotistical than the men, consider participation in associations that offer no material benefits, as pointless and as a waste of time and money.[41]

The tenor of this passage calls to mind the cogent analysis of the different implications for men and women of union efforts to mobilize workers' conduct as consumers found in Dana Frank's *Purchasing Power: Consumer Organizing, Gender, and the Seattle Labor Movement 1919–1929.*[42] Frank showed that just as men's strikes magnified the already heavy burden of household management faced by their wives, boycotts and union label shopping intensified the labor of housekeeping and the difficulties of making the budget stretch. The *Gewerkschafts-Zeitung* editorial reflects this dilemma by portraying the wife as a money-grubbing encumbrance to the conscious workingman, who might better appreciate her husband's manly devotion to the union if she got life or sickness insurance out of it.

Sartorius offers no discussion of the beneficial funds (or any other) of women's trade unions. The funds he described insured primarily, if not exclusively, against the loss to families of men's incomes. A

40. *Gewerkschafts-Zeitung,* March 15, 1880.   41. Ibid.
42. Cambridge and New York (1994).

significant exception to that proposition appears in the sickness and unemployment benefits promised by the International Labor Union (ILU), which recruited ardently among women factory operatives of New England and New Jersey and which was highly praised by the *Gewerkschafts-Zeitung*.[43] Although the once mighty union of women shoe workers, The Daughters of St. Crispin, had been virtually exterminated by 1879, the women collar starchers and ironers of Troy, New York, staged a successful strike in January and February 1880, which appeared on Sartorius's table of strikes. Their union, which had existed since 1868, boasted that it had "cared for their sick and buried their dead." Its president explained: "It was not an infrequent thing for girls employed in this business to be taken with consumption [. . .] and when any of their number had thus been taken down, they had been cared for by their own union."[44]

Women do loom large in Sartorius's discussion of relief and insurance funds that originated outside of the labor movement but covered many more working-class families than those provided by the unions. He prefaced the remarkable list of 171 institutions that aided the needy in Philadelphia alone with observations about the prominent role of middle- and upper-class women in the domain of private charities. This recognition was enveloped in his contempt for evangelical Christianity and for the public activities of women moral reformers, which he feared would corrupt even German immigrant women and thus undermine the immigrants' cultural heritage.[45] Nevertheless, he remarked, since American law concentrated on the rights of property owners, only the religious tradition kept vigorous by women served "to stress the social *duties* of wealth."[46]

43. The ILU had such a brief and strike-ridden career that it probably never put any such benefits into effect. The *Gewerkschaft-Zeitung* reported on the ILU on October 15, 1879, and offered subscriptions through J. P. McDonnell, the editor of its journal, *The Labor Standard*.

44. Carole Turbin, *Working Women of Collar City: Gender, Class, and Community in Troy, New York, 1864–86* (Urbana, Ill., 1992), 125, 264–5. The quotation is from a report by Esther Keegan to the New York Workingmen's Assembly, quoted in the New York *World*, July 3, 1869.

45. Sartorius von Waltershausen, *Die Zukunft des Deutschthums in den Vereinigten Staaten von Amerika*.

46. See Essay 5, this volume. For a discussion of the privatization of poor relief, see David Montgomery, *Citizen Worker: The Experience of Workers in the United States with Democracy and the Free Market during the Nineteenth Century* (Cambridge and New York, 1993), 71–83.

According to the author, there was "no demand for a system of compulsory public insurance in the United States."[47] Historians have not yet come to grips with this aspect of nineteenth-century political life, choosing rather to focus their attention on the materialization of demands for government social insurance after the depression of the 1890s. Sartorius von Waltershausen's explanation, based on the mobility of the population and the high earnings of skilled workers, seems inadequate to explain the absence of such demands even in the ranks of the socialists in the 1880s. He also makes it clear that company-based insurance funds were few and far between. Nevertheless, the close attention he devotes to mutual assistance funds and lodges reveals how many working people did seek protection against financial insecurity in a competitive market economy.

Race, Technology, and the Transformation of Unions

Sartorius von Waltershausen caught American trade unions not only at a moment of vigorous revival, but also in the midst of changing their structures and behavior in ways whose outcome he could only surmise. Two forces driving those changes were the reconfiguration of race in American life after the end of slavery and the rapid development of machine technology. His observations and conjectures on both those points deserve attention.

He provided evidence that black and white workers were subtly but effectively working out forms of collaboration with each other, while Chinese workers were harassed and excluded by legislation, boycotts, and crowd violence, much of it spearheaded by the organized labor movement itself. He found a union movement that had historically confined its membership to white workers and only since the end of the Civil War had fostered some experiments on admitting African Americans to white-dominated unions of their trades or, more frequently, organizing cooperation between white and black unions in the same occupations. Black workers, he noted, still resided overwhelmingly in the South and were largely confined to agriculture or to industrial occupations where "a sharp division of labor between the two races" confined them to "the more menial work." Whether future race relations in the South turned out to be harmonious or violently antagonistic, he believed, would

47. See Essay 5, this volume.

depend on whether or not the living standards and self-organization of black workers increased as rapidly as the South industrialized.[48]

Although Sartorius visited factories in Richmond, Virginia, he made no reports at all on that city's unions. This is unfortunate because Richmond was the country's most important center of African American activism in all-black unions and even in a few integrated unions (like the coopers and quarrymen). It had also produced the first black officer of a national labor congress: Warwick Reed, a leader of the tobacco workers' union, who served as vice-president of the Industrial Congress for his state in 1873; and was succeeded in that office by two other Richmond African Americans. The city was soon to emerge as a stronghold of the Knights of Labor. In contrast to other cities, where black and white Knights usually (though not always) belonged to separate assemblies, while coordinating their activities through district assemblies to which all locals sent delegates, Richmond created, at the insistence of its large black membership, one district organization for white local assemblies and another for black assemblies.[49]

He did, however, scrutinize closely the dockers' unions in several southern ports, and there he discovered much about the role of race in union organizing. His primary concern in describing the dock unions of New Orleans was to demonstrate how a Ring (properly known as the Cotton Men's Executive Council) coordinated eight major unions in the cotton export business, whose combined membership reached 8,000 at the time of his visit. Among American ports, New Orleans ranked second only to New York in the value of the exports that left its docks each year. Recent research by Eric Arnesen has shown that relations between white and black workers were often troubled (the unity among longshoremen giving way to violent attacks by whites on their black workmates during the depression of the 1890s), and constituent unions angrily stormed out of the Ring from time to time, only to return later. Nevertheless, Arnesen confirmed and elaborated Sartorius's portrayal of elaborate work-sharing rules, which extended even to the highly paid but biracial screwmen's trade a single scale of wages for workers of both races, and joint participation in all negotiations with employers.[50]

---

48. See Section I, Essay 3, this volume.
49. Rachleff, *Black Labor in the South*, 143–7.
50. See Section I, Essay 3, this volume. Arnesen, *Waterfront Workers*, 91–8, 132–4. On the ranking of U.S. ports, see Friedrich Ratzel, *Sketches of Urban and Cultural Life in North America*, translated and edited by Stewart A. Stehlin (New Brunswick, N.J., 1988), 79.

Both the strength and an important weakness of Sartorius's reporting are illustrated by his account of New Orleans. The institutionalized techniques through which workers brought order to docks, which otherwise would have been theaters of a war for survival of every worker against every other, and the role of those techniques in elevating workers' living standards, political influence, and human relations are all depicted vividly. On the other hand, the author's consistent failure to seek out the views and experiences of the workers themselves is aggravated here by his assumption that the white race was the bearer of "civilized" standards of conduct, to which black people had to be raised. Consequently, the reader is left with a white, bourgeois outsider's view of what black workers did in New Orleans, and without any insight into what their action and the complex interracial world of the docks meant to the many African Americans who found their livelihoods there.

The impact of that weakness is greatly magnified in Sartorius's discussion of Chinese immigration. Although he captured vividly the animosity of the white labor movement (and of virtually all of white society on the Pacific Coast) toward the Chinese, he made no effort to apply the methods of the German historical school to the Chinese themselves. On the contrary, he simply accepted the judgment of the Chinese exclusion movement that the Chinese "affected the whole of economic, political and moral life in the Western states" in a way that jeopardized "the efforts of European immigrants which have transformed the extensive, thinly populated Indian territories into a civilized state of the first order."[51]

To some extent, this defect was remedied by Sartorius's remarkable 1883 article on the Chinese in the United States, which appeared in the *Zeitschrift für die gesammte Staatswissenschaft*. That 111-page essay is as comprehensive as the treatment in "Trade Unions in the United States" is curt. Although the lengthy article is also informed by the belief that the cause of "civilization" requires exclusion of Chinese workers from North America, it provides both a thorough account of the harassment and exclusion of Chinese by state and federal legislation, labor movement boycotts, and mob action between 1844 and 1882 and a serious, informative effort to analyze the economic and institutional framework of the Chinese immigrant community itself. It discusses not only the patterns of self-government developed by the immigrants' asso-

51. See Section I, Essay 3, this volume.

ciations known as the *Six Companies,* but also the elaborate network of occupational societies connected to them.

Although his evidence was drawn from testimony presented by whites to congressional investigations, State Department reports, and books by European and North American visitors to China, and drew upon no Chinese-language sources, Sartorius found there the sort of material for which his training in institutional economics had prepared him. The discussion of the unions formed by Chinese shoe and cigar workers and their influence in regulating employment and raising wages is especially suggestive. The conclusion to which his economic theory led Sartorius, however, was that exclusion of Chinese was justifiable on grounds of national economy and was no longer a subject of controversy in the United States. The racist view of the world economy, with which he was to become increasingly obsessed during the subsequent decades, was already evident in this article.[52]

Moreover, the extended discussion of Chinese immigration in this article reveals a fundamental inadequacy in the methodology of the German historical school itself. Although the institutional framework of the Chinese diaspora is described at length, it has no breath of life. What migrants who crossed the Pacific Ocean wanted for their sacrifices, and what individual and collective struggles they undertook in the hope of gaining their objectives, remain completely obscured from the reader's view. Constitutions and bylaws can suggest the ways in which immigrants brought coherence to economic life, but they cannot provide the voice of the immigrants. When those regulations are presented only in the context of an argument justifying the exclusion of the Chinese, their significance for the immigrant workers themselves is doubly obscured.

Central to Sartorius's view of the restructuring of the labor movement, and even the influence of racial hierarchies and animosities, was "the relentless advance of industrial technology and the division of

52. Sartorius von Waltershausen, "Die Chinesen in den Vereinigten Staaten von Amerika." The discussion of the shoe and cigar unions is on pp. 405–8, and that of the organization of emigration, social power, agriculture, commerce, and remittances home is on pp. 398–431. For a treatment of these topics that rejects the identification of civilization with the white race, makes thorough use of Chinese-language sources, and explores the meaning of Chinese migration in China as well as in the United States, see Madeline Hsu, "Working Abroad and Faring Well: Migration, Tradition, and Change in Taishan County, Guangdong, 1904–1939" (Ph.D. dissertation, Yale University, 1996).

labor as the market expands."[53] He illustrated his point by scrutinizing recent developments in the manufacture of shoes, clothing, furniture, and meat products. In each instance, the dominance of craft workers had been undermined and the distinctions among crafts blurred. He concluded that the union movement had to change its own style of organization in response to these changes, and he explained the functions of trades assemblies and of other alliances among local unions in this context.

Of special interest to him, however, were two recent efforts to shift the very basis of the movement away from the skilled crafts. The International Labor Union was the most thorough attempt of this sort, and Carl Speyer, editor of the *Gewerkschafts-Zeitung*, was a member of its Provisional Committee. Its founders included members of the Socialist Labor Party who dissented from the party's orientation toward electoral politics and well-known leaders of the eight-hour movement from Massachusetts. They believed that the combined impact of modern technology and heavy immigration had created a force of factory operatives that could not be organized into craft-based unions, and whose numbers and importance in production threatened to undercut the strength of skilled workers who did belong to existing unions. They therefore created a general workers' union, open to workers of both sexes and every race and nationality, which proclaimed that "the wage system is despotism" but proposed to organize workers to overcome it by fighting for their immediate needs, and especially for the eight-hour day.[54]

The International Labor Union has been treated by historians largely in reference to other organizations – the socialist movement, the Knights of Labor, and the Federation of Organized Trades and Labor Unions. It mobilized effective strikes by cotton mill operatives against wage reductions in Fall River, Massachusetts, and Paterson, New Jersey, in 1878, then became involved in a number of unsuccessful textile strikes and shrank to a single branch by the end of 1881. The question of why this movement had only a transient impact, while the Knights of Labor, with a more ambiguous ideology and a structure that could accommodate virtually any style of organizing, soon emerged as the

53. See Section I, Essay 3, this volume.
54. George E. McNeill, *The Labor Movement: The Problem of To-Day* (Boston and New York, 1887), 161–4.

dominant movement in those same textile towns deserves closer attention than it has received.[55]

The Knights of Labor has been taken very seriously by historians,
just as it was by Sartorius. The membership claims that he repeats
rather tentatively (1.7 to 2.5 million in 1882) were wildly exaggerated,
but his estimate of 1,890 local assemblies chartered between 1869 and
1882, but so decimated by the economic crisis of the seventies that no
more than 345 were functioning at the time he wrote, is consistent with
the recent findings of Jonathan Garlock, who analyzed the local assemblies systematically.[56] What Sartorius has provided his readers is a
sound account of the structure and proclaimed purposes of the order
before the strike and boycott wave of 1885–7 catapulted it to national
and even international influence. He found the Knights even in 1882 the
most ambitious and distinctively American of many workers' efforts to
harness for their own benefit the social forces unleashed by the industrial expansion of the early eighties in this vast, multiracial, and multi-
national country.[57]

In sum, Sartorius made effective use of his academic training in institutional economics, his excellent introductions to knowledgeable
informants in the United States, the pioneering investigations made

55. Useful accounts of the ILU can be found in Kaufman, *Samuel Gompers and the Ori-
gins of the American Federation of Labor, 1848–1896*, 80–92; Philip S. Foner, *History
of the Labor Movement in the United States* (8 vols., New York, 1947–1988), I, 500–4;
*Friedrich A. Sorge's Labor Movement in the United States: A History of the American
Working Class from Colonial Times to 1890*, edited by Philip S. Foner and Brewster
Chamberlin, translated by Brewster Chamberlin and Angela Chamberlin (Westport,
Conn., 1977); Samuel Bernstein, *The First International in America* (New York, 1962),
290–4; and Gutman, *Work, Culture, and Society*, 260–9.
56. Jonathan Garlock, *Guide to the Local Assemblies of the Knights of Labor* (Westport,
Conn., 1982), xix. On pages 588–630 Garlock lists all assemblies formed before the
end of 1882 and membership figures for those that still existed at the end of that year.
57. The best institutional history of the Knights remains Ware, *The Labor Movement in
the United States, 1860–1895*. Among the more important recent studies are Fink,
Workingmen's Democracy: The Knights of Labor and American Politics; Stromquist,
Generation of Boomers; Kim Voss, *The Making of American Exceptionalism: The
Knights of Labor and Class Formation in the Nineteenth Century* (Ithaca, N.Y., and
London, 1993); Richard J. Oestreicher, *Solidarity and Fragmentation: Working People
and Class Consciousness in Detroit, 1875–1900* (Urbana, Ill., 1986); Susan Levine,
*Labor's True Woman: Carpet Weavers, Industrialization, and Labor Reform in the
Gilded Age* (Philadelphia, 1984); Blewett, *Men, Women, and Work;* Melton A.
McLaurin, *The Knights of Labor in the South* (Westport, Conn., 1978); Robert E.
Weir, *Beyond Labor's Veil: The Culture of the Knights of Labor* (University Park, Pa.,
1995); Rachleff, *Black Labor in the South;* Kealey and Palmer, *Dreaming of What
Might Be;* Hattam, *Labor Visions and State Power.*

available by state bureaus of labor statistics, and his voracious reading of the trade union and socialist press to offer his readers provocative insights into and rich documentation of the trade union movement of the United States as it rebounded from the protracted depression of the seventies. He captured the vitality and diversity of a movement that developed under auspicious circumstances, but without central organizations or established political creeds with sufficient influence to shape its course. He recorded the statutes and policy declarations of innumerable organizations that sought to regulate the chaotic expansion of industrial capitalism through the power not of government, but of civil society. And his own profoundly conservative commitment to social order made him appreciative of that effort from a perspective that was shared by few contemporary intellectuals in the United States.

2

August Sartorius von Waltershausen (1852–1938), German Political Economy, and American Labor

MARCEL VAN DER LINDEN
AND GREGORY ZIEREN[1]

In 1892 economist Wilhelm Lexis prepared a two-volume compendium of German universities for Chicago's Columbian Exposition, part of Germany's elaborate preparations for a triumphant return to the international competition of world's fairs after an unimpressive showing at the last American world's fair in Philadelphia in 1876. German academic interest in the United States owed its inspiration to "the astounding economic blossoming of America" in the years since the Civil War, Lexis maintained. Among the handful of experts whose work on American themes Lexis celebrated, the most prominent economist was a comparatively young University of Strasbourg professor named August Sartorius von Waltershausen. Lexis listed the professor's main research areas as trade unionism and the socialist movement in the United States, but he was also an expert on American immigration, trade and commerce, and the German-American community.[2]

The roots of the Strasbourg economist's interest in American labor and the working class originated in the Old World, not the New. Like all advanced capitalist economies in the late nineteenth century, Germany wrestled with class warfare as Bismarck pioneered the carrot-and-stick approach of banning the Social Democratic Party and offer-

---

1. Jan Gielkens (International Institute of Social History, Amsterdam) provided indispensable support for writing this essay. With remarkable resourcefulness and perseverance, he located numerous relevant documents.

  One of Gielkens's major achievements was his discovery of an untitled typescript containing the memoirs of August Sartorius von Waltershausen. This typescript (which is in the possession of Hermann and Lieselotte Wundt, Tübingen) appears as *Memoirs* in subsequent references. It was written during the years 1935–8.
2. Wilhelm Lexis, *Die deutschen Universitäten*, 1 (Berlin, 1893), 596, and "Weltausstellungen," *Meyers Konversations-Lexikon*, 2 (5th ed., Leipzig, 1896), 216.

ing social welfare programs to win the allegiance of the workers. Bismarck's policies had proven powerless to prevent the mass strikes of Ruhr coal miners in 1889 or the electoral success of the Social Democrats in the 1890 Reichstag election when they won the support of nearly 20 percent of the electorate. Indeed, the failure of his policies to manage the "social question" had contributed to his overthrow months after the 1890 election. Befitting the importance of the social question, Germany's most prominent economists devoted their careers to studying the working class at home and abroad in the hope of fashioning legislation and policies that would win the workers' loyalty to the state and nation.[3]

A second impetus for the German economist to study the United States was the impact of the Philadelphia Centennial of 1876. Europeans were stunned by the display of technological, scientific, and production-oriented inventiveness on view for all the world to see. But nowhere was the impact more dramatic than in Germany, where a public controversy broke out in the summer of 1876 over the reasons for America's brilliant industrial showing and Germany's comparatively lackluster performance. One year later, Sartorius von Waltershausen completed his law degree and embarked on the study of economics; four years later, he wrote his doctoral dissertation and embarked on a tour of the United States. Long known for political democracy and as the destination of millions of European immigrants, the United States was becoming the very image of capitalist development, a modern industrial economy unfettered by feudal remnants, useless internal borders, or redundant social classes. A European elite of academics, businessmen, government officials, social scientists, and aristocratic travelers visited America in the 1880s to see the future for themselves.[4]

A third element in the Strasbourg economist's fascination with America was implied in the alarmed response of Europeans to the Centennial and evident by the 1880s. America was certainly one of Germany's leading international competitors in trade, technology, and the quest for overseas possessions. By the 1890s, Sartorius viewed the United States

3. Michael Stürmer, *Das ruhelose Reich. Deutschland, 1866–1918* (Berlin, 1983), 335–45; Lothar Gall, *Bismarck. The White Revolutionary*, 3 (New York, 1988), 221–51; Albert Müssiggang, *Die soziale Frage in der historischen Schule der deutschen Nationalökonomie* (Tübingen, 1968).
4. C. Vann Woodward, *The Old World's New World* (New York, 1991), 16–39; on the European reaction to the Centennial, see Robert C. Post (ed.), *1876: A Centennial Exhibit* (Washington, D.C., 1976), 185.

as a "dangerous opponent," one of the three "world empires," with Russia and Great Britain, that stood in the way of Germany's legitimate aspirations on the world stage. Like the experts on the Soviet Union at Harvard and Columbia during the height of the cold war, Sartorius constantly reminded Germans of the dangers his research subject posed for them.[5]

Family Background

August Sartorius von Waltershausen was born on May 23, 1852. He belonged to a family that for generations had been firmly ensconced in the ranks of educated professionals and academicians. Known in German as the *Bildungsbürgertum,* the group included doctors, lawyers, higher civil servants, *Gymnasium* teachers, professors, and Protestant ministers. The common denominator of these professions was not wealth or income, though some in the group were certainly quite well off, but education, the enormous respect they enjoyed among their fellow citizens, and the services they performed for the German states of the eighteenth and nineteenth centuries.[6]

Georg Sartorius and Caroline von Voigt were August's paternal grandparents. Georg was born in 1765 in Kassel, the son and grandson of prominent Lutheran ministers, and attended nearby Göttingen University, where he remained to pursue a career as a writer, lecturer, and professor of economics and history. During his long career at the university he advised minor German princes, most notably at the Congress of Vienna in 1815, wrote political tracts for the educated middle-class public, and composed the first serious history of the Hansa cities of North Germany. But his most significant contribution, in the judgment of posterity, was his role as translator and popularizer of Adam Smith's *The Wealth of Nations.* An early enthusiast of classical economics and of the beginning stages of the French Revolution, Georg Sartorius was a typical early nineteenth-century German enlightened intellectual enamored of English and French Enlightenment thought. The first edition of his translation of excerpts from Smith's work appeared in 1796 as a textbook designed to initiate teachers and professors into the complex-

---

5. August Sartorius von Waltershausen, *Die Entstehung der Weltwirtschaft* (Jena, 1931), 645–7, and Manfred Jonas, *The United States and Germany: A Diplomatic History* (Ithaca [etc.], 1984), 35–64.
6. Charles E. McClelland, *State, Society and University in Germany, 1700–1914* (New York, 1980), 3 on *Bildungsbürgertum.*

ities of the British economist's thinking. He had complained that previous translations of Smith into German left him doubting that the translators had even read, much less understood, the master's work.[7]

Georg Sartorius was not an original thinker, but throughout his long career he combined the roles of historian, economist, political scientist, publicist, and court advisor. His circle of friends and acquaintances included members of Germany's literary, cultural, and intellectual elite, such as Johann Wolfgang von Goethe, with whom he and his wife carried on a long correspondence. Caroline Sartorius's inheritance from a wealthy uncle in Leipzig enabled the family to purchase in 1827 a manor house (*Schloß*) called Waltershausen near Saal an der Saale in northern Bavaria. King Ludwig I of Bavaria conferred a patent of nobility on the family permitting descendants to use the aristocratic name von Waltershausen after the family surname. Georg died the following year.[8]

Named in honor of Goethe, Wolfgang, the second son of Georg and Caroline Sartorius von Waltershausen, carried on the family's distinguished academic tradition at Göttingen. Wolfgang Sartorius was almost as well known in geology and mineralogy as his father had been in economics. Born in 1809, he taught, throughout his entire career at Göttingen, from 1842 to his death in 1876. His specialty was volcanism, especially Etna in Sicily and the volcanoes in Iceland. He undertook long scientific excursions to study these natural phenomena, sometimes in the company of his good friends and colleagues, the mathematician and astronomer Karl Friedrich Gauss and the chemist Robert Wilhelm Bunsen. Wolfgang's position at Göttingen and his scientific publications ranked him, as well, among Germany's intellectual and scientific elite; his son, August, thus grew up in an academic environment where some of the nation's most gifted persons may have shown up for Sunday dinner.[9]

7. Charles Gide and Charles Rist, *A History of Economic Doctrines*, 7th ed. (London, 1948), 122; Wilhelm Roscher, *Geschichte der deutschen Nationalökonomie* (Munich, 1874), 601, 615; Harald Winkel, *Die deutsche Nationalökonomie im neunzehnten Jahrhundert* (Darmstadt, 1977), 10, 13, 16; *Allgemeine deutsche Biographie*, 30 (Berlin, 1890, repr. 1970), 390–4.

8. *Allgemeine deutsche Biographie*, 30 (Berlin, 1890, repr. 1970), 394–5; Johann Wolfgang von Goethe, *Goethes Briefwechsel mit Georg und Caroline Sartorius von Waltershausen 1801–1825* (Weimar, 1931).

9. *Der Grosse Brockhaus*, 16 (Leipzig, 1934), 532; *Allgemeine deutsche Biographie*, 30 (Berlin, 1890, repr. 1970), 394; Götz von Selle, *Die Georg-August-Universität zu Göttingen, 1737–1937* (Göttingen, 1937), 308; Wolfgang Sartorius von Waltershausen, *Gauss: A Memorial*, trans. Helen Worthington-Gauss (Colorado Springs, Colo.,

The Göttingen connection is fundamental for understanding August's attraction to the academic study of America. Göttingen, the town where he grew up and later studied economics and history, had strong ties to the Anglo-Saxon world. Its university was founded in 1734 by the English King George II in his dual role as Elector of Hannover; Göttingen was Germany's outstanding reform university in the late eighteenth century. Göttingen pioneered changes in curriculum by moving away from the traditional medieval university faculties of law, medicine, and theology; introduced the natural sciences as components of the philosophical faculty; and stressed the combined functions of teaching and research in selecting professors. Göttingen's fame was such that Benjamin Franklin visited in 1766 to prepare plans for what would become the University of Pennsylvania.[10]

Göttingen's reputation for educational excellence and its ties to the English-speaking world attracted some of the first American students to study in Germany after 1800. Among the prominent Americans who studied there in the first half of the nineteenth century were the historian George Bancroft (later ambassador to Germany), rhetorician Edward Everett, poet Henry Wadsworth Longfellow, banker J. Pierpont Morgan, and historian and confidant of Chancellor Bismarck, John Lothrop Motley. Both Georg and Wolfgang Sartorius von Waltershausen had American students attending their lectures, so it is distinctly possible that August had met visiting Americans in his father's academic circles or during his own studies. Göttingen had one of the largest libraries in Germany, including an outstanding collection of American books, and permitted students to write their dissertations in English.[11]

Göttingen attracted American and other foreign students, too, because its faculty counted among its ranks numerous "political professors," men who spoke up for academic freedom, promoted resistance to tyranny, and expressed for their fellow citizens the hope for German

1966). Wolfgang Sartorius's research trips took years to complete and may account for the fact that he was nearly forty years old before he married; in 1848 he married Marie Emilie Lappenberg, the daughter of the Hamburg archivist and historian Johann Martin Lappenberg, a collaborator with Wolfgang's father, Georg, in a history of the Hansa cities. The couple had one daughter, Marianne Caroline, born in 1850, and one son, August, born in 1852. We are indebted to Frank Hering's research in the church archives in Göttingen for this information.

10. McClelland, *State, Society and University*, 36–47; Klaus Epstein, *The Genesis of German Conservatism* (Princeton, 1966), 106; Paul G. Buchloh and Walter T. Rix, *American Colony of Göttingen* (Göttingen, 1976), 13–14.

11. Buchloh and Rix, *American Colony*, 15–17, 116–19, 134–6, 151–5.

unification and the creation of a liberal, humane state. The "Göttingen Seven" became a *cause célèbre* in Germany in 1837 when seven professors were fired over their refusal to take an oath of allegiance to a new and reactionary constitution for the Duchy of Hannover; one of them, in fact, Joseph Tellkampf, came as a refugee to the United States and taught at Union College and Columbia University in New York before returning to Germany and serving in the Reichstag in the 1870s. Other Göttingen professors served as deputies in the Frankfurt Assembly of 1848, the very embodiment of German liberalism in the first half of the nineteenth century. Two of these professors, Franz von Holtzendorff and Georg Waitz, taught August when he was a student.[12]

Education

August Sartorius von Waltershausen did not have a happy childhood: his father's research trips sometimes lasted for years, and his mother was of little significance in his life. Moreover, Göttingen was a small provincial town with several thousand inhabitants, despite its reputation for academic excellence. Sartorius soon decided to explore the world, either by emigrating or by becoming an officer in the Prussian army.[13] His father sent him for his secondary education to a boarding school in Ilfeld near Göttingen, and he attended the Protestant *lycée* at Strasbourg (which had recently been annexed) from the fall of 1872 to the spring of 1873. In April 1873, he did his *Abitur* [final secondary school examination] shortly before his twenty-first birthday.[14] Sartorius then eagerly began his military service. In October 1873, he returned to Alsace for a year as a member of the fifth squadron in the cavalry.[15] While in the military, he met Stephan zu Putlitz and Karl von Schlözer, with whom he formed a close friendship. Putlitz died soon, but Sartorius remained very close to Schlözer for several decades until Schlözer's death in 1917.[16]

---

12. Walter P. Metzger, *Academic Freedom in the Age of the University* (New York, 1964), 111; on Tellkampf, *Parlamentarisches Handbuch für den Deutschen Reichstag* (Berlin, 1874), 143.
13. *Memoirs*, 11, 22, 48.
14. See the *vita* page of his economics dissertation, *Die wirthschaftlich-sociale Bedeutung des obligatorischen Zuschusses der Unternehmer zu den Arbeiterversicherungskassen: Ein Beitrag zur Kritik der Arbeiterfrage* (Göttingen, 1880), for biographical information.
15. *Qualifications-Attest*, dated October 1, 1874 (Waltershausen Seminar, Munich).
16. *Memoirs*, 61, 64, 348. Regarding Sartorius's friendship with Karl von Schlözer, see the

In October 1874, Sartorius rather reluctantly began his law studies at the University of Göttingen. The town bored him. "I read a lot, [especially about] geography and travel."[17] He and Putlitz took their first examination in late 1876. Next, he halfheartedly began to prepare his dissertation with the certainty that he would not pursue a legal career. In 1877, Sartorius received his doctorate in Heidelberg for two Latin essays he had written in six weeks.

At age twenty-five, Sartorius and Putlitz decided to pursue a second course of study, namely, economics. They sought out one of Germany's finest teachers of the discipline, J. A. R. von Helferich. Helferich taught economics as an abstract subject based on the revealed truths of the British Classical School, which was not fundamentally different from the economics of August's grandfather, Georg Sartorius. Helferich had taught for ten years at Göttingen in the 1850s and 1860s at the same faculty as Wolfgang Sartorius, August's father, before moving on to the University of Munich. But the personal connection here simply added to Helferich's drawing card as probably the most gifted teacher and devoted dissertation advisor in economics in Germany in the mid-nineteenth century. Other well-known economists, like Lujo Brentano and Georg Friedrich Knapp, had also studied with the master and testified to his virtues in inspiring students to pursue the subject and to his presence in the classroom. Helferich contributed nothing new conceptually to the discipline and has been largely forgotten by posterity. But his contemporaries prized his lectures for their faithful rendering of Classical School giants like Smith and Ricardo – their mathematical bent – and for Helferich's rescue from oblivion of the work of Johann Heinrich von Thünen, now regarded as one of the predecessors of the Marginalist School of economics. Intellectually, Helferich appealed to Sartorius (and possibly to Putlitz as well) in that he subscribed neither to the Historical School nor to the Manchester School:[18]

Although I had no specific objections to the Historical School and was unable to reconcile myself to the superficial approach of the Manchester School, I could hardly resign myself to either rather conspicuously acclaimed school of

letter he wrote to Karl's brother on May 20, 1925, which mentions "an unwavering friendship" that lasted "throughout 43 years" (Waltershausen Seminar, Munich).
   Stephan Gans Edler zu Putlitz (1854–83) published his doctoral thesis, *Werth, Preis und Arbeit. Ein Beitrag zur Lehre vom Werthe* (Berlin, 1880), and a monograph: *J. P. Proudhon. Sein Leben und seine positiven Ideen* (Berlin, 1881).
17. *Memoirs*, 50, 73 (quotation).
18. The German Historical School of economics developed as an institutionalist opposition to classical economics, whose approach it considered as timeless and atomistic.

economics. Instinctively, I eschewed everything considered erudite by the dominant school. The school is akin to a party in both method and spirit. Anybody who joins such a movement, as a follower rather than as a leader (which was out of the question for me as one of the younger people concerned), had to forfeit part of his personal development. I therefore went to Munich, where freedom of scholarship prevailed [. . .].[19]

Helferich advised his students to begin with Adam Smith, David Ricardo, Thomas Malthus, and John Stuart Mill before moving on to the leading German authors (Hermann, Thünen, List), and to conclude with Carey and Bastiat, possibly supplemented by Marx.[20] In turn, Sartorius recommended these same authors to his own students.[21]

The Manchester School's teachings still dominated the German economics profession in the 1860s and 1870s, though it was coming under attack from a variety of directions. Helferich's mentor, F. B. W. von Hermann, told any student who would listen to read *The Edinburgh Review* and *The Economist* in the original to improve his English language skills. Hermann also told students, "the English are further along than we Germans are," not only because they were still the world's leading manufacturers, the "Workshop of the World," but also because they had perfected their understanding of the workings of the market through Classical economics.[22]

The second economist to influence the future specialist in American labor was Georg Hanssen, another fixture of Göttingen's intellectual

The Historical School attempted to situate economic activity in its historical and social contexts. Its protagonists include an "older" generation (Wilhelm Roscher, Bruno Hildebrand, Karl Knies) and a "younger" one (Gustav Schmoller, Karl Bücher, Lujo Brentano, and others).

The Manchester School was based on classical economics (David Ricardo and others) and advocated free trade and noninterference of the state in social and economic affairs. Its German protagonists included Prince-Smith, Max Wirth, and Adolph Soetbeer.

19. *Memoirs*, 127. On Helferich (1817–92), see Walter Bräuer, "Johann von Helferich's prestaties op het gebied der economie," *Tijdschrift voor economie en sociologie*, 3 (1937), 321–49; *Encyclopaedia of the Social Sciences*, 7 (New York, 1932), 317; *Neue Deutsche Biographie (NDB)*, 8 (Berlin, 1969), 468–9.

20. *Memoirs*, 124.

21. In a letter dated March 29, 1887, Sartorius told his student Karl Johannes Fuchs: "My examination stresses the history of economics based on the premise that familiarity with the fundamental doctrines of leading political economists, such as Smith, Malthus, Ricardo, Thünen, List, and Marx, is essential for any study of political economics." (Tübingen: Universitätsbibliothek, Sign. Md 875–305.)

22. Hermann's remark quoted by Georg F. Knapp, *Einführung in einige Hauptgebiete der Nationalökonomie. Siebenundzwanzig Beiträge zur Sozialwissenschaft* (Munich, 1925), 316; on the influence of Great Britain in Germany and the prestige of Classical

life and a colleague of Wolfgang Sartorius. Hanssen was so devoted to
the university that he returned there in 1869 after accepting a call in
1860 to teach at the University of Berlin, regarded as Germany's most
renowned and perhaps the best in the world then. Unlike the classes
taught by Helferich, Hanssen's lectures were decidedly unpopular. They
were packed with dry facts and rarely conveyed any coherent conclusions. His style of delivery was "meticulous, but reserved."[23] Despite
these shortcomings, he was well regarded as a dissertation advisor, or
Doktorvater, and performed pathbreaking research in the history of
agriculture. He was happiest digging into obscure archives and specialized in the development of agriculture in his home province of
Schleswig-Holstein on the Danish border. Hanssen also taught statistics
and public finance, essential for the future civil servants who made up
the majority of students attending his lectures, and he helped establish
at Göttingen the first forestry school at any university in Germany.[24]

Hanssen belonged to a branch of the economics discipline known as
the Historical School. Like the more famous members of the "older"
Historical School – Wilhelm Roscher, Karl Knies, and Bruno Hildebrand – Hanssen first studied economics in the 1820s and 1830s from
professors trained in the Classical tradition, like Georg Sartorius and
Heidelberg's Karl Heinrich Rau. But unlike Rau, Hermann, or
Helferich, who never deviated far from the tradition, Hanssen sought to
uncover in historical archives the working out of the laws of supply and
demand and the proper role for the state. Like Helferich, Hanssen pursued his own eclectic course and did his best to avoid the conflict
between the Historical School and the Classical School. He used Rau's
Classical School textbook, *Lehrbuch der politischen Ökonomie* (first
edition, 1827), for decades the standard at German universities, while
pursuing his own research agenda in empirical and nontheoretical economic history.[25] Hanssen's most important lesson for Sartorius von

School economics, see Winkel, *Die deutsche Nationalökonomie,* 38–49, and Paul
Kennedy, *The Rise of Anglo-German Antagonism, 1860–1914* (New York, 1984).

23. G. F. Knapp, "Georg Hanssen," in *Biographische Blätter,* 1 (1895), 95–101, here 96.

24. On Georg Hanssen (1809–94): *Brockhaus Konversations-Lexikon,* 8 (Leipzig, 1931),
    169; *Encyclopaedia of the Social Sciences,* 7 (New York, 1932), 267–8; Knapp, *Ein-
    führung,* 328–50; *NDB,* 7 (Berlin, 1968), 638–9. Regarding the two periods that
    Hanssen spent in Göttingen, see H. Hanssen (ed.), "Lebenserinnerungen des Agrarhis-
    torikers und Nationalökonomen Georg Hanssen," *Zeitschrift der Gesellschaft für
    Schleswig-Holsteinische Geschichte,* 40 (1910), 1–180, 114–32, 143–9.

25. Dieter Krüger in *Nationalökonomen im wilhelminischen Deutschland, 1890–1918*
    (Göttingen, 1984), 13–15, stresses the eclectic and heterodox nature of the profession;

Waltershausen concerned "the need to rely on direct experience rather than on books and doctrines. Given the opportunity, he studied people, [such as] farmers and large landowners in the countryside [and] artisans and merchants in the towns." This approach was compatible with Sartorius's "drive to discover the world [. . .]. Out into the open air, off to distant lands, that appealed to me."[26]

August Sartorius von Waltershausen's longtime colleague at Strasbourg, Georg F. Knapp, ten years his senior, was also a student of Helferich and Hanssen. When Knapp first approached Hanssen in 1863, then still in Berlin, about learning economics under his tutelage, Hanssen dismissed the twenty-year-old with the words "Go read Rau." Hanssen eventually relented and took Knapp on, but the student's desire to pursue Historical School methodology stemmed not from his rejection of the Classical School per se but from his quest for the more applied and factually oriented style of economics Hanssen embraced. Sartorius's academic training followed a trajectory similar to Knapp's: initial studies under the auspices of a Classical School–trained professor, then further study in the Historical School methods. Sartorius's second examination field at Göttingen was history, a subject he studied with one of the deans of German history, Georg Waitz, and with Georg Pauli, a historian of England.[27]

Historicism was "in the air" of German academic disciplines at the time, as Sartorius later explained. Friedrich Karl von Savigny in Berlin was teaching law as a subject that responded to the needs of the time when it was written, as historical jurisprudence; the Brothers Grimm had transformed philology into a historical discipline. Economics was not alone as a social science in following the path of historical development to uncover the laws of change.[28]

see Joseph Schumpeter, *History of Economic Analysis* (New York, 1954), 503, on Rau's textbook, and for a general discussion of the Historical School, Georg Jahn, "Die Historische Schule der Nationalökonomie und ihr Ausklang," in Antonio Montaner (ed.), *Geschichte der Volkswirtschaftslehre* (Cologne, 1967), 41–52. For discussions of the Historical School in English, see Eric Roll, *A History of Economic Thought* (3rd ed., Englewood Cliffs, N.J., 1966), 303–11, and Howard D. Marshall, *The Great Economists: A History of Economic Thought* (New York, 1967), 183–200.

26. *Memoirs*, 108–9.

27. Georg F. Knapp, *Aus der Jugend eines deutschen Gelehrten* (Stuttgart, 1927), 125, and idem, *Einführung*, 328–35; on Pauli and Waitz, see *Brockhaus Conversations-Lexikon*, 12 (Leipzig, 1885), 758–9, and 16, 458–9.

28. August Sartorius von Waltershausen, *Deutsche Wirtschaftsgeschichte, 1815–1914* (Jena, 1921), 324, and Woodruff D. Smith, *Politics and the Sciences of Culture in Germany 1840–1920* (New York and Oxford, 1991), 67–9.

When August Sartorius von Waltershausen first enrolled as a law student at the University of Strasbourg in 1873, he had his first exposure to a Historical School professor quite unlike Hanssen at Göttingen. The Strasbourg professor who would become Germany's best-known and most influential economist in the late nineteenth century was Gustav von Schmoller, the star of the "younger" Historical School. The university there had opened in 1872 as a model of the latest German pedagogy and as an experiment featuring the newest academic disciplines. The traditional home for *Staatswissenschaft*, or economics, was in the philosophical faculty; at Strasbourg economics was lodged in the law faculty, the usual training ground for civil servants whose education, many believed, had to include an applied version of the discipline.[29]

Only thirty-six years old when called to the chair at Strasbourg, Schmoller was on the cutting edge of the field in the 1870s. He attracted enthusiastic students by the score through his energetic lectures, his statistical and empirical approaches, and his outright rejection of the deductive methods of the Manchester School of classical economics. He denied the notion that the laws of economics had been handed down on stone tablets to Adam Smith and David Ricardo, requiring their successors simply to fill in the gaps. Instead he called on his students to devote years of work on specialized monographs on all aspects of economic life across national borders and time. Only then, when all the spadework required to uncover the laws of economic development had been performed (once he estimated that thirty years of work would be required), could a true science of economics be written. A man not known for his modesty, Schmoller assumed that he would write the great synthetic work himself.[30]

Schmoller's advice to students was to learn languages, travel to foreign lands, take notes, compile statistics, and provide a historical

29. Nicholas W. Balabkins, *Not by Theory Alone . . . The Economics of Gustav von Schmoller and Its Legacy to America* (Berlin, 1988), 34–42, on the Strasbourg years, and John Eldon Craig, "'A Mission for German Learning': The University of Strasbourg and Alsation Society 1870–1918" (unpublished dissertation, Stanford University, 1973), 105, on Schmoller's impact.
30. Balabkins, *Not by Theory Alone*, 17–36. See also Friedhelm Lövenich, "'Unter Zurückdrängung der sozialrevolutionären Wühlerei . . .' – Gustav Schmollers Kathedersozialismus," *Leviathan*, 17 (1989), 527–39; Hartmut Harnisch, "Gustav von Schmoller und der gesellschaftliche Wandel seiner Zeit," in Jürgen Kocka et al. (eds.), *Von der Arbeiterbewegung zum modernen Sozialstaat. Festschrift für Gerhard A. Ritter zum 65. Geburtstag* (Munich [etc.], 1994), 560–81.

framework for studying the laws of economic development. Zealous students in his seminars were known to pound on their desks and shout "Facts, facts, more facts" in enthusiastic appreciation of Schmoller's obsession with the positivist approach to economics as a social science. Sartorius never embraced Schmoller's rejection of the Classical School, nor did he join the proposals for state-sponsored reforms of Schmoller's Verein für Sozialpolitik (Union of Social Policy), but he did learn English, French, Italian, and Spanish well enough to research in those languages and traveled extensively throughout Europe and North America. And his three volumes and numerous essays on the American labor movement past and present would have met with Schmoller's approval as building blocks in the edifice of his notion of economic science.[31]

As the first chair holder in economics at the new university, Schmoller, in fact, started a tradition of labor studies at Strasbourg that endured for a generation. Upon his arrival in 1872, Schmoller began researching the history of the weavers' and clothiers' guilds from the Middle Ages to the nineteenth century. His successor in 1880 was Lujo Brentano, Germany's acknowledged expert in British trade unionism and the English working class; Brentano's student, Heinrich Herkner, wrote a dissertation about the miseries of textile labor in the Alsatian mills, a work that set off a controversy when it was published in 1888 and prompted the extension of factory inspection laws to the new province. Schmoller and Brentano's colleague, Knapp, arrived in 1874 and published several works on agricultural labor and the impact of serfdom's abolition. Until the 1890s, the combined school of law and public policy at Strasbourg was known as one of the best, most forward-looking, and engaged in Germany.[32]

Shortly after he began his study of economics (from early August until late October 1877), Sartorius's urge to discover the world led him to travel to Southern Europe, the Canary Islands, and Tangier. His choice of destinations was based on his perspective on stages in economic history, which fully reflected the tradition of the Historical School.[33]

31. Balabkins, *Not by Theory Alone,* 57–8, and Otto Mayer, *Die Kaiser-Wilhelms-Universität Strassburg: Ihre Entstehung und Entwicklung* (Leipzig and Berlin, 1922), 29, on the students' reaction.
32. Balabkins, *Not by Theory Alone,* 36–8; James Sheehan, *The Career of Lujo Brentano. A Study of Liberalism and Reform in Imperial Germany* (Chicago [etc.], 1966), 97; Craig, "Mission for German Learning," 457–60, and Knapp, *Einführung,* 142–6.
33. Since the 1850s and 1860s, with the revival of political liberalism, Historical School economists had sought to find an intellectual middle ground between the deductive and

A political economist wishing to travel abroad could learn more in England or France than in the southern countries of my travels. Nevertheless, I feel that I made the right choice. Not yet a full-fledged political economist, I was not equipped to deal with the most advanced economies on site. Beginners should address simple problems and relationships that exist as isolated entities or are at least easy to conceptualize. [. . .] The areas I visited were still predominantly agricultural regions that relied on simple means of transport; their national economies were in far more rudimentary stages than [those of] their modern developed counterparts. Clearly, beginners are more suitable than experienced professionals for understanding other beginners.[34]

While Sartorius began this trip with Karl von Schlözer, the two parted amicably after several days. Sartorius learned the advantages of traveling alone, especially the necessity to become better acquainted with the local population.

Moreover, people travelling in groups are too apt to engage in common diversions and are less inclined to seek out other people who might teach them new things. Any traveller who sincerely wishes to learn and to advance intellectually should – except for treks through the wilderness – remain alone. Possible evening hours spent in solitude are to be used for reflection about events and for writing. The

ahistorical elements of Classical School economics and the inductive, conditional, and developmental social science that many maintained must take into account national traditions, character, and history. Woodruff D. Smith has termed this quest the "search for a science of culture." The central dilemma in the 1870s was to transform economics into an evolutionary science, especially given the popular vogue of Darwin's biological theories, which incorporated natural law and historical change in one all-encompassing package. Historical School economists began the process by sorting the historical data of economics into descriptive categories; these could be easily transformed into normative and teleological descriptions known as *stages*. Stage theories of development apparently met the test of incorporating both the inductive and the deductive, the absolute and the conditioned, the evolutionary and the nomological in perfect unison. Cultural geography, anthropology, sociology, and philosophy, as well as economics, all felt the influence of stage theorists as diverse as Herbert Spencer in Great Britain and William Graham Sumner in the United States, or of economists in Germany like Wilhelm Roscher, Bruno Hildebrand, and Karl Rodbertus. Each stage theorist had his own scheme, but all these schemes tended to fit either chronological categories or a hierarchical ordering, sometimes a combination of both. Usually Great Britain stood at the summit of the developmental pyramid, while hunter-gatherer societies outside Europe formed the base. Indeed, it was the stages of development explicit in Karl Marx's analysis that most intrigued Establishment German economists in the late nineteenth century, without accepting, of course, Marx's labor theory of value, his analysis of class, or his call for revolution. Smith, *Politics and the Sciences of Culture,* 87–99, 129–61; Edgar Salin, *Geschichte der Volkswirtschaftslehre* (Berlin, 1923), 76–94.

34. *Memoirs,* 119.

days may satisfy intellectual appetites without any other concerns, which inevitably arise in the course of group travel.[35]

Sartorius believed that he learned three major lessons from his first research trip:

First, methods for investigating conditions, such as ways to get people talking, ways to prove that one is a disinterested observer, ways to acquire various recommendations. Second came an understanding of the relativity of all economic situations. In Germany, comparisons enabled me to understand many things that I had previously taken for granted. Third, my involvement in areas outside economics, namely class, culture, and language, enabled me to understand the relationship between the different aspects of life amidst the populace.[36]

By late 1879, Sartorius had fallen in love with his cousin Charlotte Marie (Lotty) von Kap-herr. His desire to marry her encouraged him to accelerate his leisurely pace of study. At Göttingen, Hanssen allowed him to complete both his doctoral requirements and his *Habilitation* [qualifying requirements for lecturing in a university], with a single publication. Such an opportunity was highly unusual for aspiring professors like Sartorius. They could not apply for positions; they had to wait to be called by the current faculty of a department who were expected to know the qualifications, ideology, links to established scholars, and potential of those in the applicant pool. To be considered a candidate in the pool usually required a second significant scholarly work, or *Habilitation,* and a vote of the Faculty Senate (in his case, the senior colleagues of his father, Wolfgang Sartorius) entitling candidates to teach as unsalaried instructors and bear the title *Privatdozent.* Sartorius wrote his doctoral thesis cum *Habilitation* on a topic that was hotly debated at the time, namely, assistance to senior citizens and invalids. While he advocated state intervention in this area, he differed from the "Socialists of the Chair"[37] in his rejection of any form of mandatory insurance. Both Hanssen and the second reader, Adolph

35. Ibid., 120–1.
36. Ibid., 121–2.
37. The *Katheder-Sozialisten,* or Socialists of the Chair (academic socialists), agreed with the social democrats in recognizing the existence of a "social question." But while the social democrats attempted to overthrow capitalism, the Socialists of the Chair were content to work for social reform and relied on the state as it then was. The group included many adherents of the Historical School (e.g., Gustav Schmoller, Bruno Hildebrand, and Lujo Brentano).

Soetbeer (the father of German gold coinage), were delighted with this project.[38] Within months of the completion of Sartorius's dissertation, the Philosophical Faculty at Göttingen approved his *Habilitation* and appointed him *Privatdozent* that same year.

The United States of America

Before marrying Lotty von Kap-herr and establishing himself as a university professor, Sartorius embarked on a major journey across the United States. His attraction to the country was far from fortuitous. Since 1876, interest in the New World had increased dramatically. During the Centennial celebration, dozens of German officials representing government, industry, journalism, and academia came to the United States, not only to marvel at the machines and tools on display in Philadelphia, but also to register the birth of a new model of capitalist industrialization, a model with perhaps more to teach Germany than the British example could. The more than two dozen books and pamphlets on America published in 1876 and 1877 provide a measure of the intensity of Germany's sudden fascination with the United States as the future industrial colossus of the Western world.[39]

German delegations examined American railroads, factories, working conditions, worker housing, canal and waterway usage, the functions of industrial trade associations like the American Iron and Steel Association, mass production techniques, tool design, technology, the U.S. Patent Office, and the impact of protective tariffs on industry. Virtually all the commentary focused on the economic performance of the nation and little, tellingly, on the reasons Americans celebrated 100 years of independence from Great Britain, representative government, or democracy. Germans wrote virtually nothing about sectional reconciliation marking the real end of the Civil War era or much about the

---

38. August Sartorius von Waltershausen, *Die wirthschaftlich-sociale Bedeutung des obligatorischen Zuschusses; Memoirs*, 137. On Soetbeer (1814–92), see *Annals of the American Academy of Political and Social Science*, 3 (1892–3), 513–40. Gustav von Schmoller and Adolph Wagner wrote critical reviews of the study. Schmoller's response appears in his review article, "Ältere und neuere Literatur über Hilfskassenwesen," *Jahrbuch für Gesetzgebung, Verwaltung und Volkswirthschaft*, 5 (1881), 281–2; Wagner's review was published in the *Zeitschrift für die gesammte Staatswissenschaft*, 37 (1881), 677.

39. Post, *1876: A Centennial Exhibit*, 185; see the bibliography on the Philadelphia Centennial in Evelyn Kroker, *Die Weltausstellungen im 19. Jahrhundert [. . .]* (Göttingen, 1975), 216–17, for a comprehensive list of German commentary.

soon to be concluded experiment of Reconstruction in the South. What little they did write about the political dimension of the American experiment in democracy was a critical glance at the corruption of the Grant Administration, the spoilsmanship of political parties, or a re-hashing of the outlandish scale of theft practiced by the Tweed Ring in New York City.[40]

The reasons Germans focused exclusively on the economic dimension in their enthusiasm for the United States originated, first, in the general recession in the wake of the crash of 1873, which placed economic pol-icy at the top of the nation's agenda, and, second, in Germany's embar-rassing defeat in the Centennial competition for international prizes. The 1873 Panic ended nearly a quarter century of rapid economic expansion in Germany and throughout Western Europe and inaugurated another quarter century of what some have called *profitless prosperity* and oth-ers have termed the *Great Depression*. By the time the Centennial opened in May 1876, the recession was entering its fourth year, and the pro-scription of economists trained in the Classical School – for the gov-ernment to do nothing – had begun to sound hollow. German observers in 1876 came to Philadelphia looking for answers to their own economic problems, largely ignoring the obvious fact that the American economy, too, had been mired in recession since 1873.[41]

The newly formed Central Association of German Industry lobbied for changes in economic policy inspired by the American model. The Central Association published a lavishly illustrated compendium enti-tled *Die Industrie Amerikas,* arguing that tariff protection and patent laws were responsible for America's industrial greatness. The group also sent its general secretary to the United States to report back on the techniques American trade associations employed, such as lobbying,

---

40. Among the more important works on economic themes, see Georg Seelhorst, *Die Philadelphia Ausstellung und was sie uns lehrt* (Nördlingen, 1878); Arthur von Studnitz, *Nordamerikanische Arbeiterverhältnisse* (Berlin, 1877); Hermann Grothe, *Die Industrie Amerikas* (Berlin, 1877) on tariffs, patents, and Henry C. Carey; Chris-tian Mosler, *Die Wasserstrassen der Vereinigten Staaten* (Hamburg, 1877); Friedrich Goldschmidt, *Die Weltausstellung in Philadelphia und die deutsche Industrie* (Berlin, 1877). On politics, see the critical assessment of two returning emigrants: Friedrich Kapp, *Aus und über Amerika* (Berlin, 1876), and John H. Becker, *Die Hundertjährige Republik* (Stuttgart, 1876).

41. On the impact of the 1870s recession on economic policy, see Ivo Nikolai Lambi, *Free Trade and Protection in Germany, 1868–1879* (Wiesbaden, 1963); Fritz Stern, *Gold and Iron: Bismarck, Bleichröder and the Building of the German Empire* (New York, 1977), Ch. 9; Hans Rosenberg, *Grosse Depression und Bismarckzeit* (Berlin, 1967); and Helmut Böhme, *Deutschlands Weg zur Grossmacht* (Cologne [etc.], 1966).

political contributions, and public relations campaigns, to promote leg-islation favorable to their interests. The Central Association was suc-cessful in electing its general secretary, Hermann Grothe, to the Reichs-tag in 1877, where he helped secure passage of a patent law patterned after the British and American models, and helped shape in 1878 and 1879 a dramatic turnabout in German economic policy when free trade met its demise and tariff protection for agricultural commodities, tex-tiles, iron, and steel was reinstituted. By American standards the tariff protection was modest indeed, but it was the success of the tariff in the United States and the scandal over Germany's "defeat" in Philadelphia that had set the policy change in motion.[42]

The abandonment of free trade in 1879 meant far more than a sim-ple change in taxation or trade; it represented the eclipse of the Classi-cal School both as the official policy of the state and as the mainstay of the German economics profession. The American economist and pro-tectionist Henry C. Carey enjoyed a brief vogue, for instance. An engrav-ing of Carey provided the frontispiece for the Central Association's *Die Industrie Amerikas,* and his "refutation" of Ricardo's pessimistic theory of rent won admiring references to the American thinker in Reichstag debates on economic policy. One of Bismarck's ministers had stunned the Reichstag and the nation in 1875 when he proffered the solution of Classical School economists for the recession: wages and prices must fall even further; bankruptcies and unemployment must climb before the "invisible hand" righted the scales once more and economic growth could resume. Such advice was cold comfort indeed to a nation at a loss to deal with the initial successes of the Social Democratic Party in the polls of 1874 and 1877 and the growing disaffection of the working class that the election results represented. The eclipse of free trade marked the beginning of a more activist role for the state and the inau-guration of Bismarck's social welfare schemes in the 1880s to win back working-class voters.[43]

The sensation caused by the Centennial and the rapid pace of popu-lation growth and industrialization led August Sartorius von Walters-

42. Henry Axel Bück, *Der Centralverband deutscher Industrieller* (Berlin, 1902), 1, 148–72 on Grothe's activities; *Verhandlungen, Mittheilungen und Berichte des Cen-tralverbandes deutscher Industrieller,* Nos. 1–3 (Berlin and Düsseldorf, 1876–7); Her-mann Grothe, *Das Patentgesetz für das Deutsche Reich* (Berlin, 1877).
43. Winkel, *Die deutsche Nationalökonomie,* 25–8; J. G. R., "Henry C. Carey in Germany," *The Penn Monthly,* 7 (November 1876), 894–7; Siegfried von Kardorff, *Wilhelm von Kardorff: Ein nationaler Parlamentarier im Zeitalter Bismarcks und Wilhelm II, 1828–1907* (Berlin, 1936), 116–29, and Stürmer, *Das ruhelose Reich,* 208–30.

hausen and many other Germans to believe that America had surpassed
Great Britain, a fact production statistics would confirm by 1890, and
achieved a new stage of capitalist development. The logic of stage theories of economics made the conclusion inescapable that America was
a new model, and that alone made it worthy of study and analysis. C.
Vann Woodward has called this view of America in its broadest application "the Silver Screen in the West." No genius was required, furthermore, to see that clues to the resolution of Germany's own social
problems might be found in the United States.

It stood to reason that the most advanced manufacturing techniques
in the world would generate the most sophisticated working-class
response. R. Laurence Moore has demonstrated that even the European
Left shared this view of the American working class as the world's most
advanced until Haymarket, Homestead, and Pullman shattered the illusion. Sartorius planned to build a career on what proved to be an illusion, though he could not have known that in 1880 when he completed
his dissertation in economics at Göttingen, a dissertation in the deductive mode of the Classical School, and set off for the United States. He
gambled his career on the assumption that the study of the American
working class would yield valuable lessons for Germany's policy makers and win him academic acclaim and a secure position.[44]

Accordingly, Sartorius embarked on an extensive research trip
throughout North and Central America after completing his studies in
economics. He probably planned his travel itinerary on the basis of
work by Friedrich Ratzel, a founding father of modern geographic science, who had undertaken a major journey across the United States and
Mexico from 1873 to 1875. Ratzel's subsequent books about his travels were widely read.[45] Advice from Kurd von Schlözer (the German

44. Woodward, *The Old World's New World*, 16–39; R. Laurence Moore, *European
Socialists and the American Promised Land* (New York, 1970), 25–81. See the introduction to *Die nordamerikanischen Gewerkschaften unter dem Einfluss der fortschreitenden Productionstechnik* (Berlin, 1886) for the formulation of Sartorius on American modernity.

45. On Ratzel (1844–1904) see Harriet Wanklyn, *Friedrich Ratzel. A Biographical Mem-
oir and Bibliography* (Cambridge, 1961); Robert E. Dickinson, *The Makers of Modern Geography* (New York, 1969), 64–76; C. O. Sauer, "The Formative Years of Ratzel
in the United States," *Annals of the Association of American Geographers*, 61 (1971),
245–54. A description of Ratzel's American itinerary (including a map) appears in
Günther Buttmann, *Friedrich Ratzel. Leben und Werk eines deutschen Geographen,
1844–1904* (Stuttgart, 1977), 43–50.

Ratzel's major publications about his travels across America are *Städte und Kultur-
bilder aus Nordamerika*, 2 vols. (Leipzig, 1876); *Aus Mexiko. Reiseskizzen aus den
Jahren 1874 und 1875* (Breslau, 1878); *Die Vereinigten Staaten von Amerika*, 1:

ambassador in Washington, D.C., since 1872 and an uncle of August's friend Karl) may also have been an important factor.[46]

The discovery of diaries from 1880–1 (which cover most of the trip)[47] and an extensive chapter from the *Memoirs*[48] have facilitated a fairly detailed reconstruction of Sartorius's American journey. In each new city along the way, he used virtually the same modus operandi. After arriving by train or boat, he began by searching for accommodations (at a hotel or boarding house). Next, he hastened to the local German consul, bearing letters of recommendation, and asked to be introduced to local experts on relationships in industry and labor. He subsequently visited entrepreneurs, journalists, and – considerably less often – labor militants. Sartorius supplemented his research with various other activities. He spent many hours exploring natural wildlife and the countryside. He also hunted, attended the theater, and made friends with people he encountered. Figure 1 describes his itinerary.

On October 22, 1880, Sartorius von Waltershausen arrived in New York after a twelve-day crossing aboard the steamship *Suevia*. He roamed the city for nearly a month. He spoke with Alexander Jonas and Serge E. Schewitsch [Ševič], the editors of the *New Yorker Volkszeitung,* a publication founded a few years earlier. Sartorius was impressed with both individuals: Jonas espoused

Physikalische Geographie und Naturcharakter (Munich, 1878), and 2: *Kulturgeographie der Vereinigten Staaten von Nordamerika unter besonderer Berücksichtigung der wirthschaftlichen Verhältnisse* (Munich, 1880). See also Stewart A. Stehlin's edited and translated work, *Sketches of Urban and Cultural Life in North America by Friedrich Ratzel* (New Brunswick, N.J., 1988). Ratzel also wrote a study on Chinese emigration: *Die chinesische Auswanderung. Ein Beitrag zur Kultur- und Handelsgeographie* (Breslau, 1876) – a subject that Sartorius covered in detail during his travels through the United States.

46. Karl von Schlözer, *Menschen und Landschaften. Aus dem Skizzenbuch eines Diplomaten* (Stuttgart, 1926).

47. These American handwritten diaries comprise four notebooks (measuring 7¾ × 6¼ inches), including a total of 504 pages [hereafter cited as *Diaries*]. The first two are in the possession of the Waltershausen Seminar in Munich, and the last two currently belong to Hermann and Lieselotte Wundt in Tübingen. The diaries cover the periods from October 8 through December 24, 1880, and from January 11 through mid-August 1881. No entries appear between February 1 and April 26, 1881, as Sartorius (who was in Mexico during these months) was severely debilitated by a bout of typhus. In addition to his diaries, Sartorius recorded various descriptions and reflections in separate notebooks (of which we found a few) and in letters, especially to Lotty von Kapherr (which we were unable to locate).

48. *Memoirs,* Chapter XIV ("Reise nach Nordamerika [. . .]"), 139–225.

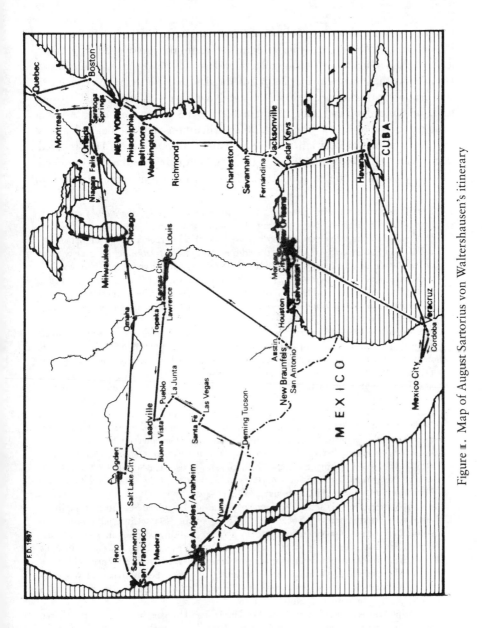

Figure 1. Map of August Sartorius von Waltershausen's itinerary

revolutionary socialism, and Schewitsch was married to the actress Helene von Racowitza (née Dönniges) – the woman for whom the famous German labor leader Ferdinand Lassalle had fought a duel (in which he lost his life) in 1864.[49] He also met the social reformer Felix Adler and attended a lecture on consumer cooperation at the Cooper Union. While in New York, he encountered various trade union leaders, including cabinetmaker Carl Speyer, cigarmaker Adolph Strasser, and typographer Jean Weil. Weil invited him to his home, which was probably the first proletarian abode Sartorius had ever entered. He observed that it was "quite an orderly dwelling" of "good quality" and even contained works by Goethe, Schiller, and Lessing.[50] Sartorius also maintained frequent

49. Karl J. R. Arndt and May E. Olson, *German-American Newspapers and Periodicals 1732–1955* (revised ed., New York and London, 1965), 406.

    Alexander Jonas (1834–1912), born in Berlin with a bourgeois background, came to the United States in 1869; initially the editor of *Die Arbeiterstimme,* he later became cofounder and editor of the *New Yorker Volkszeitung.* He actively supported women's rights and was put up twice as a candidate for Socialist Labor Party congressman. He spoke and wrote exclusively in German. Dirk Hoerder and Christiane Harzig (eds.), *The Immigrant Labor Press in North America, 1840s–1970s. An Annotated Bibliography,* 3 (New York [etc.], 1987), 514.

    Serge Schewitsch (ca. 1847–1911), originally a member of the Russian nobility, arrived in the United States in 1877. This celebrated speaker was fluent in English, German, and French. Ibid., 516; A. Dreyer, "Helene von Schewitsch (Racowitza), geb. v. Dönniges," *Biographisches Jahrbuch und deutscher Nekrolog,* 16 (1911), 198–201, and Helene von Racowitza, *Von Anderen und mir. Erinnerungen aller Art* (Berlin, 1909), 44–147 and 220–86.

50. *Diaries,* 81, 83–4, 88. Felix Adler (1851–1933) arrived in the United States at age six. He later attended Columbia University and obtained his doctorate at Heidelberg. After abandoning his plans to become a rabbi, he established the Society for Ethical Culture in 1876. This society became his life's work. *Dictionary of American Biography* [hereafter *DAB*], 11, Supplement 1 (New York, 1944), 13–14; "The Society for Ethical Culture of New York," in *1876–1896. Twenty Years of the Ethical Movement in New York and Other Cities* (Philadelphia, 1896), 35–42.

    Carl Speyer (1845–?) settled in New York in 1870. He joined Section 1 of the International Workingmen's Association (IWMA – the "First International") and cofounded the national organization of American furniture workers in 1873; he succeeded Friedrich Sorge as general secretary of the IWMA's General Council in New York; he also served as secretary of the Amalgamated Trade and International Union. Samuel Bernstein (ed.), "Papers of the General Council of the International Workingmen's Association, New York: 1872–1876," *Annali Istituto Giangiacomo Feltrinelli,* 4 (1961), 401–549, here 416, Note 3.

    Adolph Strasser (1841?–1939) was born in Austria-Hungary and came to the United States in 1871 or 1872. He cofounded the United Cigarmakers in 1872, the Social Democratic Party in 1873, and the Socialist Labor Party in 1877 and served as the international head of the Cigarmakers International Union of America from 1877 to 1891. H. M. Gitelman, "Adolf Strasser and the Origins of Pure and Simple Unionism," *Labor History,* 6 (1965), 71–82; Patricia A. Cooper, "Whatever Happened to Adolph Strasser?" *Labor History,* 20 (1979), 414–19; and Merl E. Reed, "Strasser, Adolph," in Gary M. Fink (ed.), *Biographical Dictionary of American Labor Leaders* (Westport, Conn., and London, 1984), 532–3.

contact with Udo Brachvogel, a friend of Racowitza's,[51] who edited the widely read *New Yorker Belletristisches Journal.* He was also well acquainted with prominent merchants such as Amsinck and Schwab, as well as with Charles F. Chandler, a chemist who had studied in Göttingen.[52]

From November 18 until December 6, 1880, Sartorius stayed in Philadelphia, where he met the dissident Social Democrat Wilhelm Hasselmann. Hasselmann had been expelled by the German Social Democratic Party for his insurrectionary views a few months earlier. At the time of his encounter with Sartorius, Hasselmann was working with Joh[an]n Most to establish a new party in the United States.[53] Sartorius gathered a wealth of information about the labor movement at the editorial offices of the *Philadelphia Tageblatt,* as Schlesinger (the paper's editor and a former Social Democrat) took a liking to him.[54] He also visited a

Jean Weil (1850–1915) was a German-born printer who emigrated to New York City in 1870. He helped organize the German-American Typographia and served as its secretary from 1876 to 1883. He later became the editor and manager of the *Brewers' Journal,* a trade publication. Stuart B. Kaufman (ed.), *The Samuel Gompers Papers.* Vol. 1: *The Making of a Union Leader, 1850–86* (Urbana and Chicago, 1986), 506.

51. *Diaries,* 44, 83, 91; Arndt and Olson, *German-American Newspapers,* 345–6; Racowitza, *Von Anderen und mir,* 223.

Udo Brachvogel (1835–1913) was born near Danzig/Gdańsk, studied law in Jena and Breslau, and emigrated to the United States in 1867. He initially worked with Joseph Pulitzer as an editor of *Die westliche Post* (St. Louis). In 1875 he was appointed coeditor of the *Belletristisches Journal* in New York. Brachvogel was considered a leading German-American poet. *NDB,* 2 (Berlin, 1955), 503–4; *DAB,* 2 (New York, 1929), 541–3.

52. On Chandler: *DAB,* 3 (New York, 1929), 611–13.

53. *Diaries,* 101, 104, 130. Wilhelm Hasselmann (1844–1916) was born in Bremen and studied natural sciences in Hannover, Göttingen, and Berlin. After becoming a socialist in the mid-1860s, he became the editor of the *Neue Social-Demokrat* in 1871, and was a member of the *Reichstag* from 1874 to 1877 and from 1878 to 1881. Although he was initially an adherent of Lassalle's ideology, his views became progressively more reflective of putschism. After his expulsion (while still officially a member of the Reichstag), he emigrated to the United States via London in August 1880. Following a brief stint with the anarchist movement, Hasselmann soon ceased to be of major significance. Günter Bers, *Wilhelm Hasselmann. Sozialrevolutionärer Agitator und Abgeordneter des deutschen Reichstags* (Cologne, 1973); Wilhelm Liebknecht, *Briefwechsel mit deutschen Sozialdemokraten,* 2: 1878–84, edited by Götz Langkau (Frankfurt am Main, 1988), 101–2; Max Schwarz, *MdR. Biographisches Handbuch der Reichstage* (Hannover, 1965), 339.

54. *Diaries,* 120, 124, 140, 141. At the time, the progressive *Philadelphia Tageblatt* had a circulation of about 8,000. Arndt and Olson, *German-American Newspapers,* 574–5; William F. Kamman, *Socialism in German American Literature* (Philadelphia, 1917), 46.

Sartorius's reference to Schlesinger's membership in the socialist movement in Breslau/Wroclaw suggests that this individual was Alexander Schlesinger (?–?), the brother of the more widely known Maximilian Schlesinger (1855–1902). In 1876 Maximilian became the first editor-in-chief of Breslau's radical newspaper *Die Wahrheit;* Alexander had been in charge of the advertising section. From the outset, the periodical was

mechanized bakery and spent a day at Egg Harbor, a nearby German settlement.[55]

Sartorius was in Baltimore from December 6 to 12. He visited various operations, including a dry dock, a large piano factory, a hair-processing plant, and a tobacco factory.[56] From there he traveled to Washington. The German ambassador Kurd von Schlözer (his good friend Karl's uncle) welcomed him and supplied him with additional letters of recommendation.[57] After visiting the capital, he departed for Richmond on 16 December. Again he toured various local firms, including an iron mill, a cotton mill, and factories manufacturing buckets and tobacco goods.[58] After a few days in Charleston (December 18–22) Sartorius traveled to Savannah (December 22–25), where he observed workers loading cotton onto some ships and removing the material from others.[59] On Christmas Day, he boarded a coasting steamer for Jacksonville. He used this town – the largest in Florida at the time – as his base for roaming the surrounding area (including a trip to St. Augustine). After the new year began, Sartorius traveled by train via Fernandina to Cedar Keys.[60]

Following his arrival in Havana on January 11, 1881, Sartorius explored the island of Cuba until January 24. He visited a sugar plantation and various cigar factories and studied the organizational strength of the cigarmakers' unions.[61] After four days at sea, he disembarked at Veracruz, Mexico, on January 28 and departed for Cordoba the next day. With Winkelmann (a sales representative for sewing machines) he traveled on horseback to the mountain village of San Antonio Huatusco, where he stayed with Dr. Märcker, a physician and farmer of German descent. After spending three days exploring the area and visiting the nearby Hacienda Mirador, owned by his namesake, Don Florentino Sartorius, he returned to Dr. Märcker with a high fever. A bout of typhus kept him bedridden for five weeks; he subsequently spent two weeks recuperating at the Hacienda Mirador. On April 27, Sartorius finally felt strong enough to continue his journey. He traveled to Mexico City (April 30 to May 7) and then returned to Veracruz to depart by ship.[62]

After three days in quarantine (May 13–15), Sartorius was permitted to enter New Orleans. He carefully examined the labor conditions and trade unions of

subject to major repressive measures; Maximilian was imprisoned in 1877, and Alexander "departed for America because of the threat of a trial in the press." Theodor Müller, *45 Führer aus den Anfängen und dem Heldenzeitalter der Breslauer Sozialdemokratie* (Breslau, 1925), 47–50 (quotation from p. 48).

55. *Diaries*, 127, 132–41.   56. Ibid., 157–66.
57. *Memoirs*, 149; *Diaries*, 170, 173. Understandably, this meeting does not appear in Kurd von Schlözer, *Amerikanische Briefe. Mexikanische Briefe 1869–1871. Briefe aus Washington 1871–1881* (Berlin [etc.], 1927).
58. *Diaries*, 182–5.   59. Ibid., 185–202.   60. *Memoirs*, 151–72.
61. *Diaries*, 253, 257–8, 260–2, 269–74. Sartorius wrote an essay about the unions of the Cuban cigarmakers entitled "Die Gewerkschaften der Cigarrenarbeiter in Habana," *Jahrbücher für Nationalökonomie und Statistik*, 38 (1882), 292–305.
62. *Memoirs*, 178–92; *Diaries*, 289–90, 313–14, 321–39.

the local longshoremen and was especially impressed with their powerful Ring. To compensate for the time he had lost in Mexico, he left this port city for Texas by May 18.[63] He traveled by train through Morgan City and Houston and reached Galveston (another port city) a day later. After briefly reconnoitering the town, he journeyed to San Antonio. He arrived on May 21 and encountered four conservative German experts who were studying American agricultural policy. From this Texas city, he went on a two-day excursion (May 23–24) to New Braunfels, a nearby German settlement that had been established in the 1840s.[64] The community fascinated him. He subsequently traveled through Austin across the heavily forested state of Arkansas into southern Missouri to St. Louis, where he arrived on May 27. In this city, where "great modern factories were popping out of the ground like toadstools," he visited the gigantic Beef Canning Company. He resumed his journey in early June.[65]

Sartorius boarded the Missouri-Pacific line to travel via Kansas City, Lawrence, and Topeka to Manitou Springs (a spa near Colorado Springs). On June 7, after a few nature hikes through the area, he traveled to Denver. There he gathered information about the miners and moved on to Leadville (June 8–9). This small town of rugged miners left an indelible impression.[66] He rushed through Buena Vista, Pueblo, La Junta, and Las Vegas to Santa Fe (June 11). From there, his journey took him past Deming, Tucson, Yuma, and Colton to Los Angeles and Anaheim, the nearby settlement of German winegrowers, where he enjoyed a brief respite.[67]

After traveling by train via Madera, Sartorius arrived in San Francisco on June 23. He had heard a lot about this city, the powerful trade unions "that had previously wielded dictatorial power," and the large number of resident Chinese laborers. Accordingly, he spent an entire week studying the community. He gathered information about the local labor movement and the xenophobic agi-

63. *Memoirs*, 192–4; *Diaries*, 341, 345–6, 348–51. More details about the Ring appear in Section I of Essay 3, this volume. For the New Orleans longshoremen in 1880–1, see also Eric Arnesen, *Waterfront Workers of New Orleans. Race, Class, and Politics, 1863–1923* (New York and Oxford, 1991), 60–73.

64. *Memoirs*, 196–200; *Diaries*, 363, 368–76. Following their trip, the German agricultural experts published: Rudolf Meyer, *Ursachen der amerikanischen Concurrenz. Ergebnisse einer Studienreise [. . .]* (Berlin, 1883). Sartorius reviewed this work in *Jahrbücher für Nationalökonomie und Statistik*, 40 (1883), 574–6. For more on New Braunfels, see Albert B. Faust, *Das Deutschtum in den Vereinigten Staaten in seiner geschichtlichen Entwickelung* (Leipzig, 1912), 409, and Ernest G. Fischer, *Marxists and Utopias in Texas* (Burnet, 1980), 58–75.

65. *Memoirs*, 201 (quotation); *Diaries*, 377, 382–3.

66. *Diaries*, 397, 401, 406–9; *Memoirs*, supplement "Leadville, eine junge Stadt im Felsengebirge" (12 pp.); "Eine junge Stadt in dem Felsengebirge Colorado's," *Allgemeine Zeitung*, 16 April 1882, supplement, 1554–6; see also this volume.

67. *Diaries*, 410–12, 416–18; *Memoirs*, supplement, 2; Vincent P. Carosso, "Anaheim, California: A Nineteenth Century Experiment in Commercial Viniculture," *Bulletin of the Business Historical Society*, 23, 2 (1949), 78–86.

tation by labor leader and "loudmouth" Kearney, and visited several sites, including a Chinese cigar factory.[68]

On June 29, Sartorius started his return to the East. He traveled via Sacramento, Reno, Ogden, Salt Lake City, and Omaha to Chicago, where his train arrived on July 6. Anton Caspar Hesing, the owner of the *Illinois Staats-Zeitung*, showed him the municipal waterworks. Afterward, Sartorius visited the Chicago stockyards. Understandably, his program included a visit to Milwaukee (July 10–12), given the German majority among the local population. On July 13 he reached Detroit, where he met Philip Van Patten (the national secretary of the Socialist Labor Party) and learned a lot about producer cooperatives, the Knights of Labor, and the local trade unions.[69] On July 14, he journeyed to Niagara Falls and Oneida in upstate New York. After a pleasant stay in Saratoga Springs, he crossed the border into Canada, where he visited Montreal and Quebec and took a cruise up the St. Lawrence River as far as the Chicoutimi River. He returned to Quebec on August 2. After visiting Boston for three more days, he headed back to New York. He probably arrived back in Germany in late August 1881.[70]

A New Stage in His Life

Sartorius von Waltershausen's return to Europe marked the beginning of a new stage in his life in several respects. In November 1881, he mar-

68. *Diaries,* 426–8, 431–7, 439–40, 443–5 (the quotations are from pp. 428 and 431); *Memoirs,* 221–4. As both the present volume and his major essay "Die Chinesen in den Vereinigten Staaten von Amerika," *Zeitschrift für die gesammte Staatswissenschaft,* 39 (1883), 320–431 reveal, Sartorius's distaste for Kearney's agitation did not stop him from espousing racist views of his own with regard to the Chinese in San Francisco. For more on Denis Kearney (1847–1907) and his racist agitation, see Alexander Saxton, *The Indispensable Enemy. Labor and the Anti-Chinese Movement in California* (Berkeley [etc.], 1971), 116–26, 141–53; *DAB,* 10 (New York, 1933), 268–9.

69. *Diaries,* 452–8, 460–6. Sartorius was apparently unaware that Van Patten was the secretary to both the Socialist Labor Party and the general executive board of the Knights of Labor. Richard J. Oestreicher, *Solidarity and Fragmentation. Working People and Class Consciousness in Detroit, 1875–1900* (Urbana and Chicago, 1986), 92.

Philip Van Patten (?–?) served as national secretary to the Workingmen's Party of the United States (founded in 1876) and was elected national secretary of the Socialist Labor Party in 1879. Philip Foner, *History of the Labor Movement in the United States,* Vol. 1 (New York, 1947), 566; idem, *The Workingmen's Party of the United States* (Minneapolis, 1984), 31, 37, 64, 80, 110; Howard H. Quint, *The Forging of American Socialism. Origins of the Modern Movement* (Indianapolis [etc.], 1953), 23; Bruce C. Nelson, *Beyond the Martyrs. A Social History of Chicago's Anarchists, 1870–1900* (New Brunswick and London, 1988), 45, 67, 69–70, 168.

70. *Diaries,* 467, 471–86, 504; *Memoirs,* 224–5. It is possible that Sartorius met with Carroll D. Wright (1840–1909), the chief of the Massachusetts Bureau of Statistics, in Boston. His *Diaries* mention Wright's work and his address. For Wright's activities, see

ried Lotty von Kap-herr;[71] in the two decades that followed, six children were born to the couple.[72] Despite a severe physical handicap (his right arm and leg were amputated when he was very young), Hermann, the oldest, became a very well-known composer and a highly respected director of the Akademie der Tonkunst in Munich and thus achieved even greater renown than his father.[73]

Shortly after his marriage, Sartorius began teaching American economics at Göttingen and assumed some of the responsibilities of his mentor, Hanssen, when Hanssen was permitted to retire from teaching on account of his advanced age and failing health in 1884.[74] Sartorius based his lectures on the social liberal theoreticians he had studied before his trip to the United States. Henry Charles Carey was the first such influential figure. This autodidact in economics from Philadelphia had published *Principles of Social Science* and *The Unity of Law*. The German translations, which had appeared in the 1860s, had figured on the reading list assigned by Helferich.[75] In addition to echoing Friedrich List's defense of trade barriers for boosting infant industries, Carey asserted that capital accumulation and rising wages were two facets of the same process and would facilitate the gradual automatic resolution of the social question.

The second major influence on Sartorius was the blind philosopher and vehement antisemite Eugen Dühring, who avidly propagated Ca-

S. N. D. North, "The Life and Work of Carroll Davidson Wright," *Quarterly Publications of the American Statistical Association*, June 1909; *DAB*, 20 (New York, 1936), 544–5; James Leiby, *Carroll Wright and Labor Reform* (Cambridge, Mass., 1960).

71. Marriage certificate No. 646, Dresden, November 16, 1881 (Waltershausen Seminar, Munich).

72. Hermann (1882), Imogen (1884), Senta (1885), Eberhard (1887), Siegfried (1893), and Walther (1901). Otto Sartorius, "Sartorius-Familien-Forschungen. Fünfte Fortsetzung," *Ekkehard. Mitteilungsblatt deutscher Genealogischer Abende*, 11–12 (April 17, 1935), 165–6.

73. Karl-Robert Dauler and Richard Mader, *Hermann Wolfgang Sartorius Freiherr von Waltershausen* (Tutzing, 1984), 22–3; *The New Grove Dictionary of Music and Musicians*, 20 (London, 1980), 190.

74. Sartorius's first course in American economics is listed in Sigmund Skard, *American Studies in Europe: Their History And Present Organization* (Philadelphia, 1958). Hanssen's retirement from teaching is discussed in Knapp, *Einführung*, 347.

75. Henry Charles Carey, *Lehrbuch der Volkswirtschaft und Socialwissenschaft* (Munich, 1866) – this condensed version of the *Principles* is based on the American summary *The Manual of Social Science* (Philadelphia, 1864); *Die Einheit des Gesetzes* (Berlin, 1868). On Carey (1793–1879) see J. W. Jenks, *Henry C. Carey als Nationalökonom* (Jena, 1885); A. D. H. Kaplan, *Henry Charles Carey. A Study in American Economic Thought* (Baltimore, 1931).

rey's ideas.[76] While Dühring agreed with Carey on many points, he had considerably less confidence in market forces and considered the emancipation of the working class primarily a political issue. Dühring made various political recommendations throughout his career. In the 1870s and early 1880s, however, he was known for his support for responsible trade unions that pursued a reallocation of social production while preserving the capitalist basis.[77]

Sartorius welcomed such views. Notwithstanding his lifelong support for trade unions, he firmly believed that institutionalized negotiations were a suitable and necessary means for containing the conflict between capital and labor.[78] The liberal Hirsch-Duncker trade unions (which were established in 1868–9) subscribed to this view and seemed to be serious competitors of the German social democratic organizations around 1880.[79]

In 1885, Sartorius obtained an appointment as professor of political economy at the University of Zurich.[80] His disillusionment with life in Switzerland, however, soon led him to seek a position elsewhere.[81]

By 1884, Sartorius conceived a plan for combining some of his essays into a book.[82] His first major work finally appeared in 1886.[83] This book focused on American trade unions; he neglected the political element of the labor movement as much as possible. In Switzerland he started writing a second book. This work focused primarily on social-

76. *Memoirs*, Postscript 1936, 5. Eugen Dühring, *Careys Umwälzung der Volkswirthschaftslehre und Socialwissenschaft* (Munich, 1865); *Die Verkleinerer Careys und die Krisis der Nationalökonomie* (Breslau, 1867). Carey dedicated *The Unity of Law* (Philadelphia, 1873) to "Professor Eugene Dühring – Worthy Successor of Frederic List [. . .]." See also Hermann Lambertz, *Carey und Dühring. Ein Vergleich ihrer nationalökonomischen Lehren* (Dortmund, 1926).
77. Eugen Dühring, *Kapital und Arbeit* (Berlin, 1865); *Kursus der National- und Sozialökonomie* (Leipzig, 1873). On Dühring (1833–1921), see Gerhard Albrecht, *Eugen Dühring. Ein Beitrag zur Geschichte der Sozialwissenschaften* (Jena, 1927).
78. See also Sartorius's chapter on conciliation efforts.
79. Hans-Georg Fleck, *Sozialliberalismus und Gewerkschaftsbewegung. Die Hirsch-Dunckerschen Gewerkvereine 1868–1914* (Cologne, 1994), 195–241.
80. Letter of appointment dated July 11, 1885 (Wundt Archive, Tübingen); the appointment started on October 1, 1885; *Memoirs*, 232.
81. Regarding these difficulties in adjusting, see *Die Universität Zürich 1833–1933 und ihre Vorläufer* (Zurich, 1938), 831.
82. See his letter to the publisher Carl Cotta in Stuttgart (dated October 29, 1884) announcing a book of thirty to thirty-two sheets with sections on the United States, Cuba, and Mexico; he expected to complete the manuscript by February 1885. (Archiv Cotta, Schiller-Nationalmuseum/Deutsches Literarchiv, Marbach.)
83. Sartorius von Waltershausen, *Die nordamerikanischen Gewerkschaften*.

ist movements in the United States. His conviction that emigrants from his country were the driving forces among the socialists led him to emphasize the German influences. His residence in Zurich greatly benefited this research, as Hermann Schlüter (a major publisher-in-exile for German social democracy) also lived there.[84] Schlüter provided him with the necessary American socialist newspapers, pamphlets, and brochures.[85]

In 1888, Sartorius became a professor at the University of Strasbourg. He replaced Lujo von Brentano, who had left following a disagreement.[86] There was more than luck and skill at work in winning this appointment. Sartorius made ample use of what his colleague Knapp called "the tremendous advantage [. . .] of the path made wide" for sons, nephews, and cousins of established professors. Many scholars took years to complete and win approval for *Habilitation* texts; many others spent a decade or more as miserably paid *Privatdozenten* until they won an appropriate position or gave up because of the hardship of poverty.[87] Receiving the call from Strasbourg at age thirty-six would have been unusual, though the university there had had a tradition since 1872 of recruiting promising younger scholars. Per-

84. The German social democrat Friedrich Hermann Schlüter (1851–1919) lived in the United States in the early 1870s; he returned to Europe in 1876, probably because of the Panic in America. After initially settling in Dresden, he organized the distribution of social democratic writings from abroad between 1883 and 1888. "He very successfully ran a publishing house for books on German social democracy in Hottingen-Zürich. Schlüter was of great service in establishing the social-democratic party archive. In 1882, he drafted a plan for collecting the writings of the socialist movement and zealously pursued this project in addition to his work running the publishing company after his move to Zurich." In 1888, Schlüter was deported from Switzerland. After a brief residence in London, he returned to the United States. Schlüter's publications include *Die Anfänge der deutschen Arbeiterbewegung in Amerika* (Stuttgart, 1907); *The Brewing Industry and the Brewery Workers' Movement in America* (Cincinnati, 1910); *Lincoln, Labor and Slavery. A Chapter from the Social History of America* (New York, 1913); and *Die Internationale in Amerika. Ein Beitrag zur Geschichte der Arbeiter-Bewegung in den Vereinigten Staaten* (Chicago, 1918). See *Geschichte der deutschen Arbeiterbewegung: Biographisches Lexikon* (Berlin, 1970), 399–400. See also Sartorius's letter to Georg Hanssen, dated October 14, 1887 (Biblioteka Jagiellońska, Kraków, collection autographs ad/B-280r/217/93/94).

85. *Memoirs*, 239. Sartorius and Schlüter began their collaboration in August 1887. See Sartorius's letter to Schlüter dated August 17, 1887, at the IISH in Amsterdam, Nachlaß Heinrich Schlüter, Sign. 131/1.

86. Letter of appointment dated January 4, 1888 (Wundt Collection, Tübingen); Lujo Brentano, *Elsässer Erinnerungen* (Berlin, 1917), 85–126; *Mein Leben im Kampf um die soziale Entwicklung Deutschlands* (Jena, 1931), 124–41.

87. On the academic career path, the status of *Privatdozenten,* and the *Habilitationsschrift,* see Daniel Fallon, *The German University: A Heroic Ideal in Conflict with the*

haps more unusual was the fact that in 1888 Sartorius had only one book and several less ambitious works to his credit.[88]

Political considerations may have played a role in his selection at Strasbourg. The university faced a crisis in 1887 when Reichstag election returns in Alsace sent a slate of Social Democrats, Alsatian dissidents, and Catholic Center Party representatives to Berlin, all of them more or less hostile to Bismarck and his government's rule of the province. Bismarck directed his anger from the election returns at the university for failing to Germanize the native population properly, as proponents of a new German university in Strasbourg had argued it would do in 1871. Appointments were held up, prominent faculty were allowed to depart for other university chairs without counteroffers, and the university was threatened directly from Berlin with the loss of its generous appropriation. The chief of the higher education division of the Prussian Ministry of Education, Friedrich Althoff, a onetime Strasbourg professor himself, shocked his former colleagues when he told them to adjust to the university's becoming smaller (and poorer).[89]

The dominant figures in the faculty of law and economics were Georg Knapp and law professor Paul Laband. Political differences between Knapp, one of the founders of the liberal Union for Social Policy with his friends Brentano and Schmoller, and the conservative Laband contributed to what the latter recalled in his memoirs as the petty jealousies, backbiting, and divisiveness in the department. Laband was one of Germany's best-known legal experts, a codifier of imperial law, and a defender of the view that ultimate authority in the empire lay in the hands of the emperor, not the Reichstag. Sartorius would have been an acceptable compromise choice for the chair being vacated by

---

Modern World (Boulder, Colo., 1980), 39–45; Konrad H. Jarausch, *Students, Society and Politics in Imperial Germany. The Rise of Academic Illiberalism* (Princeton, N.J., 1982).

88. Knapp, *Aus der Jugend*, 125; as the nephew of Germany's most renowned chemist, Justus von Liebig, Knapp knew the advantages firsthand; see Craig, "A Mission for German Learning," 244, on the relative youth of professors called to Strasbourg in the university's first decades. The last member of the Sartorius family to teach at Göttingen was still teaching there in 1945; see Wilhelm Ebel, *Catalogus Professorum Gottingensum 1743–1962* (Göttingen, 1962). On Knapp (1842–1926), see Ludwig Dehio, "Georg F. Knapp," *Die Grossen Deutschen*, 5 (Munich, 1968), 320–8; *NDB*, 12 (Berlin, 1980), 152–3.

89. On the crisis of 1887, see Craig, "A Mission for German Learning," 429–88, and Ernst Anrich, *Die Geschichte der Universität Straßburg* (Berlin, 1942), 134, on Althoff's remarks.

Brentano, something of a left-liberal thorn in the side of the government. With his distinguished family name and acknowledged expertise in American labor, Sartorius represented continuity in Strasbourg's labor studies orientation; more important, he was politically acceptable to Laband and Berlin.[90]

Sartorius's political credentials were impeccable. In 1884 he published a ringing defense of Bismarck's ban on the importation of American pork because of the danger it posed to public health. American diplomats, meatpackers, and Department of Agriculture officials argued that Bismarck was using the excuse of the danger of trichinosis as a means of making economic policy, or protectionism in disguise, a view generally supported by historians and commentators since then. Sartorius, with considerable evidence, provided the government with factual justification and the backing of his economist's expertise that the public health danger was real and the policy justified. He also embraced Bismarck's quest for German colonies in the mid-1880s in a speech, later published, sponsored by the Göttingen branch of the *Colonialverein,* a pressure group promoting colonial acquisitions. Those emigrants seeking to leave Germany, he maintained, should be directed to the new colonies and not to the United States, where they would be lost to the Fatherland. Politically reliable, safely conservative in his politics (right-wing National Liberal), every bit the German nationalist and patriot, Sartorius was also well connected in Berlin (through the Von Kap-herrs and Von Schlözers) and had even studied law under Laband in Strasbourg more than a decade before being called to the economics chair. For Knapp the appointment had less to offer, but it would acknowledge his debt to the man who was mentor to both, Georg Hanssen, and would permit Knapp to give up the burdens of running the Institute of Economics and Public Policy, established by Schmoller in 1874. Finally, Sartorius was also trained by Hanssen to teach two necessary subjects for the department, public finance and taxation.[91]

90. Paul Laband, *Lebenserinnerungen* (Berlin, 1918), 56; he recalled his first academic post at Königsberg (Kaliningrad) fondly, noting that there were "no divisions, no cliques, no jealousy, and no envy, as I later experienced at Strasbourg." On Laband (1838–1918), see *NDB,* 13 (Berlin, 1982), 362–3. Laband even defended the role the German military later played in the Zabern Affair in Alsace; see David Schoenbaum, *Zabern 1913. Consensus Politics in Imperial Germany* (London, 1982), 152. On Laband's dominant role in the law and economics faculty, see Craig, "A Mission for German Learning," 240.

91. August Sartorius von Waltershausen, *Das deutsche Einfuhrverbot amerikanischen Schweinefleisches* (Jena, 1884); see also Louis L. Snyder, "The American–German Pork

By accepting this appointment, Sartorius returned to German terri-
tory and was therefore subject to the restrictions imposed by the Anti-
Socialist Law. A striking description of the consequences appears in his
memoirs:

Upon obtaining the appointment in Strasbourg in the Spring of 1888, I had yet to
complete my book on American socialism. I was unable to cover current topical
writing in newspapers and literature, however, as I was denied access to such
documents under the Anti-Socialist Law. I approached the only prosecutor I knew
for advice. He recommended that I submit a petition for freedom to use the
writings for research purposes to Puttkamer's undersecretary. I first raised this
issue during a private conversation when I was granted an introduction [to this
undersecretary]. As a liberal who was receptive to such ideas, he believed that the
pursuit of objective scholarly research on social democracy could only be
desirable[92] to the state, as the fight against the intellectual characteristics of
socialism specific to that movement required intellectual means. Nevertheless, the
undersecretary did not feel competent to render a decision concerning my request,
as the matter was of national import. Accordingly, my petition for a bit of printed
matter was forwarded to Berlin. As the responsible authority there was also
uncertain of the best course of action, [the issue] reached Chancellor Bismarck,
who personally scrawled in the margin of the application: "Rejected, professors
should not be concerned with social democracy." [. . .]

I therefore had to travel to Switzerland during my vacation to make excerpts
of the most recent writings. By the Fall, too much material had accumulated for
a comprehensive perusal. While my wife managed to bring some documents in the
lining of her coat, I left behind a larger share and requested the bookstore to save
[these items] along with subsequent issues for me. A few weeks later, I received a
thick package from an unknown sender in Mulhouse in Alsace-Lorraine. It contained the prohibited American printed matter, which, like so many socialist
goods produced in Zurich, had been smuggled across the border (such as infant
cereal, condensed milk, and chocolate) or possibly transported by ship along the
Rhine without passing through customs. Thus, I became an unwilling witness to
the ineffectiveness of the Anti-Socialist Law with respect to importing prohibited
literature.[93]

Dispute, 1879–1891," *Journal of Modern History,* 17 (March 1945), 16–28, and
Jonas, *The United States and Germany,* 37–9; on German immigrants in the United
States, see August Sartorius von Waltershausen, *Die Zukunft des Deutschthums in den
Vereinigten Staaten von Amerika* (Berlin, 1885), and Gregory Zieren, "Late Nine-
teenth Century Industrialization and the Forces of Assimilation on German Immi-
grants: The Views of Economist August Sartorius von Waltershausen," *Yearbook of
German-American Studies,* 21 (1986), 127–35; on his courses in the department in
Strasbourg, see Lexis, *Die deutschen Universitäten,* 1, 602.
92. The original text has "undesirable," which apparently is a mistake.
93. *Memoirs,* 240–1.

Racism and Weltpolitik

Sartorius von Waltershausen's book about *Modern Socialism in the USA* appeared in 1890.[94] Following archival research at the British Museum in London (1892–3), he published a third major work about North America (concerning English colonial labor laws).[95] This publication marked the end of Sartorius's study of American labor; indeed, his only significant later treatment of American themes at all concerned trade, and that from the perspective of Germany's national interest. As early as 1892, in response to the highly protectionist McKinley Tariff of 1890, German officials began promoting the idea of a central European customs union incorporating Austria-Hungary, the Netherlands, Belgium, and possibly Italy in a trade bloc that could retaliate against the United States. Sartorius even argued in favor of purchasing the Danish Virgin Islands in order to create an entrepôt for German trade to the Western Hemisphere free from American interference. He clearly viewed the United States as hostile, potentially dangerous, and threatening to Germany's legitimate aspirations for a "place in the sun." By 1900 Sartorius had joined a small group of economic experts on the United States like Ernst von Halle, a propagandist for the Navy League, and Max Sering, a Berlin professor who argued that agricultural competition with the United States required German colonies in the East. All three were united in their outspoken warnings against what was sometimes called the *American Peril;* all three signed a petition circulated among German professors in 1900 to urge the Reichstag to approve a generous appropriations bill for the German navy, a move warmly supported by Admiral von Tirpitz's Navy League, of course, but which earned them the nickname "the battleship professors" by critics.[96]

After 1900 Sartorius pursued another research agenda useful for an expanding *Volk*, international migration, world trade and commerce,

---

94. August Sartorius von Waltershausen, *Der moderne Socialismus in den Vereinigten Staaten von Amerika* (Berlin, 1890).
95. August Sartorius von Waltershausen, *Die Arbeits-Verfassung der englischen Kolonien in Nordamerika* (Strasbourg, 1894). Concerning his visit to the British Museum, see *Memoirs*, 268, and a letter from the British Museum (Christopher Dale, Ass. Museum Archivist) dated July 17, 1995.
96. On the *American Peril*, see Heinz Gollwitzer, *Europe in the Age of Imperialism, 1880–1914* (New York, 1969), 172–5; Sartorius's draconian suggestions for coping

or *Weltwirtschaft*. *Weltwirtschaft* was the economic counterpart of another German pursuit after 1900, *Weltpolitik,* defined as a foreign policy engaged worldwide in promoting German trade, investments, colonial acquisitions, and national interests in general. He wrote a much admired study of capital markets abroad in 1907, delivered his Chancellor's Address at the University of Strasbourg on *Weltwirtschaft* in 1913, and completed what he believed would be his magnum opus in the late 1920s while in retirement and well into his seventies, a book now largely forgotten. In fact, only two of his many publications have proven durable over the years: his early work on labor in the United States (a nation he came to despise) and a 1921 study of the economic history of Germany between 1815 and 1914.[97]

After the mid-1890s, racism figured far more explicitly in Sartorius's work. This development was by no means coincidental. The increased popularity of *racial hygiene, eugenics,* and the like was virtually ubiquitous throughout German academia, as well as in Anglo-Saxon countries.[98] Fritz Ringer, Walter Struve, and others have noted the rise of what Konrad Jarausch calls *illiberalism* among students and professors at German universities in the 1890s, a trend Sartorius's philosophical transformation mirrored. On the eve of the Columbian Exposition he entitled his lecture course for the summer semester of 1892, "Race and Nationality in Economic Life," and argued that America's economic performance was the result of the Germanic and Anglo-Saxon elements in the population mix; America's success must inevitably falter when

with the American Peril are found in *Deutschland und die Handelspolitik der Vereinigten Staaten von Amerika* (Berlin, 1898), 68–84, and *Die Handelsbilanz der Vereinigten Staaten von Amerika* (Berlin, 1901), 56–71. On the growing rivalry, see Ragnhild Fiebig-von Hase, "Die deutsch–amerikanischen Wirtschaftsbeziehungen, 1890–1914, im Zeichen von Protektionismus und internationaler Integration," *American Studies/Amerika Studien,* 33 (1988), 329–57. On the "battleship professors," see Wolfgang Marienfeld, *Wissenschaft und Schlachtflottenbau in Deutschland, 1897–1906* (Frankfurt, 1957). Ratzel, Schmoller, Sering, von Halle, Sombart, Sartorius von Waltershausen, and Max Weber are among the 270 professors listed by Marienfeld.

97. August Sartorius von Waltershausen, *Deutsche Wirtschaftsgeschichte.* On the legitimizing functions of *Weltpolitik* in Wilhelmine Germany, see Wehler, *The German Empire,* 175–9, and Stürmer, *Das ruhelose Reich,* Chs. 8 and 9; August Sartorius von Waltershausen, *Das volkswirtschaftliche System der Kapitalanlage im Auslande* (Berlin, 1907) and his *Rektor* (Chancellor's) address, *Begriff und Entwicklungsmöglichkeit der heutigen Weltwirtschaft* (Strasbourg, 1913). See also his *Die Entstehung der Weltwirtschaft* (Jena, 1931).

98. The best overview of this trend in Germany appears in Peter Weingart, Jürgen Kroll, and Kurt Bayertz, *Rasse, Blut und Gene. Geschichte der Eugenik und Rassenhygiene in Deutschland* (Frankfurt am Main, 1992), 27–187.

the "inassimilable" African, Southern European, and Hispanic elements numerically overwhelmed the descendants of the original Northern European groups. He persisted in his old-fashioned use of the word *socialism* to mean any policy or movement tending to interrupt the natural workings of the market in lectures on the United States as late as 1897. In the 1880s he had published most of his American labor studies, first as articles in the country's best-known economics journal, *Jahrbücher fur Nationalökonomie und Statistik;* under the editorship of Johannes Conrad, the host and friend of dozens of American economics students at the University of Halle, the journal accepted submissions from economists of all persuasions – Classical School, marginalist, and Historical School alike. In the 1890s and beyond, Sartorius's journal of choice for his work was the *Zeitschrift für Socialwissenschaft*, a decidedly conservative publication edited by the economist Julius Wolf, whom he had come to know and appreciate in Zurich.[99] Wolf became controversial in the 1890s because he supported the pressure exerted on Prussian universities by Reichstag deputy and Saar industrialist Freiherr von Stumm to deny chairs of economics to avowed liberals.[100]

After World War II the eminent Austrian-American economist Joseph Schumpeter insisted that economists in Germany and Austria had been immune from the racial interpretations that infected the social sciences in the 1890s and beyond. Schumpeter, however, reckoned without Sartorius, or another part-time American expert, Werner Sombart, for that matter. Hans-Ulrich Wehler was closer to the mark when he noted, "from the mid-1870s onward, racialist views sprouted in German domestic politics like so many poisonous fungi."[101]

As indicated earlier in the section about his journey to the United States, Sartorius seems to have been influenced by Friedrich Ratzel, another right-wing National Liberal, imperialist, and social Darwinist.

99. *Memoirs*, 243.
100. Fritz K. Ringer, *The Decline of the German Mandarins: The German Academic Community, 1890–1933* (Cambridge, 1969); Walter Struve, *Elites Against Democracy: Leadership Ideals in Bourgeois Political Thought in Germany, 1890–1933* (Princeton, N.J., 1973); and Jarausch, *Students, Society, and Politics,* 276; on Johannes Conrad (1839–1915), see Schumpeter, *History,* 580; on the 1892 lectures "Race and Nationality in Economic Life," see Lexis, *Die Deutschen Universitäten,* 615; on Julius Wolf (1862–1937) and the conservative *Zeitschrift für Socialwissenschaft,* see Rüdiger vom Bruch, *Wissenschaft, Politik und öffentliche Meinung: Gelehrtenpolitik in Wilhelminischen Deutschland, 1890–1914* (Husum, 1980), 300–17. Sartorius and Julius Wolf remained in contact until their twilight years (see the correspondence at the Waltershausen Seminar, Munich).
101. Schumpeter, *History of Economic Theory,* p. 615; Wehler, *German Empire,* p. 105.

The man who coined the term *Lebensraum* believed that the fittest nations and races had to expand their geographic scope and push out the native, less fit inhabitants in the process. He thought that he was seeing just such a conflict between the races in California in the 1870s, a conflict ended in 1882 by the passage of the Chinese Exclusion Act. As Woodruff Smith has established, Ratzel's notions of the diffusion of races and nations were quite popular among German social scientists, with or without their overtly racist implications. Ratzel, in fact, was more inclined to use the term *das Volk* in its cultural, national, or even linguistic sense than with its purely racial meaning.[102] Strasbourg was an intellectual breeding ground for the new wave of racism. Karl-Ludwig Schemann, who also worked there, engaged in unrivaled efforts to propagate the works of Gobineau, the French father of racist theory. Schemann translated Gobineau's *Essai* into German, established a Gobineau Association (1894) and a Gobineau Museum (1906), and included a two-volume biography of Gobineau among his published works. Sartorius was on good terms with him.[103]

These circumstances led Sartorius to assert that the racial relationships underlying production, distribution, and consumption formed the basic problem rather than these economic processes as such. He claimed that race alone could explain why some peoples attained great affluence and others did not:

Previously, theories of political economics attributed little significance to racial factors. The discipline generally overlooked such differences, and the resolution of their problems reflected assumptions by abstract economists, even in historical

102. Schumpeter, *History,* 612; on Ratzel, see Smith, *Politics of Cultural Sciences,* 129–61; idem, "Friedrich Ratzel and the Origins of Lebensraum," *German Studies Review,* 3 (1980), 51–68, and *The Ideological Origins of Nazi Imperialism* (New York, 1986), 141–52. Sartorius's earliest American studies also reflect the influence of Wilhelm Wundt's *Völkerpsychologie;* see the discussion of Wundt in Smith, *Politics of Cultural Sciences,* Ch. 6.

103. Ludwig Schemann, *Gobineau: Eine Biographie,* 2 vols (Strasbourg, 1913–16); idem, *Quellen und Untersuchungen zum Leben Gobineaus,* 2 vols. (Strasbourg, 1914–19). Concerning Schemann, whose life spanned exactly the same years as Sartorius's, see Weingart, Kroll, and Bayertz, *Rasse, Blut und Gene,* 94–6; Martin Broszat, *Der Nationalsozialismus. Weltanschauung, Programm und Wirklichkeit* (4th ed., Stuttgart, 1961), 81; Frank Thieme, *Rassentheorien zwischen Mythos und Tabu* (Frankfurt am Main [etc.], 1988), 119; Kurt Nemitz, "Antisemitismus in der Wissenschaftspolitik der Weimarer Republik: Der 'Fall Ludwig Schemann'," *Tel Aviver Jahrbuch für deutsche Geschichte,* 12 (1983), 377–408. Their cordial relationship is apparent from sources including Sartorius's letter thanking Schemann for the copy of his book *Gobineaus Rassenwerk* (letter dated December 22, 1909: Freiburg im Breisgau, Universitätsbibliothek, Nachlaß Schemann, Sig. IV B 1).

research on structures of corporations and businesses and the formation of economic classes. Eventually, this approach detracted from the discipline's ideological wealth. The problem can be rectified only by regarding the assorted permanent varieties of human beings as active economic factors.[104]

For example, Sartorius, who was becoming an increasingly ardent supporter of Nietzsche's *Wille zur Macht* ("will to power"),[105] doubted that "the colored races would be able to advance to sophisticated versatile economic activity."[106]

The expression of such views did not impede the course of Sartorius's career. In May 1913 he was appointed rector of Strasbourg University for a year.[107] A few years later, at the end of the Great War, Sartorius, his family, and all his German colleagues were forced to cross the Rhine Bridge after the French authorities took control of Alsace-Lorraine and the university, which they closed on one day's notice. The natives hurled rotten fruit and epithets at them as they made the humiliating crossing back to Germany. In 1918, Sartorius and others had to fight for the return of their possessions and books from the French and for acknowledgment of their pension rights from the German government.[108]

Sartorius von Waltershausen, who had already lost part of his wealth, returned to Germany a poorer man (although he was far from destitute).[109] After some meandering, he and his wife Lotty bought a rather modest house in Gauting to the south of Munich. Their primary reason for choosing this place of residence was that their son Hermann was rising to fame as a composer in the Bavarian capital.[110]

104. August Sartorius von Waltershausen, "Beiträge zur Beurteilung einer wirtschaftlichen Foederation von Mitteleuropa," *Zeitschrift für Socialwissenschaft*, 5 (1902), 557–70, 674–704, 765–86, 860–94, here 684.

105. "The desire for power drives every social being." Sartorius von Waltershausen, "Beiträge," 559.

106. Ibid., 685.

107. *Memoirs*, 294–303; August Sartorius von Waltershausen, *Begriff und Entwicklungsmöglichkeit der heutigen Weltwirtschaft*, Strasbourg, 1913.

108. *Memoirs*, 341–3; Erich Kostermann, *Rückkehr der Strassburger Dozenten, 1918–19* (Halle, 1932).

109. In 1907 the firm F. Lappenberg in Hamburg (owned in part by Sartorius von Waltershausen) had filed for bankruptcy. This "rather drastic" financial loss obliged him to sell Kempfenhausen, the manor house on the Starnberger See that he had bought fifteen years earlier. The quotation appears in a letter from Sartorius to his friend Bernhard Naunyn, dated October 15, 1907 (Staatsbibliothek Preußischer Kulturbesitz, Berlin, Handschriftenabteilung, Collection Darmstaedter 1926, 127). The deeds of purchase and sale are at the Waltershausen Seminar in Munich.

110. *Memoirs*, 345.

Sartorius, who had earned five government awards between 1906 and 1918,[111] received several honors from the Weimar Republic as well. In May 1922, in honor of the fiftieth anniversary of Strasbourg University, the University of Frankfurt am Main appointed him a *doctor honoris causa;* he became a professor with an endowed chair at the University of Heidelberg in 1927; the trade academy in Leipzig designated him an honorary member in 1933.[112] None of this favorable recognition, however, subdued Sartorius's sense of bitterness. This sentiment is manifested in his final works, which contain numerous antisemitic observations. In 1933, when his esteemed son Hermann had to retire early for criticizing national socialism, both parents expressed disapproval of Hermann's views and refused to defend him in any way.[113]

Nevertheless, Sartorius did not become an unmitigated champion of Hitler. Shortly before his death, he described national socialism as a highly volatile system that might have been avoided through prudent policy. Eight months before *Kristallnacht,* he condoned antisemitism ("without disregarding humanity") but considered economic autarky an unrealistic objective.[114] His *reluctant* support for the new regime may be the reason that his death on July 31, 1938, went virtually unnoticed.[115]

111. See the distinctions presently in the possession of Mr. and Mrs. Hermann and Lieselotte Wundt in Tübingen.
112. See the records dated May 6, 1922 (Frankfurt am Main), and February 26, 1927 (Heidelberg), at the Wundt Archive.
113. Dauler and Mader, *Hermann Wolfgang Sartorius Freiherr von Waltershausen,* 15.
114. *Memoirs,* postscript of March 1938, 12–16; quotation on p. 15.
115. See the death notice in the *Münchner Neueste Nachrichten,* August 1, 1938, and the brief obituary in the *Frankfurter Zeitung,* August 4, 1938.

3

The Trade Unions in the United States of America

AUGUST SARTORIUS VON WALTERSHAUSEN

I. Factors Helping and Hindering the Trade Union Movement[1]

Heinrich Semler, the eloquent analyst of North American agriculture, comments in his well-known book on overseas grain competition on the prevalence of economic and social organizations in the United States. He sees this as a major reason for its people's economic success. Ninety-nine out of every 100 Americans belong to some association or another and 95 belong to a sickness or death insurance fund, he avers.[2] This phenomenon certainly cannot be attributed to any natural inclination by this young nation, which makes it tend toward a greater degree of socialization than other nations, since U.S. citizens not born in the country and even recent immigrants are just as enthusiastic about joining clubs, societies, and associations as the people who have lived there for generations. This trait should be seen within the context of the overall economic character of the American people. Just as this is the outcome of various natural conditions and social and political institutions, which also influence the immigrants who have started a new life in the New World, the widespread phenomenon of the associations should be seen as the outcome of the same underlying causes. It should be remembered that no more than 50 years ago even those regions now considered the most developed on the continent were characterized by the colonial conditions that still obtain in a number of states and territories today. So the notion of cooperation and the productive strength that

1. "Die Gewerkvereine in den Vereinigten Staaten von Amerika (I)," *Jahrbücher für Nationalökonomie und Statistik*, Neue Folge, Bd. 6 (1883), 517–60.
2. [Heinrich Semler, *Die wahre Bedeutung und die wirklichen Ursachen der nordamerikanischen Concurrenz in der landwirthschaftlichen Production*. Mit einem Vorwort herausgegeben von C. Wilbrandt (Wismar, 1881), 161.]

derives from it have added importance for a nation that is still dwarfed by the wide expanses of uninhabited land. People would be at the mercy of the powerful forces of nature unless they cooperated with others in cultivating and developing the land.[3] The observation that the new territories were not settled, as they had been in Europe in previous centuries, by communities but by individual and family endeavor is wide of the mark. To our ancestors the village community and common ownership must have seemed the most effective forms of association. While it is true that the modern American settlers have brought the awareness of the productive significance of private property with them from Europe, and are therefore organized in privately based economic units, they nevertheless embark on their colonization work jointly, usually on the basis of voluntary agreements. Anyone who has seen colonial settlements develop will confirm that the farmer is followed by the craftsman and the shopkeeper is not far behind. Often the railroad leads the way and connects the apparently isolated farm with civilization in the East. And the farmer produces for a wider market from the outset: he would be truly isolated if he tilled his land for subsistence only.

Life in the new settlements is characterized by a high degree of social equality. Personal abilities and achievements determine a person's status in the community, to which each person is expected to make a useful contribution. Differences in wealth are small and labor power is a person's greatest asset. The high value attached to labor creates a social equality and thus provides the ideal condition for the development of cooperative associations. The greater the similarity between the members, the more likely an association will thrive.[4]

The impact of the government on a nation's economic life is smaller the more it still retains a colonial character. Conditions in America's West are different from those in the East. The absence of government channels initiative into self-help in the form of mutual assistance. Poor relief, for instance, is organized by individuals. The whole insurance system – the many lodges are a case in point – is organized on a voluntary and cooperative basis. All railroads and telegraph lines are in pri-

3. Just as every economic theory is rooted in the country in which it has been developed, Henry C. Carey's ideas on economic cooperation and associations also clearly owe much to American conditions. See H. C. Carey, *The Past, the Present, and the Future* (Philadelphia, 1818); *Principles of Social Science* (Philadelphia, 1858–1859).
4. When Semler suggests to German farmers that the cooperation among American farmers could be a model for them, he forgets that the mix of large, medium-sized and small holdings is quite different in Germany; he also ignores the fact that American farmers have very similar levels of education, marketing interests, and consumption patterns.

vate hands. Even the administration of justice and the protection of property and persons are often provided on the basis of agreements among the citizens.

The predilection to form associations rooted in the above factors and others has also influenced the origins of workers' combinations, in particular trade unions. In these associations, which were initially aimed at improving wage levels, the notion of strength in numbers was further developed on the basis of unique aspects of the American experience. For one thing, capital has surely never been accumulated at a faster rate than in the eastern United States over the last 30 years.[5] Capital accumulation has been most pronounced in enterprises employing large numbers of wageworkers, such as the large factories and railroad companies. This concentration of capital and the social power it represented triggered a stronger reaction among the American working class than in other countries, which was expressed in a wide range of associations and alliances. It also explains the continual urge to create new forms of association. Many workers' associations did not survive the 1873–8 depression because of inadequate organization and weak demand for labor. But as soon as capital dared to embark on new ventures again and gained new strength, workers founded new associations in an effort to protect themselves against the pressures exerted by employers.

It is not so much in the major cities but at the more isolated production sites, in the silver-, copper-, and coal-mining districts for instance, that workers have been quick to form social combinations. This is because they represent virtually the whole political community in these localities and thus already have common interests. Except for a few craftsmen, shopkeepers, saloonkeepers, and mining-company directors,

---

5. According to a report by the director of the U.S. Mint to the U.S. Treasury, the population and national wealth increased as follows between 1825 and 1880:

	Population (in millions)	National wealth (in $ millions)
1825	11.2	3,273
1849	22.5	6,918
1861	32.1	17,013
1875	44.0	34,074
1880	50.2	43,300

During this period the population grew in a ratio of 1:2:3:4.5, while the national wealth increased (in terms of exchange values) in a ratio of 1:2:6:11:13.5. [No source is cited for this report.]

the mining communities are dominated by several hundred usually unmarried miners, who provide their own police, justice, health, and
funeral services. They also use their collective strength against the mineowners. Exploiting their monopoly position given by the mines' isolation, they are able to secure very high wages. Such wage demands can
only be realized through concerted action, and a trade union is the
necessary result. The miners' union in Virginia City, Nevada the site of
rich silver-ore deposits, was able to jack wages to $5 for a 10-hour day
in 1879 – when business was still flourishing and labor hence in strong
demand – and keep them at that level for a considerable period. To
prevent competition, the miners also insisted that no Chinese workers be
allowed to work outside the city. This agreement was all but given the
status of law and was enforced with near-terrorist methods. (In the city
the Chinese were, of course, indispensable as cooks, launderers, servants,
and waiters.) Newly arrived miners were allowed to work on probation,
for four weeks, after which the union decided whether they could stay
or had to go. Anyone who did not submit to the union leaders had no
hope of finding permanent employment in the mines. When the number
of arrivals threatened to depress wages, the influx was stopped. To give
force to such rules the revolver, America's national weapon, is quickly to
hand in isolated places. In Robinson Camp, twenty miles from Leadville,
Colorado, the boom town which had a population of around 40,000
eighteen months after its foundation, three managers appointed by the
mineowners were shot dead by members of the tyrannical miners' union
within the space of a year, out of revenge or in an attempt at intimida-
tion after its excessive demands against the owners were not met.[6]

Another factor which has helped American trade unions to flourish
is the use of British models. By the time the first American unions were
formed, British trade unions had already gained extensive experience in
their struggles with factory owners. The transfer of knowledge occurred
through emigration by British unionists to the United States, through
the close connections between the labor presses on either side of the
Atlantic, and through contact between union representatives at major
conventions. But one should not conclude from this that the institutions
in the two countries are broadly similar. Rather, even though they often
rely on British experiences, the American unions have been molded by
the specific characteristics of American life. On the one hand, they have
moved on from the narrow base of the British craft unions and their

6. *Allgemeine Zeitung*, 26 December 1881.

resemblance to guilds; on the other hand, they have not yet been able to develop the stable and solid support structures typical of the British unions. The American workers' associations are thus, uniquely, pragmatically progressive on the one hand and not sufficiently conservative on the other. Both aspects result from the volatile but technically highly advanced nature of the U.S. economy, which could not have spawned a union movement along British lines.

Against the above-mentioned positive factors, there are also a number of factors which have inhibited the development of specifically American unions. The first obstacle to effective unionization is the heterogeneity of the working population in terms of race and nationality. It is well known that the workers' question overlaps to some extent with the Negro question in the southern states and largely coincides with the Chinese question in the western states. What interests us here is the attitude of the white trade unions to the race issue. In general it can be said that they have tried to reconcile the differences between whites and blacks while at the same time devoting considerable energy to widening the gulf between Americans and Asians (i.e., Chinese). An accommodation with the Negroes is understandable in that thus far the unions have had nothing to fear from the efforts and skills of the blacks, but also because since the emancipation of the slaves the material aspirations of the blacks have become more similar to those of the white working class. The Chinese, on the other hand, were not able to adapt to the European-American civilization during the thirty years they were allowed to come to America; instead, in accordance with the situation obtaining in their home country, they were willing to work for wages which the unions could never have accepted.

As is only to be expected from people who were released from slavery only twenty years ago, the blacks' spending on the essentials of life are still lower than those of the white working population. In the major cities, especially in the thriving cotton-exporting ports, where personal antipathies are often overcome by common economic interests, there have been some signs that wage levels between the two races are converging.[7] The situation is very different in the isolated districts in the South, where the way of life of black unskilled workers has changed little in recent decades. But since they are all engaged in agriculture, a sector which has no unions, we need not concern ourselves with them here.

---

7. In Savannah, a gang of six black screwmen (who stow the cotton bales on the ships) earned $21 in 1881 compared to $26 for a white gang. In New Orleans white and black cotton weighers earned the same wage at this time.

In the cities competition from blacks has tended to be only a marginal problem for white workers because of the sharp division of labor between the two races. Wherever Negroes and Caucasians live in proximity, the former as a rule perform the more menial work. They are the roadsweepers, drivers, loaders, and shoeblacks; in the cigar factories they carry out the simple task of stripping the tobacco leaves (i.e., taking out the midribs); and in the skilled trades they are only used for the ancillary tasks. They have established a significant presence in only a few higher positions. In addition to the dockers discussed below, women work as maids, especially caring for children, and men as hotel and restaurant staff. The shortage of service staff in the United States is far greater than the overall labor shortage because white Americans, reflecting the country's social and political values, seek to avoid any service relationships that involve a personal dependence. The job of servant, although far freer than in Europe and to some extent a position of trust (as in Europe), is not sought after. It is gladly left to the blacks, whose political and social history differs from that of the whites.

Competition between the two races will take on a different dimension when the agricultural southern states, where most of the Negroes still live, develop an advanced manufacturing system. Modern technology calls for unskilled labor. Both races are equally suited to the execution of simple operations which can be learned in a few days. If the Negroes have not reached the standard of living of the Caucasians when the factory system takes root, then the South will experience the kind of struggle that has become inevitable in the West and which has come to a temporary conclusion with the prohibition on Chinese immigration. That similar conflicts cannot be ruled out in the South is evidenced by the tensions that erupt in those situations where whites and blacks work alongside each other in large numbers. This is the case in the ports of New Orleans, Charleston, and Savannah, where the divide between the races clearly hinders the development of trade unions. The two different groups are not easily brought together in a cooperative association, and the employers benefit when they are opposed by a disunited workforce. As mentioned above, it is in New Orleans that the unions, despite the occasional outbreaks of tension, have been most successful in overcoming the racial divide. Although largely motivated by self-interest, they have fulfilled a civilizing role by raising the level of black labor. The efforts of New Orleans's dockers, to which we will return below, are aimed at including members of both races in the union and securing equal wages for all members.

In Savannah there are two segregated trade unions in the cotton industry. They do cooperate to some extent, however, to prevent open competition between them. In the northern states the race issue does not figure strongly as a labor question. To prevent any problems from arising on this score, the cigarmakers' union and others have determined that membership cannot be based on race.[8]

Racial tension between Chinese and Caucasians has only surfaced in a small part of the Union, primarily in California, Oregon, and Nevada. The union movement has never really flourished in the West, no doubt largely because of the competition from Chinese workers. This explains the unions' bitter hatred of the *yellow peril*. The Chinese workers formed their own unions, which were characterized by strong internal discipline and were always prepared to take whites' jobs. The differences in lifestyle and culture precluded any understanding between the two groups. In fact it was not even imaginable as long as the Chinese saw themselves as temporary migrant workers on American soil. They came to the States to earn money and always intended to return to China eventually.[9]

8. For instance, article 2, section 1, of the constitution of the Pittsburgh cigarmakers' union states: Every person over the age of 17 regardless of color "may become a member of this organization." [The impression left by these remarks that trade unions in the North were generally open to black members is very misleading. A survey of relations between black workers and the labor movement after the Civil War can be found in Philip S. Foner, *Organized Labor and the Black Worker, 1619–1973* (New York, 1974), 17–107.]

9. See August Sartorius von Waltershausen, "Die Chinesen in den Vereinigten Staaten von Amerika," *Zeitschrift für die gesammte Staatswissenschaft*, 39 (1883), no. 2, 320–431. [Although this article deals extensively with the anti-Chinese movement in the United States and also with the institutional structure of the Chinese immigrant community, the author's justification of the Chinese exclusion movement and the paucity of information he provided in the present article concerning the lives, aspirations, and organization of the Chinese in North America make it important to call attention here to the extensive historical research which has been published during the last two decades. Among the most noteworthy recent studies of Chinese workers, which should be read in conjunction with this text, are the following: Sucheng Chan, *This Bittersweet Soil: The Chinese in California Agriculture, 1860–1910* (Berkeley, CA, 1986); Lucie Cheng and Edna Bonacich, eds., *Labor Immigration under Capitalism: Asian Workers in the United States before World War II* (Berkeley, CA, 1984); Chris Friday, *Organizing Asian American Labor: The Pacific Coast Canned-Salmon Industry, 1870–1942* (Philadelphia, 1994); Yuji Ichioka, "Asian Immigrant Coal Miners and the United Mine Work-

At the moment the composition of the population in terms of nationality is more important to the success of trade unions than race. In
general it can be said that the nationalities, following certain inclinations, also tend to have their own spheres of economic activity and are
thus not invariably in competition with each other. At the same time,
however, specific groups within the nationalities are drawn to certain
trades, and the unions have had to acknowledge this fact and deal with
the issues flowing from it.[10] A major problem for the unions arising
from the mix of nationalities is linguistic diversity. While American
English is of course the dominant language in business life and every
immigrant therefore has no choice but to use it, there is no doubt that
most unskilled immigrant workers, unless they arrived at a very young
age, never quite gain a full command of the language of their adoptive
country. They certainly learn to negotiate with their employers about
wages and conditions, can get what they need in the street and on the
railroads, and may well read an American newspaper; but they often
cannot make fluent conversation, follow a rapidly delivered speech,
or participate in a discussion in English. In the major cities, where
the majority of workers are, of course, concentrated, immigrants can
find sufficient numbers of compatriots with whom they can converse in
their native language. They will move into the same area (all major
American cities have German and French neighborhoods as well as,
in many cases, Swedish, Norwegian, Polish, etc. neighborhoods), they
visit restaurants, cafes, and places of entertainment run by their compatriots, they marry women from their own country, and they regularly
read newspapers in their native language. Only the second generation,
which no longer respects the customs and language of their elders,
becomes truly American.

ers of America: Race and Class at Rock Springs, Wyoming, 1907," *Amerasia Journal,*
6 (1979), 1–24; Ronald Takaki, *Strangers from a Different Shore: A History of Asian
Americans* (Boston, 1989); Renqiu Yu, *To Save China, to Save Ourselves: The Chinese
Hand Laundry Alliance of New York* (Philadelphia, 1992). The basic study of the anti-
Chinese movement is Alexander Saxton, *The Indispensable Enemy: Labor and the Anti-
Chinese Movement in California* (Berkeley, CA, 1971).]

10. In Chicago the occupational divisions among the nationalities are as follows: Americans by birth: businessmen, middlemen, agents, brokers, carriers, rentiers, factory
owners, public servants, scholars, technicians, engineers, sales people, ironworkers and
steelworkers; Germans and Scandinavians: craftsmen, shopkeepers, servants, sales-
men, brewers, woodworkers; Canadians, Bohemians, Poles, and Irish: roadmen, railroad workers, maids, day laborers; Italians: fruit sellers, restaurant keepers, roadmen,
musicians, ragmen.

Urban workers from a particular trade can organize themselves in several ways: they can form mixed unions comprising all nationalities, general unions with distinct national sections, or separate unions based on nationality. Workers will choose the first option when the nature of their trade means they are not very numerous. This applies, even in the largest cities, to the blacksmiths, woodcarvers, coppersmiths, brushmakers, paperhangers, shoemakers, wiredrawers, trunkmakers, broommakers, and some others. These mixed unions are by far the most numerous. With a few exceptions English is the dominant language in all of them. The meetings present a problem, however. Many of the immigrant members do not understand the comments from the chair and cannot follow the debates, and only a few can take part in them. All too often this leads to mutual suspicion among the members and the emergence of special-interest groups within the union, which feud with each other and so undermine the all-important unity. Tensions within the union are also exacerbated by the various nationalities' divergent opinions on how to advance the labor question. Many German union members tend toward socialist views and demand radical measures, while the British immigrants generally want to introduce the principles guiding the home country's unions and to shift the movement's emphasis away from campaigning for higher wages toward regulating benefits for the members. The American-born members believe they alone have the answers. They regard the European immigrants as novices, who should first acquaint themselves with the way things are done in their adoptive country.

In general American workers are less than enamored of the influx from Europe. They have been known to use the press to try to deter immigrants by putting their own circumstances in a negative light. They have had little success in this, however, because those social forces interested in recruiting cheap labor – the employers – are in a better position to paint a rosy picture of American life. During the debate on the federal bill to ban Chinese immigration, opponents of the measure argued that it would set a dangerous precedent for the assessment of future immigration from Europe. If the Chinese would be kept from U.S. soil essentially in the interests of working people in the West, then what would stop workers in the East from demanding the same with regard to the labor influx from Europe, it was argued. When strikes broke out in the Pennsylvania coal fields in the spring of 1882, the mineowners turned to New York, as they had done during previous disputes, and hired large numbers of recently arrived European immigrants. The strikers certainly did not welcome the replacement workers with any greater warmth than the San Francisco mob reserved for the arrival of a steamship heaving with Chinese workers.

But the parallel drawn between the prohibition of Chinese immigration and a possible ban on European immigration is not pertinent. The Chinese have been excluded not so much because their arrival aggrieved the existing working population but because it affected the whole of economic, political, and moral life in the western states. Precisely the opposite is true of European immigration. It is the efforts of European immigrants which have transformed the extensive, thinly populated Indian territories into a civilized state of the first order. And this is as true today as it was 100 years ago. Admittedly the conditions of working people in the major cities and elsewhere are occasionally adversely affected by the often unexpected waves of European arrivals. But these effects are generally temporary and tend to disappear as quickly as they emerge. There is still a good chance of finding work. Millions of European farmers can still establish themselves, estimating the remaining mineral reserves in the mountains is not even possible at this stage, and huge forests are still awaiting rational exploitation. In short, there are ample opportunities to provide large numbers of people with a secure existence. Even today it is still clear that no matter how high the level of immigration from Europe, the demand for labor consistently exceeds the supply (except in recessionary times) and any congestions in the labor market are relieved within a short period. The impact of European immigration on the United States is comparable to the impact of the introduction of new labor-saving machinery in Europe in this century. Initially this depressed wages, but after a transitional period, the overall economy expanded and the temporarily displaced labor found itself in a more favorable situation than before the innovations. As the U.S. labor force grew, it was able to develop previously untouched natural resources. This in turn stimulated enterprise, boosted the accumulation of capital, and provided the basis for additional demand for labor. The unions which call for restrictions on European migration thus show little foresight. They should instead concentrate on recruiting to their organizations every new arrival on American soil as a matter of urgency.

The second means by which the unions accommodate the diversity of nationalities is by setting up special *national sections*. This is of course only possible when the number of workers in a particular trade and in a particular locality reaches a significant level. These sections – English,

French-, and German-speaking, etc. – are organized on the same principles and are held together by a central committee, but generally they operate their own support funds for sickness and death. The members of these national sections look for work with the same employer if possible, which facilitates mobilization in case of an industrial dispute. The costs of a strike initially fall to the section concerned, and only when its resources are exhausted do the other sections extend a helping hand. Given this subsidiary support commitment, it is understandable that every strike requires the approval of the central committee or of a general assembly of all members.[11] These national sections should not be confused with the union sections set up in specific localities. Because American cities are built very spaciously and the distances between neighborhoods are often considerable, the large labor unions organize separate local meetings to deal with current business; their decisions are then communicated to the central committee.[12]

The third form of union organization – nationality based – is rare. It occurs when the nature of the trade justifies such a division, as among printers,[13] some of whom work in German and others in English, or when the number of workers in a trade is so large that individual national groups consider themselves strong enough in every way to defend their interests on their own.[14] Just as the American unions are affected by immigration from the East (i.e., from across the Atlantic), so they are

11. In New York, for instance, the custom shoemakers have English-, French-, and German-speaking sections and the cigarmakers have German- and English-speaking sections. In Chicago the carpenters and joiners also have German and English sections. In St. Louis there is the Stonemasons' Union No. 1 and the German Stonemasons' Union No. 2. These unions' statutes are drafted in several languages. In some cases union newspapers also take account of the linguistic plurality. Thus *The Carpenter,* published in St. Louis in 1881, contained articles in German as well as English, and *The Cigarmakers' Official Journal* of New York occasionally publishes official union announcements in German.

12. Article 6 of the constitution of the Furniture Workers' Union No. 1 in Chicago states: "a. Because it does not seem practical, given the size of Chicago, for all members of the union to meet regularly at one place, sections will be created in the various parts of the city.
b. All nationalities are authorized to create their own sections; similarly separate branches, like wood carvers, pianomakers, turners, etc., can form their own sections."

13. The statutes of the German-American Typographia Union No. 7 state: "Every printer who has command of German and is based in New York and its vicinity may, provided he meets certain conditions, become a member of this association."

14. For instance, besides the strongest German union, the furniture makers, which includes cabinet makers, carvers, turners, upholsterers, pianomakers, gilders, varnishers, etc., there are also American unions of pianomakers, upholsterers and varnishers.

adversely affected by "emigration" from the eastern states to the West. The annual exodus from the major cities to the new states and territories opened up for settlement is indeed a migration on a massive scale. Without doubt the huge expanse of cheap land has been highly beneficial to the United States' economic and social development. During recessionary times it has allowed redundant or lowly paid workers to find relatively lucrative employment as farmers in the West. In heading west these people also helped those who remained behind in the cities, since they could count on regular work and could secure sharply higher wages even during a modest tightening of the labor market. This prevented the emergence of a Marxist *reserve army of labor* that would have returned to the labor market as the economy improved and thus curbed wage rises. But many workers are drawn to the West not only when times are difficult but also when the economy is strong. Wages are higher during boom periods, and with earnings of $2 and outgoings of $1 an unmarried man can quickly save enough money to take up a homestead. Many who feel hemmed in by their status as wageworkers are likely to heed Horace Greeley's oft-quoted advice to "go west, young man, and grow up with the country" and become free farmers on their own land.[15]

These conditions have no doubt been conducive to the United States's economic development, although their impact has diminished in the last decade as a result of overcropping, widespread land speculation, and increased immigration. They have also hampered the union movement in several ways. Many workers join unions to protect their current wages and conditions. But in doing so they do not abandon their ambition of moving out of wage labor altogether. Such justified hopes are not confined to owning one's own farm. There are also many other opportunities in the newly settled territories – at least still in the Far West – to earn a living as craftsmen and shopkeepers, as well as agents and carriers for many big companies. No branch is overcrowded, and there is a strong demand for all these skills.[16]

15. The crucial importance of cheap land to North America's social development is the key to Henry George's proposal for the abolition of private groundrent. The easy accessibility of land, which is decreasing from year to year and in many states has almost disappeared, is to be made permanent, in effect, by the forfeiture of rent [to the community]. In *Progress and Poverty*, vol. 9, chapter 1, George argues that the implementation of his "single tax" (on unearned rent income) will cut land prices, end speculation, and leave land in the hands of those who want to cultivate it. Precisely these conditions prevailed 15–20 years ago in all states west of the Mississippi.

16. The loss in union membership due to the westward migration is not offset by European immigration. European immigrants do not join unions immediately and are therefore initially perceived as competitors.

Some people are even absorbed into the political system. (This is true across the country, not just in the new settlements.) Many manual workers are tempted to give up their jobs and try their luck in the public sector, to stand for election to one of the many public offices. All these factors combine, then, to dent the unions' membership levels. This no doubt explains why these workers' associations are more interested in raising wages and shortening working hours than in setting up structured mutual assistance funds. Support for the elderly or the disabled is only rarely on the agenda, since this requires long years of experience to calculate benefits as well as a large and stable premium-paying membership.

But the overriding problem the trade unions face, and which has already sparked an attempt to restructure the labor movement, arises from the relentless advance of industrial technology and the division of labor as the market expands. Skilled work or any learned material-processing work is steadily declining in importance, and increasingly workers only need to learn a few simple operations to perform their factory job. As industry develops in this direction, it becomes more difficult to demarcate the trade unions. And as work demands even out, competition between those dependent on the same kind of livelihood intensifies. An inevitable side effect is that boys, women, and girls enter into competition with adult men in selling their labor.

Traditionally the trade union movement has been seen as a means of helping and organizing skilled workers and as a way of solving part of the labor question. But this interpretation is surely no longer valid as workers' social status levels off. It also fails to acknowledge that the advance of modern technology constantly creates new impulses for the conflict between capital and labor. The labor question is becoming generalized, as is the means of responding to it. On the one hand, this makes life easier for a government concerned for the well-being of its citizens and which wants to regulate working conditions. It also encourages the emergence and facilitates the success of broadly based, numerically large, centrally led voluntary and general trade unions. On the other hand, it tends to intensify the opposition between the haves and the have-nots and exposes large numbers of people to revolutionary ideas. Just as new technology was largely responsible for the demise of the guilds, so modern technology will also deal the death blow to the craft unions. This is not meant as a criticism of the development of self-help workers' associations, but only a pointer to their likely future. Traditionally the most powerful unions are those able to limit competition by restricting the number of apprenticeships and whose members require years of training before becoming fully qualified in their trade. This kind of occupational exclusiveness is becoming increasingly rare, however, and unskilled labor is responsible for an ever larger share of industrial production.

Like the old guilds, the craft unions did not only draw their strength from being able to control their trade; they also relied on geographical isolation. But this too is being eroded by the rapid expansion of the means of transportation in this century. It is now possible, for instance, for a craft union strike in a city to be broken by a group of unskilled workers brought in from elsewhere. With every improvement in the transportation system it becomes cheaper for employers to hire replacement workers from elsewhere.

Let us now look at some illustrations of how craftsmen are displaced by large industry. With few exceptions, shoes are mass produced in factories in America. The form of production implies no loss of quality: on the whole consumers enjoy the same standards of comfort, elegance, durability, and price as in Europe. The shops are so well stocked that customers have a very good chance of finding something suitable. The factories also take special orders, so they can accommodate every style and fashion as well as individual customers' wishes. A special order is fitted into the mass production process in the following way. The manufacturers provide the retailers with printed forms or cards, on which they can specify, in around 20 categories, the size and width of the shoe or boot and the type of leather, sole, heel, and laces. The cards are sent to the factory, where the supervisor marks on the back the names of the workers responsible for fulfilling the special aspects of the order. Some of the work is the same for every item, so at this point the special orders can be treated as part of general production. The card stays with the boot or shoe from the start of production to its completion and shows the worker how he should proceed at the various stages. Only a small number of factory workers are engaged in this way, since most goods are not custom orders but are destined for the warehouses. Those who work on custom orders usually have a number of different ones to fulfill at any one time. In most large cities the factories use retailers as their agents, and they receive many special orders. For this reason specialist workers are therefore unlikely to run out of work. Nor is it necessary for the orders to be fulfilled within a working day. Since even specialized footwear is completed in large quantities every day, customers can still be served quickly even if there are several delays in production. Little time is lost when a worker moves from one order to another, since he only has to adjust his own machine (for leather size, eyelet position, seam type, etc.) or repeat his operation more or less often (single or double soles, heel height, eyelet number, etc.).

In the large factories in Massachusetts, where 300–400 workers produce 3,000 pairs of boots or shoes per day, the division of labor is so far advanced that a shoe has passed through the hands of 64 workers by the time it is ready for sale.[17] Most use special, steam-driven machines. One cuts the soles by machine, a second presses them, a third rips the sides for the seam, a fourth smooths it down, a fifth fits the second sole. No fewer than ten men are involved in the production of the boot heel; even more work on the preparation of the uppers. Within the factory a whole floor contains only sewing machines, and another contains all the polishing, lacquering, and pressing equipment for the otherwise finished goods.

The tailoring trade has been subject to a similar process of disintegration, although it has not yet progressed as far as in the shoe industry. In America ready-to-wear clothes are far more common than in Germany. The main stores in New York, Philadelphia, Boston, and Chicago have a number of large halls containing thousands of garments sorted by color, cut, strength, and size. Most Americans buy their clothes from these establishments. The extraordinary choice means that customers usually find something suitable. The major clothing shops have branches in the smaller towns, which are supplied from the main warehouses according to demand. Alternatively there are agents or independent retailers who have regular contact with the main depots. Considering the size of the United States and its diverse population in terms of race and nationality, it may be thought remarkable that the production and distribution of clothes are so standardized and generalized. But this phenomenon is not surprising given that fashion rules even more tyrannically in the New World than in the Old and that, broadly speaking, income differentials are smaller in the United States than anywhere else. The existence of a large middle class creates a uniform consumption base, and only a relatively small section of the population has the option of choosing between buying clothes in one of the large shops or ordering them from a tailor at perhaps two or three times the price. The characteristic rapid spread of new patterns and materials

17. See *Investigation by a Select Committee of the House of Representatives Relative to the Causes of the General Depression in Labor and Business; and as to Chinese Immigration* (Washington, 1879) [hereafter cited as *Causes of the General Depression*], 429.

can be explained in part by the Americans' affection for anything new and in part by the general social equality (which, in the young countries at least, means that people's desire to go one better on others can only be expressed in such externals). Either way it sets the conditions under which mass and standardized garment production becomes profitable.

By no means are all clothes produced in factories, however. More commonly the work is split up, with the buying and cutting out of the materials controlled by manufacturers and all other operations generally performed by home workers. A detailed division of labor is evident in the cutting out of material, with specialized workers responsible for dresses, pants, jackets, etc.; for each type of garment different people are responsible for making the designs, drawing the patterns, and cutting materials (often using machines in the latter case). The boss tailors take the cut items home and finish them with family members or wageworkers. Such workplaces are fitted out the same everywhere.[18]

In both the shoe-making and tailoring trades, craftsmen who can make a whole item or supervise its production have a better chance of making a living in the eastern states than in the western territories. Most wealth is concentrated on the Atlantic seaboard, and the wealth gap is wider there than in other parts of the continent. Proficient workers can find sufficient work among the more affluent consumers. But it should be noted that only high-grade work is properly appreciated and rewarded, so that the number of people actually employed in this field is very small. Moreover, numbers are declining because the factories are improving both in quantitative and qualitative terms. Besides catering for the less well off, there is a constant demand for repair work.

The above-mentioned tailoring workshops can also take care of garment repairs, while every town and city has a number of cobblers to repair shoes and boots. These are either qualified shoemakers who have been condemned to this subordinate position by competition from the factories or those who are not sufficiently skilled to supply the rich customers. In passing it should be mentioned that generally the repair of garments or shoes does not proceed as in Germany. Anything that has been torn or damaged in some other way is often thrown

18. See *Fourth Annual Report of the Bureau of Labor Statistics, to the General Assembly of Ohio, for the Year 1880* (Columbus, 1881) [hereafter cited as Ohio BLS, *Fourth Report*], 276. "The description of one of these factories [in Cincinnati] applies to all. It possesses six large sewing machines, four tables, two irons to iron the dresses, two pairs of scissors and a buttonhole machine. The value of all this equipment is $200." [This is not a correct reference for the quotation.]

away, in part probably because mending it is very expensive and therefore not worthwhile and in part no doubt also because of the general
profligacy in consumption typical of America. Experience shows, here
as in other areas, that as people find it easier to earn money, they save
less. Against this the Americans are very economical in production, in
particular with regard to the most expensive factor of production,
human labor. It is above all the cost of the latter that has spurred the
development of the factory system and the invention of labor-saving
machinery. It also seems the main reason why craftwork has disappeared much faster in the New World than in the Old. Modern technology has, of course, also brought about tremendous changes in
Europe, but in North America it has propelled the whole economy
from one phase into the next much more quickly.[19]

Let us also look at some other trades which in the past were the preserve of craftsmen but are now dominated by unskilled workers. Many
aspects of the butcher's trade, for instance, have already become de-
skilled. The killing and cutting up of a hog at a large slaughterhouse at
the Chicago stockyard involves fifteen people performing different
tasks. Since up to ten hogs can be killed and cut up every minute, this
amounts to 150 simple operations! A maximum of 13,000 hogs can be
processed during a day and night cycle in a single establishment. Ham
and sausage making is similarly subjected to an advanced division of
labor. Machines are used in several stages of the processes to simplify
human labor. The large hog and cattle slaughterhouses produce processed meat for dispatch elsewhere, as well as fresh meat for local consumption. Because of the competition from slaughterhouses, the previously independent butchers have become meat traders, and most
journeymen and apprentices and less prosperous master butchers have
become factory workers. The butchers' trade unions comprise those few
workers who still need a number of years to learn their trade, despite
the existence of the slaughterhouses and their advanced division of
labor. For all the others there is no point in combining into a union,
since they have no leverage when taking strike action as a last resort.
Employers are, of course, not compelled to hold on to their employees,
and in the large cities strikers can easily be replaced with other unskilled
workers.

19. The overexploitation evident in American agriculture is also *partly* traceable to this
cause. Expensive labor encourages the use of machines. Because the capital invested in
them often depreciates rapidly as they are overtaken by new inventions, farmers are
forced into the relentless exploitation of the cheap natural resources.

The cabinetmakers' trade has undergone a similar process of atomization. Today there are only a few workers who can make a whole table, chair, or chest of drawers. The various components are made by individual workers, with the use of machines, and put together by others who cannot make the component pieces and often are not even in a position to see their colleagues at work. To save on transportation costs, for instance, large wood-processing factories have been set up in the forests of Pennsylvania, near a railway line of course, in which the constituent parts of the furniture are worked up to the polishing, varnishing, decorating, and assembly stages. The final stages of production are carried out in main cities (above all in Philadelphia), where the markets are for the end products. So the rural establishments do not produce masses of sawn wood but instead dispatch standard processed pieces, which means that waste wood does not have to be transported and that transportation costs can be spread across higher-value goods. Finishing the goods off on site is not economical either, however, on transportation-cost grounds, because it is relatively expensive to transport items of furniture in bulk.

The division of labor has been carried even further in a particular branch of furniture making, namely, piano making. Nearly every one of the piano's many components is made by a different worker. Steam-driven planes, saws, and drills take care of most of the work. Then there are various operations to wind and tighten the strings. Ten to fifteen workers are responsible for varnishing the instrument. Altogether some seventy people are involved in the manufacture of a grand piano. In the iron and steel industry the differentiation of activities is similar to that in the wood-working industry. While years ago the machinebuilder or toolmaker had to be an expert with the lathe, drill, vise, hammer, file, and chisel, these days a single machine will shape and smooth more metal in a day than a skilled worker could in a week or a month.

Many more examples can be provided, since there is hardly any trade, excepting the personal services such as barbers and hairdressers, etc., which has not been affected by modern technology in one way or another.[20] Let us add that no fewer than 17,620 patents were granted

20. ["It applies to every trade, not even excepting stone cutting. In stone-cutting they have got little knives which put the face on the stone. That is a branch of the introduction of machinery to stone-cutting. It is what they call the patent hammer." *Causes of the General Depression*, 430.]

in Washington in 1881, which gives an indication of American inventiveness and makes a further displacement of individually multiskilled workers highly likely in the future.

Despite the many handicaps outlined above, the American unions have been able to secure a number of significant successes in terms of wages and conditions, especially at times of economic prosperity. This is due primarily to the shortage of labor typical of the colonial countries. The more isolated a production site, the more difficult it is for the employer to resist the demands of his workforce. Compared to the developing western territories, the trade unions in the eastern states and especially in the populous cities are in a much weaker position during an industrial dispute because of the competition of unskilled workers. It is here that new voluntary labor organizations have emerged which have more or less abandoned trade exclusiveness and, reflecting the leveling of the working class, set themselves up on a much broader basis. Within these efforts four trends can be discerned.

1. The Formation of Central Labor Assemblies Which Are Not Concerned with the Trade of the Constituent Unions.   Their main objectives are, firstly, preventing competition among unskilled workers, and secondly, given that the sociopolitical effect of strikes is steadily diminishing with the leveling down of individual training, enabling union members to unfold concerted political action.

In England, Wales, and Scotland, *trades' councils* have been set up in many cities. In 1878 they numbered 21 and claimed a membership of 132,056. These local associations have no influence on the internal affairs of the individual trade unions, but have set themselves the task of campaigning for specific demands inside and outside Parliament. The trades' councils hold the annual Trades' Union Congress (the twelfth was held in Edinburgh in 1879), which discusses political tactics for the coming year and possible legislative measures to protect workers.

This form of organization was initially copied in the United States and later spread under the name *trades and labor assembly*.[21] Their constitutions, first of all, set out the goals of political action. These include

---

21. I have examined the statutes of the trades assemblies of New York, Chicago, Cincinnati, Detroit, and San Francisco. Similar associations exist in St. Louis, Washington, Pittsburgh, Boston, Minneapolis, Milwaukee, Cleveland, Buffalo, Denver, Indianapolis, Cheyenne, Wyo., Newark, N.J., Leadville, Colo., New Haven, Conn., Saint Joseph, Mo., Columbus, Ohio, Allegheny, Pa., and Fall River, Mass.

shortening of the working day by law, protection of child and women's labor, introduction of factory inspectors in those states that do not yet have any, abolition of the truck system, abolition of competition from prison labor, abolition of the tenement system in all pertinent branches of the economy,[22] establishment of a bureau of labor statistics in states that do not yet have one, and, in San Francisco before 1882, introduction of legislation banning Chinese immigration.

To stop workers from competing with each other, it is imperative to combine all workers in a city in individual unions and to bring these together in a trades assembly. Since 1879 efforts in this direction have met with considerable success. But it is doubtful whether these unions are now strong enough to survive a prolonged economic recession. The major crisis of the 1870s, which was responsible for the demise of most unions that did not have a structured insurance system, also destroyed many local centrals. That these achieved relatively little in terms of legal reforms was mainly due to the political ineptitude of their leaders, who time and again allowed themselves to be tricked by unscrupulous professional politicians. The trades assemblies do not confine themselves to promoting cohesion among the unions. Unlike their British models, they can interfere in the unions' internal affairs during strikes or inter-union disputes. The first power is particularly important in creating an all-embracing bond and preventing competition. Political campaigns are worth little to workers who are fighting for their material existence. Support and assistance during a strike is what they need as a basis for securing their incomes. The detailed rules governing the trades assemblies differ from city to city. The assemblies as a whole have also gone through various constitutional phases.

The trades assembly's function as arbiter in disputes within affiliated unions is set out only in general terms, and comes into play only when an internal dispute cannot be resolved through the union's existing conciliation and arbitration procedures.[23] The trades assembly's authority as arbiter arises from its power to expel, as an ultimate sanction, a

22. The latter is a particularly important issue in New York City, where very oppressive home production, especially in cigar making, is organized in large tenements owned by manufacturers.

23. For example, the constitution of the San Francisco trades assembly states that "In case of a dispute within a union, a committee of arbitration will be set up whenever possible" [retranslated from German]. Some constitutions are silent on this matter, but provide for arbitration procedures for disputes between the assembly and its affiliated unions.

union from the local central. Expulsion would have serious consequences for the union concerned.

In case of industrial disputes between unions and employers, the
trades assemblies recommend a compromise and offer assistance in the
conduct of negotiations to this end. If the dispute cannot be settled, they
will support a strike provided they have explicitly endorsed it. Under
some statutes the unions are obliged to submit every proposed strike
action to the assembly for endorsement; under others they are free to
invoke the assembly's help or not. Some statutes stipulate the grounds
on which an assembly can endorse a strike. The constitutions of the
individual centrals also diverge in terms of the type of support they provide in case of strikes, as the texts below show.

a. Detroit: "In case of strikes approved by the Council, subscription
lists will be issued to the officers of all Unions and other responsible
persons, and voluntary contributions collected for the benefit of the
strikers. The moral support of the Council will be pledged in the form
of proper resolutions, published in the daily papers and otherwise, and
every possible effort will be made to influence public opinion in favor
of the workmen involved. Should the articles manufactured by the
employers concerned be of such kinds as are principally sold in Detroit
or vicinity, the public in general, and working people in particular, will
agree to refuse to purchase them, but to buy instead those
manufactured in establishments whose employees are fairly paid."[24]

b. Cincinnati: "In the event of a conflict between employers and
workers it is the duty of individual unions to bring the matter before the
Assembly. If a strike is approved by the latter, all trade unions should be
directed to support it. The level and the type of contribution offered is
to be determined by the individual unions. Should one of the latter
refuse to contribute, it will be excluded from all support on the occasion
of its own strikes."[25]

c. San Francisco: "If a strike is deemed necessary, the Assembly
should appoint a committee of three persons to advise the union
involved. Moreover, should the Assembly resolve to provide financial
aid, and if the strike continues, a per capita assessment should be levied

24. [*Constitution, By-Laws, and Rules of Order of the Council of Trades and Labor
Unions of Detroit, Mich.* (1889). This is the earliest version we have found.]
25. [Retranslated from German.]

on all affiliated unions, so that the strike can be carried to a successful conclusion, and the workers not need to suffer want."[26]

d. New York: "Sec. 1 All strikes, which are properly called by individual organizations which are affiliated to this union, shall be assisted, provided they are called under the following circumstances: a) against a reduction of wages, b) for an increase of wages, c) against an effort to break the union, d) against an effort to lengthen the hours of labor.

Sec. 2 The assistance shall begin in the third week after the strike has been reported to the President and the Recording Secretary; however, an organization which applies for assistance must have been affiliated with this union at least three months.

Sec. 3 The amount of the assessment shall not exceed 15 cents per week, moreover the organization which is on strike shall not be assessed. Each union shall pay for all members which are listed in its monthly report.

Sec. 4 The amount to which striking members shall be entitled, shall not exceed three dollars per week [. . .].

Sec. 6 All organizations shall pay the sum of 10 cents per member into the reserve fund. Said fund shall be used exclusively for strikes. In the event that the fund sinks below 10 cents per member, the shortfall shall be made up.

Sec. 7 Any organization whatever which fails to pay the assessments for strikes or the reserve fund within four weeks shall be suspended until the assessment is paid; moreover, the union shall receive no assistance before the passage or one month after all arrears have been made up."[27]

All we wish to say here about the organization of the trades and labor assemblies is that the affiliated unions are entitled to a number of delegates proportional to their numerical strength, that they have to pay monthly or quarterly dues on the same basis, and that there are several standing officials (president, vice-president, secretaries, treasurer, ushers, auditors), as well as ad hoc committees to deal with special matters.

These local centrals have made several attempts to set up a national

26. [Retranslated from German.]
27. [*Constitution of the Amalgamated Trade and Labor Union of New York and Vicinity,* taken from the *Gewerkschafts-Zeitung,* 20 July 1880, and retranslated from German. In 1881 the relevant provisions of the New York constitution were modified to approximate those applying in Cincinnati.]

association. Some statutes made this an explicit objective.[28] A national labor convention was held in Pittsburgh in November 1881, at which the Federation of Organized Trades and Labor Unions of the United States and Canada was founded. The national and international (i.e., including Canadian) unions nominate delegates to the annual conventions. The meetings hear reports of the federation's main activities, and the organization of unions and trades assemblies, and express views on the political activities for the coming year. The federation's *legislative committee* is a standing committee of five members, which is responsible for day-to-day administration. Every worker affiliated with the national federation pays a quarterly subscription.

2. Local Centrals of Various Trade Unions Whose Members Are Involved in the Production of the Same Goods.

Given the advance of the division of labor, there is a wide scope for this type of association.

Let us look first at cigar making. Four types of workers are employed here: the strippers, wrappers, cigarmakers, and packers (sorters). Each occupation is organized in a separate union. It is, of course, incontestable that by combining in some way, rather than acting on their own, the four unions are in a much stronger position to oppose the employers. When a union takes unilateral strike action, other workers in the industry can be induced to take over at least part of the strikers' work during the transition when full replacements are not immediately available. This happened during the great cigarmakers' strike of 1877 in New York, when strippers and wrappers were retrained and took the jobs of the striking cigarmakers. If the four branch unions link up in some way, this can be prevented. Not only that, when one union goes on strike, the others can take solidarity action and thus put strong pressure on the employer.

At the moment union centralization of this kind is most developed in the southern cotton-exporting ports. It is therefore instructive to examine the situation of workers there.[29] The cities of New Orleans, Savannah, Charleston, Norfolk, Virginia, and Galveston, Texas, are purely commercial centers with negligible industrial bases, and only the most

---

28. For instance, the Detroit assembly statute states that "in particular, links should be established with trades assemblies, councils and unions in other cities with the aim of providing mutual support."

29. See also August Sartorius von Waltershausen, "Production und Verladung der Baumwolle in den Vereinigten Staaten [I–II]," *Allgemeine Zeitung*, 23 and 24 June 1882.

elementary crafts and construction work are performed there. Most workers are employed in the cotton trade.

Apart from the small number of workers involved in the highly mechanized ginning (during which the cotton seeds are removed from the fibers) and cotton oil preparation, most of the manual workers in New Orleans are engaged in the various activities ranging from unloading the bales from the riverboats or railways to their loading onto seagoing vessels. In New Orleans, the most important cotton market, the division of labor has advanced furthest. Eight different jobs can be distinguished: (a) the longshoremen, who unload the cotton from the riverboats and freight cars and load from the wharf into the seagoing vessels; (b) the draymen, who transport the bales from the unloading sites to the large cotton yards, where the cotton is stored, classified, weighed, and pressed in preparation for export, and who then transport the cotton to the seaport; (c) the yardmen, who unload the cotton at the yards and bring it into the covered halls for pressing and weighing; (d) the cotton classers and markers, who sort the bales by quality and stamp them accordingly; (e) the scaleshands, who put the bales on the weighing scales and pull them away when they have been weighed; (f) the weighers and reweighers, who weigh the bales; in the past there were only weighers, who were often in cahoots with one or another buyer; their work is now checked by the reweighers, so that the buyer and seller are both represented at the scales; (g) the pressmen, who work the steam presses (cotton is pressed provisionally on the plantation; to make sea transportation economical, the bales are reduced to a third of their size in the steam presses; at the same time the sack, which is now too wide, is pulled together and sewed together with a few stitches, and the iron hoops are removed and replaced with new ones that fit the new compressed mass; in the past hemp ropes were used, but these often tore owing to cotton's expansivity and proved impractical); and (h) the screwmen, who stow the bales in the seagoing vessels; what matters here is to distribute the cargo equally within the ship, to fasten it so that it cannot move during the journey, and to use the hold as efficiently as possible; the heavy bales are rolled by hand to their allocated place and then squeezed together with *screws* (hence the workers' name). The screwmen have a special position among the dockers. The piecework which is common among the other classes of workers is not suitable for the screwmen, since this could encourage bad packaging, and in any case it is not possible to supervise their work in the unlit holds. The screwmen are organized in white or black *gangs* of six to eight members and led by a foreman. Because the work is heavy and highly skilled, they receive the highest wages in the United States: between $6 and $7 for a ten-hour day. It should be borne in mind, however, that married workers have no income in the summers, when there are no cotton transports; the unmarried workers often head north to New England and Canada in the summers to look for work in timber transporting.

The wage increases which all eight classes of workers have secured in recent years are in no small part due to the excellent organization which binds all of them together. Every class has its own union, which provides a sickness and accident insurance system and maintains links with counterparts in the other cotton-exporting ports. The eight unions, which had around 8,000 members in May 1881, together form a Ring. This is headed by an executive committee composed of one or two members from each affiliated union. Strikes or any other action against the employers must be endorsed by this committee. The individual unions' constitutions state that every person, regardless of color, may be admitted to the union when they have worked in their branch for a year and are of good character. Although the race issue does lead to tensions between white and black workers, the separation between blacks and whites has been avoided in New Orleans by the formation of joint unions, as mentioned earlier, in order to prevent one group of workers from undercutting the other.

Generally speaking, the Negroes are less forceful than the whites in disputes between employers and workers, have been more willing to accept wage offers, and have thus exerted some downward pressure on the income of all workers. After joining the union, workers can no longer accept individual job contracts, and there are special rules to guard against this. Thus the constitution of the weighers' and re-weighers' union states that "no member of the association will accept work at a lower rate of pay than the person who previously performed the same task" and "that on punishment of expulsion from the association no member will seek or accept a job from which another member of the association has been dismissed, unless in both cases the executive committee has given its permission in writing after a detailed investigation of the matter in hand."[30] Under the classers' constitution, a union member is obliged to call on other union members if he has too much work and may only turn to nonunion labor if no union member is avail-

30. [Retranslated from German.]

able. Members pay an initial fee of $5 and then a monthly subscription
of $1. The accumulated funds, generally administered by a treasurer,
are used to support strikers and pay sickness benefits. The latter, set at
$5 per week, are not paid until a member of the executive committee
has personally confirmed a member's illness. Any member who falls six
months behind in his payments forfeits union membership and has no
claim on previous contributions. Disputes among the members are settled by the executive committee and, failing an acceptable outcome, are
decided by the general assembly. Differences of opinion during the cotton weighing are settled by another union member, who submits his
judgment to the parties concerned in writing.

The Ring of these unions has been greatly strengthened in recent years
by committed solidarity and ruthless actions. It has become a powerful
adversary for the cotton traders and exporters. While it is usually the
workers who complain about the demands imposed by employers, in
New Orleans the employers complain about a workers' tyranny. Because
of the close ties among the workers, employers cannot break a strike by
hiring other workers. When, for instance, the longshoremen go on strike
(with the approval of the Ring's executive committee), their relatively
unskilled task could in theory be performed by other workers; but since
they usually also belong to the Ring, the employers cannot entice them.
They can only turn to nonunion workers. But they are few in number,
and in any case do not dare to oppose the powerful union at the moment.
And even if the employers find replacement labor, they still face major
problems. For if other longshoremen are brought in to unload the cotton from the riverboats, there will be no draymen or drivers to take the
cotton to the yards, since their union will also call a strike on the order
of the executive committee. The employers thus face eight successive
strikes, and in this situation their chances of victory are slim indeed.

Once the union Ring secured high wages for its members, it became
active in the political sphere. This was all the more likely since a majority of the white workers are Irish, who have a special affinity with political demonstrations, campaigns, and conspiracies and can stand and fall
as one man on the strength of their common racial, national, and religious identity. Largely in response to their pressure, the Louisiana state
legislature adopted a law banning seamen from foreign ships from
working in the wharf. In Texas the unions tried to get a similar measure
adopted, but they failed because they consisted of different nationalities
and were not as united as those in New Orleans. But they are still a

potent force in Galveston, as the following terms agreed to between the employers and the Cotton Screwers' Association suggest: (a) a nine-hour working day; (b) a minimum daily wage of $6 in the wharf and $5 outside (the port of Galveston is silting up, so lighters have to be used to load large ships on the open sea); (c) for those working outside, working time starts when they board the lighter and ends when they disembark again; they are paid in full regardless of whether they can work or not (adverse weather sometimes disrupts normal activities); (d) union members must be employed whenever they are available, whether they are more capable than nonmembers or not; (e) a gang of five workers may stow a maximum of seventy-five bales per day, while no minimum is guaranteed; a full day's pay is paid whether seventy-five bales are stowed in four hours or thirty bales in nine hours.

The negotiations between the union representatives and the merchants or ship captains are conducted by a special type of agents, the so-called boss stevedores. These do not negotiate on an individual basis but also belong to an association. For the workers the existence of these middlemen has the advantage that they gain early information about the general demand for their labor. To the merchants they offer a means of ensuring that the cotton is actually loaded, since the agents are responsible for this. And they are almost indispensable to ship captains who are not familiar with conditions in a strange port.

At times the boss stevedores take joint strike action with the workers. One such case occurred in Savannah in the fall of 1880. It emerged that the ship captains paid the stevedores less than the London merchants had been willing to pay but nevertheless charged them the full amount. To put a stop to the captains' fraud, the stevedores delegated one of their number to travel to England to reach an agreement with better terms for himself, the workers, and the English merchants. When he returned to Savannah, he began to negotiate directly with the workers on his own initiative, ignoring his union. The workers were initially happy to accept the improved terms, but they were persuaded by the other agents that the new contract would be illegal. The upshot was a joint strike in which the two groups called on the captains to break off all links with the self-seeking stevedore. The strike collapsed after several days, however, since the boss stevedores fell out among themselves and the workers were not really committed to the cause. The boss stevedores' association was then dissolved but was reconstituted shortly afterward.

3. Local But Centrally Led Associations of Workers From Different Trades for Which an Independent National Union Organization Is Not Practical.

Such an organization was the International Labor Union of America (ILU), which was fairly prominent in 1879 and 1880, gaining a foothold in New York City and then in Fall River, Lowell, Clinton, and Worcester, Massachusetts, Saginaw, Michigan, Omaha, and Paterson and several other towns in New Jersey. The main task this organization set itself was to unite the great mass of unskilled workers, to stop them from competing against each other, and to ensure that during strikes the employers did not replace striking workers with newly trained ones.[31] The ILU also admitted unions which did not have a nationwide membership and as purely local organizations were too weak to resist employers. It also included so-called mixed unions, which brought together craftsmen who were not sufficiently numerous to form separate unions. This organization, which carried the label "international" because it accepted workers of every nationality and race as members, consisted of separate branches with their own statutes (of course, in line with the main program) and their own sickness insurance schemes. For strikes and emergencies, such as unemployment, there was a central fund,[32] into which each member paid an initial fee and monthly contributions. All strike action had to be endorsed by the executive committee. There was also a propaganda fund, into which each member paid 2¢ per month.

The ILU's general declaration of principles reflected socialist ideals and terminology, probably because of the large number of German members. But the practical objectives it outlined were fairly moderate.[33] It read as follows:

Resolved:

1st. That the wage system is a despotism, under which the wage-worker is forced to sell his labor at such price and under such conditions as the employer of labor shall decide.

---

31. As the *Gewerkschafts-Zeitung* of 15 October 1879 noted: "It does not help the skilled laborers to look down on the unskilled laborers, because the latter are dangerous competitors to the former, and their competitive strength increases daily as the division of labor keeps pace with developments in industry and improvements in machinery."

32. There is also a contingency fund, administered by the executive committee. Five-sixths (originally four-fifths) of this is used to support strikes and lockouts, and one-sixth (one-fifth) to support members in exceptional cases of distress.

33. A member of the ILU executive committee told the author "that the United States is not a country for the social democratic movement, because under the capitalist mode of production manual workers could do better if they would only stand together. I could make some theoretical observations on social issues, but they would have about as much practical relevance as scientific studies on the origins of the sun."

2nd. That political liberty cannot long continue under economic bondage; for he who is forced to sell his labor or starve, will sell his franchise when the same alternative is presented.

3rd. That civilization means the diffusion of knowledge and the distribution of wealth; and the present system of labor tends to extremes of culture and ignorance, affluency and penury.

4th. That cultural progress depends on measures improving the knowledge and wealth of the workers.

5th. That as the wealth of the world is distributed through the wage system, its better distribution must come through higher wages, and better opportunities, until wages shall represent the earnings and not the necessities of labor; thus melting profit upon labor out of existence, and making co-operation, or self-employed labor, the natural and logical step from wage slavery to free labor.

6th. That all attempts to anticipate co-operation in advance of societary conditions are exotics or mere hot-house growths that are kept alive for a time through the sheer force of character and self-sacrificing leadership attempting them, and are as foreign to an atmosphere of cheap labor and a world of wages as the plants of the tropics are in a northern clime.

7th. That the first step towards the emancipation of labor is a reduction of the hours of labor, that the added leisure produced by a reduction of the hours of labor will operate upon the natural causes that affect the habits and customs of the people, enlarging wants, stimulating ambition, decreasing idleness, and increasing wages.[34]

The immediate demands were restricted to the following: "The reduction of the hours of labor; higher wages; factory, mine, and workshop inspection; abolition of contract [and] convict labor and [the] truck system; employers to be held responsible for accidents by neglected machinery; prohibition of child labor; the establishment of labor bureaus."[35]

4. The Most Widespread Workers' Organization These Days Is the Order of the Knights of Labor.[36]

On the one hand, this has diverged appreciably from the union movement, and on the other, as a specifically American phenomenon in the social struggle between capital and

---

34. [George E. McNeill, *The Labor Movement: The Problem of To-Day* (New York: M. W. Hazen Co., 1887), 161–2. The fourth point is not reproduced in McNeill and has been retranslated from the German.]

35. [Ibid., 162.]

36. T. V. Powderly, "The Organization of Labor," *North American Review*, 85 (August, 1882), 118–26; also Arthur von Studnitz, *Nordamerikanische Arbeiterverhältnisse* (Leipzig, 1879), annex 11, which does not do justice to the Order in terms of either its composition or its goals, but sets out its constitution accurately; Henry W. Farnam, *Die amerikanischen Gewerkvereine* (Leipzig, 1879; reprint Vaduz, 1988), 28; August Sartorius von Waltershausen, "Die bedeutendste Arbeiterorganisation in den Vereinigten

labor, it is far removed from European social democratic and anarchist theories and agitations. The union origins of the Order have survived only in the third type of association outlined above: unions which are unable to form national organizations are recognized as local assemblies when they have a certain number of members. The Order of the Knights of Labor differs from the ILU in that its political objectives are less ambitious, membership is not restricted to wage earners, and its organization is secret. The Order was founded in Philadelphia in 1869. Because it was a secret society, the public became aware of the Knights of Labor, which was already gaining strength, only four years later, during the trials of the Molly Maguires,[37] a group based in the coal-mining districts of Pennsylvania and dedicated to violent action. The Order seems to have been established at the instigation of the Philadelphia cloth and linen weavers.[38] But as it became clear that political action required a broad popular base, craftsmen and factory workers from all branches of industry soon joined the organization. In terms of numbers it expanded exponentially. Just as the American experience has shown that small businesses are inexorably swallowed up by bigger rivals and that the drive toward the concentration of capital is an accelerating process, the same, remarkably, can be observed among workers' associations. Over the years small locals or nonpolitical associations have been forced to subordinate their objectives to those of the large labor organizations and have eventually been absorbed by them. This fully explains the bitter antipathy that many surviving unions feel toward the Knights of Labor and the smears directed at the Order.

During the depression of the 1870s workers suffered substantial wage cuts and in many cases lost their jobs altogether. Many lost confidence in cooperation and unionization, which had not been able to stem the onslaught on wages and conditions. Membership of the Knights of Labor, which had peaked at 80,000, had fallen to around 12,000 by 1878. But many locals survived, and when the economic

Staaten von Amerika [I–II]," *Politische Wochenschrift*, 1882, no. 4, 29–30, and no. 5, 37–8. The following analysis is based largely on the constitution adopted in Reading, Pa., in 1878, a copy of which the author has gratefully received from the Chicago *Arbeiterzeitung*.

37. [1876–8.]

38. [The nine founders of the Knights of Labor were garment cutters. The Order soon grew to embrace weavers, among others, in Philadelphia. See Norman J. Ware, *The Labor Movement in the United States, 1860–1895: A Study in Democracy* (New York, 1929), 22–36.]

recovery set in and workers' confidence in cooperation returned in the wake of successful strikes, membership numbers soared again. The Knights of Labor claim to be represented in all states of the Union, but their strongholds seem to be in Pennsylvania, Ohio, Indiana, and New York. No reliable estimate can be given of the Order's total membership. It claims 2.5 million, while social democratic forces suggest a figure of 1.7 million. In the summer of 1881 a leading member spoke of 1,680 local assemblies, while in August 1882 a writer clearly familiar with the organization spoke of 1,890. By the end of that year another 210 assemblies were supposed to have been founded. This is certainly possible, since in the past the union movement gained in strength at times of economic prosperity and with the extraordinarily rapid expansion that characterizes all aspects of American social life. Even so, it is unlikely that all these 1,890 assemblies are still functioning. To bolster their strength, the Knights of Labor apparently number their new assemblies consecutively, regardless of whether older assemblies are still active. The demise of many assemblies can be explained in part by the impact of the economic crisis during 1873–9 and also by the fact that American workers often organize themselves only on special occasions – during a wage dispute, for instance. At such times the Knights of Labor will provide support. But when the dispute with the employers has been settled, they tend to disappear into the background again. So it is quite possible that the Order has no more than 345 functioning assemblies at the moment.

Because of their centralized leadership structure the Knights of Labor are ideally suited to engage in political action. The Order has the ear of part of the press, publishes its own newspapers (e.g., the *National Labor Tribune* in Pittsburgh and the *Progressive Age* in Chicago), and has substantial financial resources. Its achievements have nevertheless been modest thus far. The reason for this is that it has not been able to develop its own politics and act as an independent force. Instead it has sometimes allied itself with the Republicans and at others with the Democrats in the hope that it could realize its objectives through either one of the two major parties. At elections it has either supported "the best man," i.e., the person it thought could be relied on to further the cause energetically in Congress or in the state legislature; or it has resorted to so-called pressure politics, i.e., negotiating with the parties and pledging support to the party which had promised the most. The Knights' fond hopes were frequently dashed, however, and they were forced to recognize time and again that America's professional politicians are largely motivated by self-interest and see politics as no more than a sordid business. There are indications that recently some Knights of Labor leaders have decided to break off all ties with the established parties and instead want to forge ahead independently and more purposefully.

The Knights of Labor adopted a set of objectives at a convention in Reading, Pa., on 1–4 January 1878. They are set out in the preamble to the constitution. It runs as follows:

The alarming development and aggression of aggregated wealth, which, unless checked, will inevitably lead to the pauperization and hopeless degradation of the toiling masses, render it imperative, if we desire to enjoy the blessings of life, that a check should be placed upon its power and upon unjust accumulation, and a system adopted which will secure to the laborer the fruits of his toil; and as this much-desired object can only be accomplished by the thorough unification of labor, and the united efforts of those who obey the divine injunction that "In the sweat of thy brow shalt thou eat bread," we have formed the * * * * * with a view of securing the organization and direction, by co-operative effort, of the power of the industrial masses; and we submit to the world the objects sought to be accomplished by our organization, calling upon all those who believe in securing "the greatest good to the greatest number" to aid and assist us:

I. To bring within the folds of organization every department of productive industry, making knowledge a stand-point for action, and industrial and moral worth, not wealth, the true standard of individual and national greatness.

II. To secure to the toilers a proper share of the wealth that they create; more of the leisure that rightfully belongs to them; more societary advantages; more of the benefits, privileges, and emoluments of the world; in a word, all those rights and privileges necessary to make them capable of enjoying, appreciating, defending, and perpetuating the blessings of good government.

III. To arrive at the true condition of the producing masses in their educational, moral, and financial condition, by demanding from the various governments the establishment of bureaus of Labor Statistics.

IV. The establishment of co-operative institutions, productive and distributive.

V. The reserving of public lands – the heritage of the people – for the actual settler; – not another acre for railroads or speculators.

VI. The abrogation of all laws that do not bear equally upon capital and labor; the removal of unjust technicalities, delays and discrimination in the administration of justice; and the adopting of measures providing for the health and safety of those engaged in mining, manufacturing or building pursuits.

VII. The enactment of laws to compel chartered corporations to pay their employees weekly, in full, for labor performed during the preceding week, in the lawful money of the country.

VIII. The enactment of laws giving mechanics and laborers a first lien on their work for their full wages.

IX. The abolishment of the contract system on National, State and municipal work.

X. The substitution of arbitration for strikes, whenever and wherever employers and employees are willing to meet on equitable grounds.

XI. The prohibition of employment of children in workshops, mines and factories before attaining their fourteenth year.

XII. To abolish the system of letting out by contract the labor of convicts in our prisons and reformatory institutions.

XIII. To secure for both sexes equal pay for equal work.

XIV. The reduction of the hours of labor to eight per day, so that the laborers may have more time for social enjoyment and intellectual improvement, and be enabled to reap the advantages conferred by the labor-saving machinery which their brains have created.

XV. To prevail upon governments to establish a purely national circulating medium, issued directly to the people, without the intervention of any system of banking corporations, which money shall be legal tender in payment of all debts, public or private.[39]

As the above program shows, the objectives pursued by the Knights of Labor are not restricted to improving wages and conditions. It is therefore understandable that their members are not exclusively wage earners but also include tradesmen, independent artisans, and others. Since there are plans to set up consumer cooperatives, contacts with the retailing sector will prove rather useful. The Order's broad base also means that disputes between member wageworkers and employers can be discussed and settled in the local assemblies. In most cases the Order's authority is such that it can enforce the decisions of the arbitration body. According to the statutes at least three-quarters of an assembly's membership have to be wage earners. All persons involved in the sale or distribution of spirits, as well as lawyers, doctors, and bankers, are barred from membership. These four groups of people are regarded as the enemies of the working class: liquor sellers because they undermine family life, lawyers because they are often unscrupulous, selfish politicians, doctors because they charge exorbitant prices for quack remedies, and bankers because they monopolize money and credit to the detriment of the working class. Stockbrokers and professional gamblers are not accepted either. The Order has no other restrictions on membership. No one may be refused membership on grounds of race, nationality, religion, or membership in other organizations. Some members of the Socialist Labor Party also belong to the Knights of Labor. The socialists opposed the Order until 1881 because they con-

39. [*Constitution of the General Assembly, District Assemblies and Local Assemblies of the Knights of Labor of North America,* as revised September 1883.]

sidered its secrecy inappropriate and its program not radical enough. But since then they have changed their stance, no doubt partly because they have become aware of the Order's overall numerical strength. They now join it for the purpose of preparing the ground for the socialist utopia. They are unlikely to succeed, however, since American workers will not waver from the specifically American and will not accept party programs drawn up in Europe and inspired by circumstances quite different from those obtaining in the United States today.

The Order seeks to include all components of the working class and thus differs fundamentally from the trade union movement. In modern conditions, in particular the advanced division of labor, it considers the latter inadequate and aims to put something more inclusive in their place. As it succeeds in incorporating the large masses of the working people, the argument goes, competition among wageworkers will disappear and the arbitration of disputes between capital and labor it advocates will be brought nearer. Such procedures function best when both sides have an equally strong social power base, when both sides are free to accept or reject proposals from the other. Under these conditions both sides have to make concessions until one can go no further. At this point it is nonsensical for the other to press its demands, since it too must be interested in further cooperation.

The constituent associations of the Knights of Labor are not occupationally based but geographically based: they bring together the members living in a certain locality. The main unit of the organization is the local assembly. It may be structured in very different ways, depending on the circumstances. In the large cities, where workers of the same trade are amply represented, there are trade-based assemblies. But these should not be confused with trade unions, since they have no special links to the trade locals in other towns but only with the other Knights of Labor local assemblies within the same district. Other local assemblies are organized on the basis of nationality and language. In this way workers can be properly informed about the Order's objectives and can express their views on the issues of the day. In smaller towns these distinctions cannot be made, of course, and there workers from different trades and nationalities belong to the same local assembly. In the larger cities many trades with few members are also often combined in a single assembly.

The tier above the local assembly is the district assembly, which is set up as required and must represent at least five local assemblies, which may be in different counties or states. They send 1 delegate for every

100 members to the district assembly. The district assemblies arbitrate disputes in the local assemblies and hear appeals on members' grievances (the local assemblies serving as courts of first instance, as it were). The district assemblies elect delegates to the general assembly. This is the "highest tribunal" for adjudicating disputes. It also has the power to amend the constitution by a two-thirds majority; the lower-tier assemblies only have limited powers to adopt certain implementing regulations. It issues traveling cards to enable members to transfer from one local assembly to another, issues passwords and signs of recognition for the members (to identify each other), charters new assemblies, dispatches district organizers to set up new branches, and so on. A five-member executive board is responsible for managing the funds, ensuring that the Order's objectives are respected, that the constitution is being honored, and that the "grand master workman" or president is fulfilling his duties.

As mentioned, the Order of the Knights of Labor is a secret society.[40] The primary reasons for the secrecy are that it prevents workers from being dismissed for joining a social organization and that workers' decisions and strengths are kept from the employers, who thus cannot anticipate their demands. It is also in the Order's interests that those workers who are not members and arrange their own wages and conditions, the so-called scabs, do not find out what happens within the organization. Furthermore, it has to be said, among English-speaking workers there is also a tendency toward mystery mongering, toward lodges with ceremonial sessions and vestments, secret symbols, and so on. All these aspects are typical of the mutual insurance associations in the United States, such as the Freemasons, Odd Fellows, and Red Men. The Knights of Labor deliberately seek to emulate these. All the secrecy does have some undeniable drawbacks. For one thing, it alienates workers who have no time for formalities and religious overtones (which are all too evident in the membership oath).[41] And when, inevitably, some of

---

40. As can be gleaned from the above, many of the supposedly secret elements of the Knights of Labor have become public knowledge. But the internal discussions within the Order are kept secret long enough to ensure that they do not compromise the members.

41. According to the *Gewerkschafts-Zeitung* of 20 June 1880, the words of the membership oath are as follows: "I solemnly swear before God to obey and adhere to the laws and the constitution of this assembly, and that I will never divulge by word or by deed anything about the assembly or about a member. That I will never reveal the name of any member, and that I will never reveal anything that was done by a member of the Order either inside or outside of the assembly. That I will sustain and defend the Order

the deliberations do leak out, they often do so in a distorted form, so that outsiders can easily get the impression that there is something illegal going on behind closed doors. This reflects badly on the Order. Practice has borne out the Knights of Labor's approach, however, since they are by far the strongest workers' organization ever formed on American soil.[42]

Finally, we should point out that the Knights of Labor's organization and the political demands they have formulated are not only aimed at ending the misery inflicted on manual workers as a result of the advances of new technology and the factory system. They also believe that the state should take on the technical and industrial training of workers. Workers should be better educated generally and be able to develop their special skills, so that even though they are employed to perform simple operations, they are familiar with the whole production process and can be deployed from time to time in different operations of the factory. By introducing them to a variety of tasks in this way, workers are not only protected from physical and mental atrophy, but also acquire the skills

in its full dignity, and that in case of danger I will assist, to the extent of my ability, any branch of the Order in upholding our rights against oppressors. That I will assist any member, employer or worker, to the best of my ability, should the need arise. Should I betray in any way the solemn oath, which I am making, I will accept the consequences of my willful perjury, according to the judgement of this assembly. 'So help me God!'"

[In Ware, *The Labor Movement in the United States, 1860–1895,* 74–5, a rather different oath is reproduced, with no indication of its source. It reads: "I [. . .] do truly and solemnly swear [or affirm] that I will never reveal by word, act, art or implication, positive or negative, to any person or persons whatsoever, the name or object of this Order, the name or person of any one a member thereof, its signs, mysteries, arts, privileges or benefits, now or hereafter given to or conferred on me, any words spoken, acts done or objects intended; except in a legal or authorized manner or by special permission of the Order granted to me.

I do truly and solemnly promise strictly to obey all laws, regulations, solemn injunctions and legal summons that may be sent, said or handed to me.

I do truly and solemnly promise that I will to the best of my ability defend the life, interest, reputation and family of all true members of the Order, help and assist all employed and unemployed unfortunate or distressed Brothers to procure employment, secure just remuneration, relieve their distress and counsel others to aid them, so that they and theirs may receive and enjoy the just fruits of their labor and exercise of their art.

All this I swear [or affirm] without reservation or evasion to do and perform until death or honorable discharge [an accepted resignation] and bind myself under the penalty of the scorn and neglect due to perjury and violated honor as one unworthy of trust and assistance. So help me God and keep me steadfast unto the end. Amen."]

42. [See Powderly, "Organization of Labor," 124: "Had that body been organized openly, public opinion and the opposition it would meet with from other labor societies, would have prevented its growth."]

to become foremen or eventually start their own businesses. That it is not so much the technical division of labor that damages workers, but more the pervading social conditions and legal frameworks, is shown particularly clearly in the United States. Although the division of labor has advanced furthest there, the appalling factory conditions evident in Europe are not as glaring because the workers' plight is ameliorated by shorter working hours, higher wages, and other improved conditions. The theory of the so-called dark side of the division of labor can be valid only as long as the existing distribution of incomes is immutable, as some believe, or should be immutable, which even more people regard as the quintessence of economic wisdom. Highly developed technology and a highly detailed division of labor can be ruinous for many sections of the population under certain social conditions. But their impact is wholly beneficial if the social context in which the production of goods takes place is sufficiently broadened.

We believe we should stress this view here since the development of voluntary labor unions in America is inspired primarily by the desire to adapt the situation of wageworkers to the modern relations of production.

II. Strikes[43]

A comprehensive history of strikes in North America has yet to be written. Actually, it is unlikely ever to be written for the period covering the last 30 years, during which the conflict between labor and capital on the other side of the Atlantic Ocean has come to the fore. This is because many strikes have not even been recorded, and any reports based on reminiscences of the parties involved in the struggles are bound to be tainted by inaccuracy and one-sidedness. Nor can press reports provide a basis for a comprehensive record of labor disputes, since the back issues of the newspapers concerned, even the very titles themselves, have since long vanished. Leaving aside the few newspapers that represent powerful interests and are richly financed, the United States press reflects the country's overall economic output: enormous quantity combined with extreme instability.

The picture is not much better with regard to longer-term statistical information on strikes. Only a few states have set up bureaus of labor

43. "Die Gewerkvereine in den Vereinigten Staaten von Amerika (II)," *Jahrbücher für Nationalökonomie und Statistik*, Neue Folge, Bd. 7 (1883), 315–44.

statistics, which have made some relevant surveys, while the federal government has only occasionally addressed the labor question in the context of other issues. But a comprehensive statistical survey is the only means by which one can gain a clear view of the strikes' causes, consequences, usefulness, and perniciousness. For that which appears in the social life of nations as a mass phenomenon, but at the same time one constituted of many individual episodes, can clearly be appreciated only in its entirety. One can examine individual strikes as typical of the many specific cases only when one already has an overall picture. Taking the opposite line and generalizing from a few examples on the basis of personal preoccupations testifies to a method which, given the manifold circumstances and causes of social phenomena, should be employed with the greatest caution.

G. Phillips Bevan has provided a valuable statistical paper on strikes in the United Kingdom in the 1870s.[44] One of its salient points is that strikes were most common during both upturns and downturns in economic activity – in other words, at times of irregular production. Thus the conflict between capital and labor intensified during the boom years of 1872–3 and during the depression of 1878–9.[45] This phenomenon is hardly surprising, since in both phases of the economic cycle changes in production trigger a considerable shift in the respective social power of the two opposing sides. During an upturn employers (capital) are in more urgent need of more workers (labor) than in the previous period of broadly balanced production and consumption, while during a downturn the roles are reversed and capital confronts labor as the far stronger power. The longer a depression lasts, the more it is felt by propertyless workers. Many will lose their jobs, their meager savings will run out, and their health deteriorates.

Now the wage increases and wage cuts that occur during upturns and downturns, respectively, are only the first act in the struggle between capital and labor. At these times both sides drive up their demands in order to exploit their position of relative strength. This

44. Phillips Bevan, "The Strikes of the Past Ten Years," *Journal of the Royal Statistical Society*, 43 (1880), 35–54; "Discussion on Mr. Bevan's Paper," ibid., 55–64.
45. The number of strikes recorded in Britain between 1870 and 1879 was as follows:

1870	30	1875	245
1871	98	1876	229
1872	343	1877	180
1873	365	1878	268
1874	286	1879	308

approach inevitably triggers a reaction from the other side, which finds its external forms in the workers' strike and the employers' lockout.

Broadly speaking, it is possible to predict the outcome of strikes during both an upturn and a downturn. During the former, strikes tend to produce a favorable result for the workers, while during the latter they tend to be lost.[46] This is the second general conclusion that can be drawn from Phillips Bevan's figures.[47] (It must be said, however, that here the figures are not as convincing as in the case of strike frequencies.) Do the conclusions drawn from British experiences apply to the United States as well? On the basis of the available – although, as mentioned, not very extensive – material, we can confirm this.

The link between the economic cycle and strike activity can be illustrated by the history of labor problems in the coal-rich Tuscarawas Valley in Ohio. This has been covered in detail for the twelve-year period between 1869 and 1880 in the 1880 report by the Ohio Bureau of Labor Statistics. Below we outline the main events that interest us in this context.

The year 1869 had been a relatively successful one for those involved in the coal industry. But early the following year the demand for coal fell, and some mineowners announced wage cuts. The subsequent strike failed and the strikers were replaced by workers recruited from outside the region. The economic situation improved in 1871, coal prices edged up, and wages were raised marginally again. Because the employers were unable to realize substantial profits in the circumstances, the

46. This appears to confirm the theory that the size of the wage fund and the supply of and demand for labor exclusively determine fluctuations in wage levels. It could be argued that the strikes achieved what would have happened without them anyway. Against this it should be noted that our conclusion applies to a majority of cases but is by no means a general rule. It would be claiming far too much to posit a "law of nature" here. At the same time, one can also imagine that during prosperous times the number of potential victories by the employers is depressed because they do not want to interrupt production and might well grant wage increases they would not have without industrial action by the workers, and that during the bad times wage cuts could have been avoided without this creating a serious problem for the employers. Evidence that these factors are at play is provided by the observation made in America that proposals for arbitration (in which wages are in effect set on the basis of prevailing market conditions) tend to be rejected by employers during the downturns and by workers during the upturns. These issues will be discussed in greater detail in a later paper.

47. According to Phillips Bevan's figures, 18 strikes were won and 11 lost in 1872–3, and 6 were won and 115 lost in 1878–9. If these figures are typical, they imply that in Britain capital is relatively stronger during the downturns than labor is during the upturns. As we will show, this does not apply to the United States, where, compared to Britain, the demand for labor generally outstrips the supply.

workers accepted the small increases and used their additional resources to set up the Miners' and Laborers' Protective Union, whose
aim was to secure improved working conditions in the forthcoming
prosperous years. In the spring of 1872 demand for coal soared, a wage
claim was accepted, and a second increase followed a strike, which
closed the mines for two weeks. In November another strike over wages
was in the offing, but the owners, faced with high demand for their
product, gave in to the union's demands. At this point the workers felt
particularly strong and made the employers feel their muscle.

Some lodges in the district commenced to exercise tyranny, and in some instances
even went so far as to take control from the hands of the superintendents of
mines, and dictate to them who should and who should not be employed. Some
of its prominent members went to those who happened to be employed in a mine,
not members of the organization, and demanded of them to join the union or quit
the mine: it went further in January, 1873, and ordered a suspension of operations
throughout the Tuscarawas Valley, to aid the miners of the Mahoning district to
gain their price.[48]

The employers then tried to break the union by creating dissatisfaction,
mainly by announcing wage cuts and wage increases on several occasions. A number of strikes characterized labor's excesses, against which
the resentful mineowners believed it necessary to form a strong united
front.

The workers' actions met with varying success, until in 1873 the deep
recession set in, which lasted until late 1879. Soon wage cuts were
announced at several mines in the valley. But since they were not excessive, the workers accepted them. For a while, problems between owners
and workers were dealt with by arbitration. The arbitration procedure
was introduced at the behest of the national coalminers' union. A large
proportion of the valley's miners joined this organization after the local
body had been shattered by the economic crisis. (As we will see below,
the national union did not survive the recession either.) After wages fluc-
tuated for some time, the owners announced a deep cut in August 1875,
which led to a strike. Industrial peace was restored after a compromise
was agreed to which provided for smaller cuts than were originally
intended by the owners. The following March another wage cut was
announced and a new strike was called. This time there was violence,

48. Ohio BLS, *Fourth Report*, 78.

and the militia was called in. The strike was lost because in the prevailing economic climate it was easy to find cheap outside labor to replace the strikers. The employers, embittered by the agitation of their workers and able to set working conditions unilaterally owing to the surplus of labor, acted no differently from the workers when they had had the upper hand in 1872–3. They exploited their advantage to the full. Arrogantly and against the prevailing economic conditions, they decreed further wage cuts and tightened working conditions. Workers were banned from holding meetings, and the existing union was dissolved. In 1878 the miners were at their lowest point. They were now expected to put the hewn coal through a screen, so that only the remaining amount would count toward the usual piecework payment. This measure was tantamount to a new wage cut, and the workers tried to respond by work stoppages. Any real success was out of the question, however, since the economic climate had not improved. The workers returned to work and had to suffer the added humiliation of the supervisors dismissing those comrades who had led the actions. They walked out again and stayed out for fourteen weeks, but the strike achieved nothing.

In the fall of 1879 there were at last the first signs that the economic crisis was coming to an end. Coal prices firmed and the miners immediately submitted a wage claim. Soon after it was accepted they set up a new union, the Miners' Protective Association, and made plans for further wage rises. When they were refused, strikes were called, which lasted into 1880. Some workers accepted a compromise with a modest wage increase, while others stayed out. It looked as if there would again be violence, but the strike was called off after another intervention by militia troops. Nevertheless, because business was much better, higher wages were granted and the above-mentioned screening system was abolished. After a period of industrial peace, the final strike in the period under consideration was called in 1881. It brought victory. During the economic upturn the Knights of Labor, a secret association which had made a name for itself after scoring successes in Pennsylvania, gained a large following among the Tuscarawas miners. (The Knights' appeal was based not least on the widely held view that the failure of previous attempts at unionization had been due to the fact that they had been an open, not a secret, organization.) For 1881 the Ohio Bureau of Labor Statistics reported twenty-two miners' strikes in the state. Of these, twelve were won, two were settled by negotiation, and only six were lost.

Analyzing this period, we can draw conclusions similar to those based on the British evidence. Most strikes happen during economic upturns and downturns. The second social law – that strikes tend to be won in the former period and lost in the latter – is also confirmed. The value of the evidence is also enhanced by the information on strike causes it provides. When demand for an industry's products, in this case coal, is up, the purpose of strike action is to push through wage increases; when demand is down, strikes are called to prevent wage reductions. In the first case the workers are generally successful; in the second they fail. Both sides seek to press their advantage whenever their social power allows it. In so doing they aggravate class conflict and class hatred. The arrogance of one side creates resentment in the other. As a consequence steps are taken to find a compromise, which both sides accept to calm the situation.

The second rule is evidenced more reliably because it is based on mass observation, in Table 1. This has been drawn up on the basis of newspaper reports and information from the Ohio and Missouri bureaus of labor statistics. The information covers a period of particular interest from the point of view of strikes, namely, the first ten months[49] of the economic recovery after the prolonged recession. In the summer of 1879 there were some indications that the phase of overproduction had definitely come to an end, and in the fall this was confirmed and demand for labor was growing everywhere.

This list is obviously not comprehensive. There is no doubt that more strikes occurred in the United States in the period under consideration. I am confident, however, that all major strikes in the states of New York, Pennsylvania, Maryland, New Jersey, and Illinois are listed, and that hardly any strikes have been missed from Ohio. Despite the shortcomings, I still believe that the list offers some valuable insights. Most pertinently, it clearly confirms the two rules set out above. In so doing it helps to provide a sounder basis for a field that is as yet little examined.

Another criticism that could be made of Table 1 is that the information covers not years but only a few months. In defense it must be said that the months in question broadly coincide with reviving economic activity and are hence of particular interest in the context of the issues under discussion here, and that within the ten-month period

49. [Sartorius von Waltershausen speaks twice of a ten-month period, but his table covers eleven months.]

Table 1   *Strikes in the United States from 1 November 1879*
to 1 October 1880

Month	Workers' occupation	Cause	Location	Result
November 1879	Furniture workers	Working hours	New York	Lost
	Female weavers	Wage claim	New York	Won
	Dockers	Wage claim	Boston	Won
	Packinghouse workers	Wage claim	Chicago	Won
	Cigarmakers	Wage claim	Wheeling, WVA	Won
	Miners	Wage claim	Straitsville, OH	Won
	Pianomakers	Wage claim	New York	Won
	Dockers	Wage claim	Boston	Won
	Furniture workers	Working hours	five towns	Won
	Dockers	?	Brooklyn, NY	Won
	Iron and steel workers	Wage claim	Pittsburgh	Settled
	Pianomakers	Wage claim	Baltimore	Settled
	Dockers	?	Baltimore	Won
	Cigarmakers	Wage claim	New York	Won
	Dockers	?	New York	Won
	Rubber workers	Wage claim	New Brunswick, NJ	Won
	Tanners	?	Cincinnati	Won
December	Furniture workers	?	New York	Settled
	Weavers	Working hours	Paterson, NJ	Won
	Horse shoers	?	Chicago	Won
	Weavers	Wage claim	Easton, PA	Won
January 1880	Hatmakers	?	Reading, PA	Won
	Coopers	?	Baltimore	Settled
	Miners	?	Pittsburgh	Settled
	Packinghouse workers	Union issue	Chicago	Lost
	Miners	Union issue	N. Straitsville, OH	Won
	Coalminers	Wage claim	Ohlton, OH	Won
	Coalminers	Wage claim	East Palatine, OH	Lost
	Coalminers	Wage cut	Coalport, OH	Lost
	Coalminers	Wage claim	Steubenville, OH	Settled
	Coalminers	Wage claim	Jamesville, OH	Lost

Table 1   *(cont.)*

Month	Workers' occupation	Cause	Location	Result
	Sewing-machine operators	Wage claim	Cleveland	Lost
	Coopers	Wage cut	Cleveland	Settled
	Coopers	Wage claim	Steubenville, OH	Won
	Sectionhands	Wage claim	Steubenville, OH	Lost
	Iron and steel workers	Union issue	Springfield, IL	Lost
February	Iron and steel workers	Wage claim	Pittsburgh	Won
	Collar-factory workers	?	Troy, NY	Won
	Iron and steel workers	Wage claim	Pittsburgh	Won
	Boilermakers	Wage claim	St. Louis	Won
	Pianomakers	Wage claim	New York	Won
	Furniture workers	Wage claim	Brooklyn, NY	Won
	Stovemolders	Wage claim	Pittsburgh	Won
	Joiners	Wage claim	San Francisco	Won
	Coalminers	Wages payment	Mineral Point, OH	Lost
	Coalminers	Wage claim	Vienna, OH	Settled
	Coalminers	Wage claim	[Churchill, OH]	Won
	Tanners	Wage claim	Cincinnati	Lost
	Cash register workers	Wage cut	Cincinnati	Won
	Typographers	Union issue	Cleveland	Lost
	Rolling-mill workers	Wage claim	Cleveland	Won
	Cigarmakers	Union issue	Cleveland	Lost
	Ironmolders	Factory organization	Cleveland	Settled
	Typographers	Union issue	Cleveland	Settled
	Cigarmakers	Wage claim	Newark, NJ	Lost
	Rolling-mill workers	Working conditions	Steubenville, OH	Settled

Table 1   *(cont.)*

Month	Workers' occupation	Cause	Location	Result
	Farming-equipment workers	Wage claim	Springfield, IL	Settled
	Glassworkers	Wage claim	Bellaire, OH	Won
March	Dockers	?	New York	Won
	Stonecutters	Wage claim	St. Louis	Won
	Iron and steel workers	?	Pottsville, PA	Settled
	Machinists	Working hours	Cincinnati	Won
	Shoemakers	Wage claim	Cincinnati	Won
	Shoemakers	Wage claim	Cincinnati	Won
	Shoemakers	Wage claim	Cincinnati	Won
	Wagonmakers	Wage claim	St. Louis	Won
	Cigarmakers	Union issue	Cincinnati	Settled
	Ironmolders	Factory organization	Cleveland	Settled
	Furniture-workers	?	New York	Won
	Pianoworkers	Wage claim	New York	Settled
	Coalminers	Working conditions	Zaleski, OH	Won
	Ironmolders	Wage claim	Cleveland	Won
	Bricklayers	Wage claim	Cleveland	Won
	Stovemolders	Wage claim	Cleveland	Won
	Stovemolders	Wage claim	Cleveland	Settled
	Stonecutters	Working hours	Cleveland	Won
	Porters	Working hours	Cleveland	Settled
	Ironmolders	Wage claim	Cleveland	Settled
	Teamsters	Wage claim	Cleveland	Won
	Ironmolders	Wage claim	Hamilton, OH	Settled
	Plow-factory workers	Wage claim	Hamilton, OH	Won
	Ironmolders	Wage claim	Dayton, OH	Settled
	Ironmolders	Wage claim	Dayton, OH	Lost
	Ironmolders	Union issue	Leetonia, OH	Won
	Ironmolders	Wage claim	Lorain, OH	Settled
	Paper-mill workers	Wage claim	Franklin, OH	Won
	Ironmolders	Wage claim	Painesville, OH	Settled
	Tailors	Wage claim	Youngstown, OH	Settled

Table 1   *(cont.)*

Month	Workers' occupation	Cause	Location	Result
April	Stovemolders	Wage claim	Salem, PA	Won
	Bricklayers	Wage claim	Cleveland	Won
	Coalminers	Wage claim	Longstreth, OH	Won
	Coalminers	Wage claim	Monongahela, PA	Won
	Iron and steel workers	Wage claim	Pittsburgh	Settled
	Cabinetmakers	Wage cut	San Francisco	Lost
	Tailors	Wage claim	Pittsburgh	Won
	Carpenters	Wage claim	St. Louis	Won
	Railway employees	Wage claim	Baltimore	Won
	Pianoworkers	Wage claim	New York	Settled
	Coalminers	Wage cut	Pomeroy, OH	Settled
	Coalminers	Wage cut	Teegarden, OH	Lost
	Coalminers	Working conditions	Brookfield, OH	Lost
	Freightloaders	Wage claim	Cincinnati	Won
	Ironmolders	Wage claim	Cleveland	Lost
	Screw-factory workers	Working conditions	Cleveland	Lost
	Railway station workers	Wage claim	Toledo, OH	Settled
	Iron and steel workers	Wage claim	Pittsburgh	Lost
	Iron and steel workers	Wage claim	?	Lost
	Trunk makers	Wage claim	?	Won
	Cigarmakers	Wage claim	?	Won
	Miners	Wage cut	Pennsylvania	Lost
May	Bricklayers	Wage claim	St. Louis	Won
	Weavers	Wage claim	Philadelphia	Lost
	Stonecutters	?	Quincy, IL	lost
	Cigarmakers	Wage cut	Pittsburgh	Lost
	Stovemolders	Wage cut	?	Lost
	Coalminers	Wage cut	N. Harrisburg, PA	Lost
	Coalminers	Wage cut	Connellsville, PA	Lost
	Nail-factory workers	Wage cut	Belleville, IL	Lost
	Coalminers	Wage cut	Churchill, OH	Lost

Table 1 *(cont.)*

Month	Workers' occupation	Cause	Location	Result
	Ironmolders	Wage claim	Cleveland	Lost
	Coalminers	Wage claim	Tuscarawas, OH	Lost
	Iron and steel workers	Wages payment	Jackson, OH	Lost
	Stovemolders	Wage cut	Cincinnati	Lost
	Messenger boys	Wage claim	Cleveland	Lost
	Stationary engineers	Working conditions	Marion, OH	Lost
	Rolling-mill workers	Working conditions	Youngstown, OH	Settled
	Cigarmakers	Wage cut	New York	Lost
	Pianoworkers	Wage cut	New York	Lost
	Stonecutters	Working hours	Chicago	Won
	Cigarmakers	Wage claim	Baltimore	Won
June	Cigarmakers	?	Troy, NY	Won
	Capmakers	Wage claim	New York	Won
	Buttonmakers	?	Brooklyn, NY	Won
	Stonemasons	Wage claim	New York	Won
	Dockers	Wage claim	New York	Lost
	Streetcar workers	Wage claim	New York	Won
	Iron and steel workers	Wage claim	New York	Lost
	Dockers	Wage claim	New York	Won
	Dockers	Wage claim	Buffalo, NY	Lost
	Calico printers	Wage claim	Lowell, MA	Won
	Coopers	Wage claim	Chicago	Won
	Pipelayers	Wage claim	Chicago	Won
	Ironmolders	?	Cincinnati	Won
	Coalminers	Wage cut	Logan, OH	Lost
	Glassworkers	Apprentice-ships	Steubenville, OH	Lost
	Coalminers	Wage cut	Coshocton, OH	Lost
	Coalminers	Wage cut	Steubenville, OH	Lost
	Coalminers	Working conditions	Teegarden, OH	Settled
	Coalminers	Payday	Pike Run, OH	Won

Table 1   (cont.)

Month	Workers' occupation	Cause	Location	Result
	Coalminers	Payday	Wellston, OH	Won
	Rolling-mill workers	Wage claim	Cincinnati	Won
	Horse shoers	Wage claim	Cincinnati	Won
	Cash register workers	Foreman	Cincinnati	Won
	Coopers	Wage claim	Cincinnati	Won
	Iron and steel workers	Union issue	Cleveland	Lost
	Rolling-mill workers	Wage claim	Pittsburgh	Won
	Rolling-mill workers	Wage claim	[Hubbard, OH]	Won
	Rolling-mill workers	Wage claim	Youngstown, OH	Won
	Rolling-mill workers	Wage claim	Girard, OH	Won
	Rolling-mill workers	Wage claim	Niles, OH	Won
	Rolling-mill workers	Wage claim	Warren, OH	Won
	Rolling-mill workers	Wage claim	Massillon, OH	Won
	Rolling-mill workers	Wage claim	Akron, OH	Won
	Rolling-mill workers	Wage claim	Cleveland	Won
	Rolling-mill workers	Wage claim	Columbus, OH	Won
	Rolling-mill workers	Wage claim	Jamesville, OH	Won
	Rolling-mill workers	Wage claim	Alekanna, OH	Won
	Rolling-mill helpers	Wage claim	Youngstown, OH	Won
July	Coalminers	Wage cut	Martins Ferry, OH	Settled
	Stovemolders	Wage cut	Portsmouth, OH	Lost
	Stovemolders	Wage cut	Hanging Rock, OH	Lost

Table 1 *(cont.)*

Month	Workers' occupation	Cause	Location	Result
	Cigarmakers	Wage claim	New York	Lost
	Furriers	Wage claim	New York	Won
	Capmakers	Wage claim	New York	Won
	Ironmolders	?	Reading, PA	Lost
	Coalminers	Wage cut	Coshocton, OH	Won
	Coalminers	Payday	Mineville, NY	Won
	Coalminers	Union issue	Cambridge, OH	Lost
August	Railway workers	Wage claim	St. Louis	Won
	Cabinet-makers	Working conditions	New York	Lost
	Coopers	Wage claim	New York	Won
	Stonecutters	Wage claim	New York	Won
	Plasterers	Wage claim	New York	Won
	Shoemakers	Wage claim	Philadelphia	Won
	Sawmill workers	Working hours	Rock Island, IL	Won
	Coachdrivers	Working conditions	Indianapolis	Won
	Cigarmakers	Wage claim	New York	Lost
	Cigarpackers	Wage claim	New York	Won
	Capmakers	Wage claim	New York	Won
	Coalminers	Wage claim	Coalton, IL	Settled
	Stovemolders	Wage cut	Cincinnati	Lost
	Coalminers	Wage claim	Aetna, OH	Settled
	Hodcarriers	Wage claim	Cincinnati	Lost
	Coopers	Wage claim	Cincinnati	Won
	Ironmolders	Wage claim	Springfield, OH	Settled
September	Coalminers	Wage cut	Salineville, OH	Lost
	Coalminers	Working hours	[Churchill, OH]	Won
	Horse-collar makers	Wage claim	Cincinnati	Lost
	Coalminers	Employment contract	Corning, OH	Won
	Typographers	Wage cut	New York	Lost
	Stovemolders	Wage claim	Cincinnati	Won
	Coalminers	Union issue	Yellow Creek, OH	Won
	Coalminers	?	Steubenville, OH	Won
	Ironmolders	Wage claim	Cincinnati	Lost
	Ironmolders	Wage claim	Cincinnati	Lost

some production fluctuations occurred in the United States which are reflected in the outcome of the strikes and thus also provide detailed proof of the posited rules.

Some 205 strikes are listed. Of these, 111 were won by the workers, 34 were settled by some compromise, and 60 were lost. Most of the settled disputes broadly resulted in an improvement in working conditions. Nineteen of the thirty-four compromised strikes were called to back a wage claim, two over factory organization, three over working conditions, two over trade union issues and one against an extension of working hours, and only three against a wage cut. (In four cases the cause of the strike could not be determined from the available information.) So it can be said that of the 205 strikes during the economic upturn, 137 produced an outcome favorable to the workers. (The conciliated strikes against wage cuts and extended working hours and those whose cause is not known have been added to the unfavorable outcomes.) Analyzed by cause, 121 strikes were called to back a wage claim, 26 against wage cuts, 8 over working hours, 11 over trade union issues, specifically over the dismissal of union activists, and 20 for other reasons; the strike cause could not be determined in 19 cases.

The evidence from Table 1 also leads to the conclusion that strikes called to back a wage claim were generally successful, while those opposing a wage cut were generally lost. Of the 121 of the first type, 80 were won, 19 were settled (and thus resulted in a certain increase in earnings), and only 22 were lost. Of the twenty-six strikes against wage cuts, twenty-one were lost, three were settled (and thus resulted in some loss of earnings), and only two were won. In this case the rule holds true even more than in the first. In wage claims the deviation from the norm is 22.2 percent, while for wage cuts it is only 9.3 percent.[50]

It is also worth noting that sixteen of the twenty strikes called in May were lost. This again confirms the general rule. After output steadily increased from November 1879 to April 1880, there was a temporary slowdown in May. This was because producers had overreached themselves and had not taken sufficient account of the fact that, in the wake of the long recession, people's capacity to consume had not yet fully recovered to absorb all the new products. A person recovers from a serious illness only gradually, and there is a strong chance of a relapse if he

---

50. [Apparently Sartorius von Waltershausen made a mistake while calculating the "deviations from the norm." In the first case he gives 22 / (80 + 19) = 22.2%; this seems to imply that the second calculation should be 2 / (21 + 3) = 8.3% and not 9.3%.]

is treated like a healthy person too early. So too with the economy. If the May strikes are excluded from the figures, it turns out that 133 of the 185 strikes during the upturn had a positive outcome for the workers.

From the available information we can draw a conclusion that may be worth bearing in mind in the context of the labor question. Why is it that employers allow a wage claim to escalate into industrial action so quickly, and why is it that workers are so quick to oppose a wage cut by withdrawing their labor? Surely it would be better if both avoided what damages them, since success or failure seems largely predetermined. Shortsightedness and overconfidence on both sides often lead to strikes, while a negotiated settlement would give both sides what is appropriate in the prevailing economic circumstances. On the basis of this view, one might draw the conclusion that supply and demand are the sole determinants of wages and that social action cannot alter workers' earnings in any way. But anyone who argues that wages would be raised as much and as quickly without the workers resorting to strikes should not forget that it is only the social power created by union organization that forces employers to put up wages in line with rising profits in the first place. The demand for labor power and the supply by the individual worker are mediated by a social force, a coalition of those offering their labor, which by withholding it intensifies the tension between labor supply and demand. Without this concerted force, wages would no doubt rise when goods prices rise, but certainly not in line with them. The distribution of wages and profits does not simply conform to a certain inescapable logic; it is also determined by the social organization of the interested parties. And generally speaking, that party which can exploit its natural and social strength at any one time will carry off the prize in a dispute. In that sense strikes have largely predictable outcomes and are, on this assumption, futile.

The correct conclusion to draw from the futility of strike action in situations where unions exist is that conciliation or arbitration procedures, which lay bare the true state of market conditions, represent a better way forward. We will return to this peaceful way of settling industrial disputes in a forthcoming paper, when we will try to show, on the basis of the American experience, the advantages it offers.

One aspect revealed in the above history of the Tuscarawas strikes should not be overlooked, namely, the junctures at which workers' associations are formed. Our brief survey shows that during periods of relative calm, i.e., at times of a broad equilibrium between production and consumption, no new unions are founded, while during periods of instability, i.e., both the downturns and upturns in economic activity, the workers are attracted to forming unions. In the first case, workers are urged to associate with their fellow oppressed as the best means of overcoming their isolation and protecting their interests. And in the second case, a similar view is understandable, namely, that only by joining forces are the workers able to press their advantage in what is a favorable situation for them. The history of the American trade unions shows that the overwhelming majority of them were set up during periods of growing demand for labor. It is true that unions were also formed in all parts of the country at times of economic difficulties, but these efforts are frequently nipped in the bud by stronger counterforces. Among these inhibiting factors are, firstly, the employers' ability to recruit nonunion labor to keep their workplaces running. At these times, labor supply exceeds demand and production has been scaled down (compared to the previous more buoyant period). So the employer can pick his workforce and insist on nonunionization as a condition of employment. Another impediment to union organization is the lack of financial resources. These are needed not only to print the statutes and circulars, hire meeting halls, etc., but above all to set up a support fund, an essential means of ensuring the union's cohesion. The lack of such funds seems to have been the key reason for the demise in the mid-1870s of most of the unions set up over the previous two decades. In the autumn of 1879 the idea of unionization gained a new lease on life. Reviving old traditions, workers founded local and soon afterward national associations. Among the latter the following had been disbanded during the previous period: the unions of the coachmakers, painters and lacquerers, machine builders, bricklayers, coopers, miners, shoemakers (Knights of St. Crispin), and ironmolders. The other nationals had lost most of their branch associations during the 1870s and so retained only a small membership. Moreover, it was the associations which had not developed beyond the local level that had been the first to go under.[51]

---

51. The Missouri Bureau of Labor Statistics reported the existence of nineteen unions in the state as of 1 January 1881. Of these fourteen had been founded in 1879 and 1880, while only five had survived from the previous recession. In Ohio there were around 160 unions with 40,000 members at the start of 1881. Most of these had also been founded in either of the two previous years. During 1881 another fourteen new union foundations were reported to the state's Bureau of Labor Statistics. In New York City there were around 30,000 union members in the summer of 1881 compared to just under 5,000 in 1877. The city's cigarmakers' union had 3,300 members in 1881 com-

Sometimes unions are formed as a direct consequence of strikes. Unity is, of course, the overriding prerequisite for victory in industrial disputes. Otherwise the employers can resort to the tested ploy of dividing the workforce by giving in to or accommodating one section and opposing another. Strikers who accept the employer's proposals against the majority of the union membership are called *scabs* (or *rats, knobsticks,* or *wage killers*) and are despised as traitors to the workers' cause. If a strike succeeds despite their defection, they can be certain of their former comrades' revenge. The winners will insist, as a condition of returning to work, on the dismissal of the traitors. If the strike is lost, the scabs will stay on but they will never be forgiven by the others. The reason workers nevertheless, time and again, break ranks is simply that during a strike individuals often endure great hardship and some workers, if they are forced to choose, will put their families before their colleagues. Such people will not gain the respect of the employers, incidentally, since workers whose actions precipitate the defeat of their comrades are despised by those who use them in the same way that traitors in war are despised.

The scabs should not be confused with "blacklegs." These are workers recruited from elsewhere to replace the strikers. They are hated as much as the scabs, and the strikers will use every opportunity to create problems for them. A miners' leader from the Tuscarawas Valley told an official of the Ohio Bureau of Labor Statistics about the following act of vengeance:

The only ripple in the affairs of mining during that fall and winter, was an attempt made by the "blacklegs" working at the Brewster Coal Co.'s South Mine to inaugurate another strike. To this end they assembled in the blacksmith shop, and called the old hands to their meeting, requesting them to join hands and make a demand for an advance of ten cents per ton; but the latter looked upon it as a "little too thin," and during the meeting reminded the "strangers" that they could put no confidence in the men that had only a few months previous so shamefully sold them, and taken their places, whilst they were striking for what they thought were their just dues. A few mornings afterwards, on arriving at the face of the workings, "the strangers" were sadly surprised to find all their tools missing, and well, Dame Rumor blamed many, but convicted none: they appealed to the company to refurnish them tools, but apparently their mission was ended, a fact that the mine owners were not backward in making known to them.[52]

pared to only 380 the year before. The German typographical union had 1,200 registered members across the United States before the recession, but this figure had dwindled to 250 by 1879.
52. Ohio BLS, *Fourth Report,* 76–7.

In addition to the above-mentioned method of splitting a minority of their workers from the majority, American employers rely on a number of other ploys during or after strikes. Among these are the use of *blacklists,* on which are entered [the names of] those workers who are known as union leaders or agitators. The list is compiled for a group of firms and sent around to all of them. Its purpose is to induce the proscribed workers to leave their current jobs and exclude them from employment elsewhere. Blacklists have been used even when there are no employers' associations, but in these situations they have rarely become permanent arrangements. The workers complain most bitterly about the way in which blacklisting is used. They accuse the employers of intriguing against workers to give them an excuse to dismiss them or using some pretext to deprive diligent workers of their livelihoods.[53] In assessing this institution, one has to acknowledge that the employers have a legitimate right to maintain order in their factories and workshops and to remove elements intent on sowing discord between capital and labor. This can also be justified in economic terms as being in the interests of production. On the other hand, one cannot ignore either that through the blacklist employers can impugn the characters of people they may dislike for one reason or another and thereby possibly destroy their livelihoods. This is because the other participants in the employers' cartel have no means of determining satisfactorily why one of them wants to put an individual worker on the blacklist. So one can certainly argue that blacklisting is a two-edged sword, which carries risks that are hardly offset by the benefits. One strong argument against blacklisting is that it has led to many long strikes. There is little doubt that this institution has been responsible for as many strikes as have been averted by the removal of dissatisfied and unruly workers. The above table of strikes [Table 1] indicates where strikes were called in response to blacklisting and other union-related issues.

Another means which employers use to try to break the power of a union is described in the *New-Yorker Gewerkschafts-Zeitung,* which published a graphic report in September 1880 of a seventeen-week strike by the Stovemolders' Union of Cincinnati.[54] We reprint it here in full:

The wage contract agreed between the firm [i.e., W. C. Davis] and the union expired on 4 April this year. The firm immediately announced a 10 percent wage

53. Some examples are given in Massachusetts BSL, *Thirteenth Report,* 1882, 345–8.
54. *New-Yorker Gewerkschafts-Zeitung,* 20 September 1880.

rise. The union fell into the trap and accepted the rise without negotiation. The firm then rapidly built up stocks and felt so sure of its position that on 4 May it summarily withdrew the wage rise announced a month earlier. The union then called a strike throughout the trade. On 4 July the smaller firms sued for peace and accepted the union's demands. But Davis, which has millions of dollars in the bank and controls the market, refused to give in. It boasted of its huge financial reserves and thought it could starve the 150 union members it had employed until the strike into submission. But at this point it became clear what a union can achieve.

After the scabs had made such a mess of their work that most of it had to be melted down again, Davis was in danger of losing its customers unless it could supply better goods. At last negotiations opened between the two sides. The firm offered a 25 percent pay rise instead of the earlier 10 percent, but on condition that the scabs would remain.

The union recognized this ploy for what it was: an attempt by the employer to ensure that the scabs would be trained by the returning strikers, who could then be dismissed when the scabs had been brought up to scratch. The union instead called for restoration of the original 10 percent rise, dismissal of all scabs and reinstatement of all union members in their old jobs. The millionaire refused to budge. But based on its exemplary organization the union was able to stand its ground and responded: do or die. In the end the firm preferred concessions to bankruptcy. First, however, Davis demanded that the union be disbanded. But he had miscalculated. On 24 August the firm had to accept the union's demands.

Such dubious practices by the employers are mirrored by similar improprieties on the part of the workers. The difference is, however, that while the employers remain within the letter of the law, the workers resort to violence. The political and geographical situation in the United States makes it difficult for the authorities to oppose raw outbreaks of passion energetically and effectively. For one thing, many of the production sites are isolated. Sawmills, mines, steelmills, and smelting works are often so far removed from the country's populous cities and main transportation routes that an employer cannot count on the support of law-abiding citizens. Then there is the lack of organization among the military forces. The regular army, about 25,000 strong, is dispersed among the forts in the western territories to protect the settlers against Indian attacks. The militias are undisciplined and woefully undertrained forces led by elected officers, and their members in some cases may well have strong sympathies with the violent strikers.[55]

55. On the standing army and the militia, see Friedrich Ratzel, *Die Vereinigten Staaten von Nord-Amerika*, vol. II: *Politische Geographie* (Munich and Berlin, 1880), 494–6. And on the inadequate military assistance during strikes, see Thomas A. Scott, "The Recent Strikes," *North American Review*, 125 (September 1877), 351–62.

The great railway strikes in Pennsylvania [of 1877] have been widely – and at times well – reported elsewhere, so we need not dwell here on the violence they generated.[56] We only want to point out that socialism had little to do with these events. In New York, Chicago, and St. Louis the socialists only expressed their sympathies with the strikers in long speeches at meetings held after the events. But they took no action. Among those arrested in Baltimore was the local branch secretary of the Socialist Labor Party. This gave some newspapers an opportunity to claim that the violence had been initiated by the socialists. But it was shown that the socialists had only called a meeting among themselves to decide on their position after the violence had started. And although some believed it was time to launch the "great social revolution," the majority recognized that the dispute centered on passing sources of dissatisfaction. The meeting therefore decided that the party should adopt a passive attitude. Subsequently there was no evidence of the party's involvement in the strikes, just as the strikers did not use any socialist slogans.

After the violent disturbances, some members of Congress wondered whether it was not time to increase the size of the standing army to prevent such occurrences in the future. James A. Garfield, who was later elected president, also supported a proposal to this effect. But a majority of the congressmen rejected a bill providing for the creation of a 100,000-strong army. A key argument against the measure was that it violated the spirit of the Constitution and could infringe upon the freedom of the individual.

Mention should be made in this context of the Molly Maguires, a widespread secret society which over several years spread fear and terror – through the revolver – among comrades and adversaries alike in the coal-mining districts of Pennsylvania. In America the rise of this violent organization is often attributed to the impolitic labor legislation of the state of Pennsylvania. The suppression of the unions gave rise to a secret organization and the oppressive antilabor laws gave rise to violence, it is claimed. In other words, if trade unions had been allowed to function freely, their unnatural excesses would never have surfaced. Underlying this view is a perceived general rule which has considerable

---

56. See Cucheval Clarigny, "La grève des chemins de fer aux Etats-Unis," *Revue des deux mondes*, 23 (1877), 560–79, 763–804; Eugène Petit, "La grève des chauffeurs aux Etats-Unis," *Journal des économistes*, 48 (1877), 360–74; and Farnam, *Die amerikanischen Gewerkvereine*, 33–4.

support among the educated in America, and certainly has some truth in it, namely, that emergency laws and other forms of political repression will generate revolutionary activities, while equality and freedom allow reason to prevail. From this many draw the conclusion that socialist and revolutionary movements will not thrive in North America, since the citizens' freedom to realize political and social ideas in practice is sufficient to exclude anything that bears the stamp of unreasonableness. Acts of violence during strikes are certainly not premeditated, as the workers themselves testified often enough once the strikes were over. Raw passion in social struggles is either the result of bitterness and anger, which can arise either through political interference in the affairs of the people concerned or by measures taken by other social groups which the oppressed class regards as violations of its rights; or it is the result of bad motives such as greed. Both roots are evident in the Molly Maguires. As far as the secrecy aspect is concerned, there are secret labor organizations in the United States, such as the Glassblowers' Union and the Knights of Labor, which do not exert excessive political pressure on their members. This form of organization is preferred by some unions for the simple reason that they want to conceal their existence and activities from their political and social adversaries. And lastly, the fact that socialism is not the force in the United States that it has become in Europe can be explained entirely in terms of the favorable economic conditions obtaining in the New World. The freedom of association does not seem a relevant issue, since it also exists in France and existed in Germany during the formative years of the social democratic movement.

But let us return to the violence during the strikes. It manifests itself in two ways. It may be directed against the workers who have been recruited to replace the strikers – this is the more common situation – or against the employers and their assistants. Acts of the first type occur at times of economic upturns as well as downturns. The newspapers report many instances. We cite some typical cases here.

In 1874 the Norddeutsche Lloyd shipping company had work for only 200 of the 600 members of the longshoremen's union at the port of Hoboken, New Jersey. The union demanded wages of 40¢ per hour and alternating employment of its members. Such a high claim would enable all members to earn a decent living. But the company refused to accept these rates and hired other workers in New York, which had no shortage of labor. When the recruits arrived at the docks they found the entrances blocked by striking longshoremen, who used violence to stop the newcomers from getting to their workplace. The siege continued for three weeks, until the strike fund had been almost depleted and the branch chairman had absconded with the remaining money. The authorities refused to deploy the police or militia troops as long as there was no destruction of property. In the meantime, the Norddeutsche Lloyd management had found a way of circumventing the siege by using a steamship to ferry workers directly from New York to the dock's waterside. Throughout the strike it housed and boarded the workers in the large steamships docked at the time.

Not infrequently strikers go beyond this defensive position and move on to the attack. This will result in full-scale battles between citizens protecting property and the workers. In the summer of 1880 miners in Leadville, Colorado, called a major strike in support of an eight-hour working day. It sparked the foundation of the Miners' Union and a newspaper called *The Crisis*. Because the employers refused to give in, the workers' leaders decided to resort to violence. A large group of people armed with revolvers, guns, and sticks sought to force an improvement in conditions by threatening the indiscriminate destruction of property. The rest of the town's population – nonstriking miners, craftsmen, tradesmen, etc. – also armed themselves and formed their own regiments. For several days Leadville was divided into two camps. When the strikers fell out among themselves, the streets were witness to vicious fighting. Order was restored only after some ringleaders were arrested and convicted.[57]

In major strikes in the main cities both employers and workers try to get the public on their side. Both see public opinion as a valuable ally, and influencing coverage in the political newspapers becomes the first objective. Whether the public takes an interest in an industrial dispute depends largely on whether it is directly affected by it. This is the case, for instance, with strikes that disrupt railway and streetcar transportation. On an occasion of a strike in St. Louis, the *Irish World* editorialized:

To one who makes the labor question a subject of constant study, it is extremely interesting and suggestive to take up the papers from day to day and read the reports of strikes in different parts of the country. Strikes have become an established element in our social life. Although they rest upon no scientific and radical basis, as a means of protest on the part of labor, they nevertheless accomplish much good. As between tyrannical corporations and their employees, it has become

---

57. For a more detailed description of the working population of Leadville, see August Sartorius von Waltershausen, "Eine junge Stadt in dem Felsengebirge Kolorado's," *Allgemeine Zeitung*, Supplement, 16 April 1882, 1554–6.

understood that the general public stands as a sort of jury or court of arbitration. The justice of the respective claims of the two parties is canvassed and discussed on every corner and in every household, and I notice with pleasure of late that in several instances the public, and even the dominant press, have taken sides with the workingmen against their employers. Public opinion, which in this country is all powerful, is thus made to bear on the controversy, and the tendency now seems to be to make the general public a party to the strike. All this looks well and promises much. Out of it is liable to grow a general understanding, that in oppressing labor, corporations must be made to understand that the public has a right to demand justice as an interested party.

The tendency is in full accord with Republican systems, where the people are supposed to be sovereign. Strikers at present have to rely solely on contributions from their fellow-toilers, in their struggles with employers. When it becomes a settled fact that the general public is necessarily a party to a great strike, the public will raise funds to support the strikers in case they are in the right. Where the party against whom the strike is instituted is a public carrier, as in the case of a railroad corporation, the disturbed traveling public, by virtue of whose subsidies and franchises the corporation exists, has of late expressed itself emphatically as having the right to demand that the corporation shall deal justly with those whom it employs.[58]

That public opinion is able to have a decisive influence was shown during the Cincinnati streetcar workers' strike of 1881.[59] Before the strike, conductors earned $1.75 for a fifteen- to sixteen-hour day, drivers $1.50, and hostlers $1.25. The claim was for a 50¢ increase across the board. This was widely considered reasonable by the city's people, but the management of the consolidated streetcar company declared it could not meet the claim. A strike was called, and all streetcar transportation was suspended from one day to the next. There was violence on only one occasion, when people who wanted to stay at their posts were forced to leave their cars. But the men involved in this violent action were not company employees but outsiders. On the evening of the first strike day the workers' leader urged his members to refrain from violence as well as from drinking, since this could jeopardize their cause. At the same meeting the following letter from a prominent Cincinnati citizen was read out:

To the Chairman of the Meeting of Street Railway Employes: Draw on me fifty dollars, if necessary, to maintain the strike. The public owes the company

58. [*Irish World*, 14 May 1881.]
59. For a detailed description, see *Fifth Annual Report of the Bureau of Labor Statistics, to the General Assembly of Ohio, for the Year 1881* (Columbus, 1882) [hereafter cited as Ohio BLS, *Fifth Report*], 207–12.

nothing. Were it not for the corruption of the Council and Board of Public Works, they would have no right to run cars on our streets. It is the duty of the public to assist this strike.[60]

Two days later an attempt was made to get several streetcars on the road under police protection. The strikers gathered in a public square, and when the cars approached they lifted them off the tracks and sent the horses back to the stables. The police officers, who had only been sent along to protect the company's property, did not intervene since no property was damaged. Expressions of sympathy and offers of financial support for the strikers came from various citizens, one of whom donated $200.

A number of major companies signed a petition addressed to the streetcar company which stated that the wages paid to the streetcar drivers and conductors were inadequate given the long hours they worked and in many cases did not stretch to supporting a family. The companies therefore requested the chairman and directors of the streetcar company to accept the workers' "reasonable" demands.

At a strikers' meeting another petition was drawn up. It called on the public not to travel on cars that were staffed by strike breakers. And a prominent citizen who had offered a substantial amount of money was sent a thank-you note. A large public meeting was held in the city's east end that evening. The chairman opened the proceedings by declaring that the purpose of the meeting was of interest to every taxpayer, who had given the transit company its right of way, and to every working person in the community. He expressed his pleasure that the public had expressed its sympathy for the strikers in such large numbers. He said the strikers' claim was fair and just. Several speakers reiterated this sentiment but also urged the strikers to conduct their dispute in an orderly and peaceful manner. The meeting adopted the following resolution: "Resolved, That it is the sense of this meeting that the citizens of the East End will not patronize the street cars, if the present conductors and drivers are discharged, nor until this strike is satisfactorily settled."[61]

Two days later the company decided to give in to the strikers and offered them a compromise. Wages would be raised by 25¢ and hours would be cut. On the evening of 18 April the proposals were discussed at a meeting of citizens and strikers in a meeting room adjoining the mayor's office. After long deliberation the chairman of the citizens'

60. Ibid., 209–10.   61. Ibid., 211.

committee reported that the streetcar workers had unanimously decided to accept the proposal. At the end of his report to the citizens' meeting, the mayor declared: "Gentlemen: I thank you. In behalf of the men, women and children of Cincinnati, I thank you. You have made a manly fight, and your conduct throughout has been manly. Once more I thank you for your wise determination."[62] The same evening the citizens of the east end held another meeting to express their sympathy with the strikers. Resolutions were adopted declaring that it was the firm and freely arrived at conviction of four-fifths of the citizens that the demands of the honest, hard-working, and loyal streetcar employees should be granted.

Let us examine in conclusion what the unions' constitutions have to say about strike action. There is no similarity of views. Rather, they range from the conservative to the fairly radical. The former manifest themselves as a more or less principled aversion to strikes and the obstacles put in their way, such as the nature of the strike ballots, the imposition of certain time limits, and so on. Unions at the other end of the spectrum explicitly provide for strikes in their constitutions and set simple formalities for their approval. In general it can be said that the democratically run unions are more moderate, while those with centralized constitutions are more militant. This is no doubt related to the fact that support from the strike fund – essential to the success of any industrial dispute – is more difficult to obtain when those who have collected the money also dispose of it than when a union president or executive makes the decisions as an administrator of other people's money. It is worth noting, however, that the statutes do not always offer a clear guide to a union's behavior, since experience shows that some apparently disciplined unions in practice do not take much account of their moderate rules.[63]

Here we restrict ourselves to the contents of unions' constitutions.

1. When a local branch of the *Iron Molders' Union of North America* proposes strike action, it must be approved in a general meeting by two-thirds of the eligible members attending. Such a majority seems sensible, since frequently all members of a local branch are affected by the strike. The corresponding secretary informs the president of the international union that a decision to this effect has been taken. The latter gives each branch the

---

62. Ibid., 212.
63. For an example, see Farnam, *Die amerikanischen Gewerkvereine*, 15.

opportunity to vote on the matter. When they approve the strike by a two-thirds majority, the president collects regularly support funds from the branches. These are distributed as stipulated by the constitution, $5 a week for unmarried strikers and $7 for married ones. In conjunction with the international executive the president has the power to declare a strike lost, at which point the financial support stops. But the strikers must be given two weeks' notice of such a decision.

In terms of demands this union is one of the most moderate in the United States. It generally abides by its "platform of principles" drawn up by its most outstanding president, William H. Sylvis.[64] It has an aversion to the strike weapon on principle and will approve strikes only in exceptional cases and as a necessary evil, when all other means of settling a dispute have been exhausted.

2. When members of a local branch of the *Gewerkschafts-Union der Möbel-Arbeiter Nord Americas* (Furniture Makers' Union) are planning industrial action, they are obliged to communicate their reasons to the branch assembly and await its majority decision. The constitution urges members to approve a strike only when all other means of peaceful settlement have been exhausted. Once the local branch has backed a strike, it must inform the trades assembly it is affiliated with and the national union's headquarters immediately. The actions of the first have already been mentioned, and the second is obliged to examine the situation in detail and report the result of its inquiry to its branches, which then make a final decision. If the strike is approved at this stage, all local branches must be informed within five days of the vote. The strikers are initially supported by their own strike fund and later by the all-union fund. The national executive has the right to levy additional funds from the local branches if the strike funds become depleted.

3. If members of the *Cigar Makers International Union of America* feel aggrieved by their employer and consider strike action justified, they must turn in the first instance to the local branch to which they affiliated. Decision making within these [branches] is not uniform across the union. The Pittsburgh branch statutes, for instance, stipulate that any strike action proposed by more than fifteen workers must receive a two-thirds majority at a specially convened general meeting. Only then will the union pay out a $1 a day strike benefit. If the proposal does not secure the required majority, the workers in question are free to withdraw their labor but then cannot count on support from the union funds. If the number of workers considering action is less than fifteen, the executive has the sole right to decide whether to back the strike or not.

64. See James C. Sylvis, *The Life, Speeches, Labors and Essays of William H. Sylvis* (Philadelphia, 1872), [284–95]. The book has a dedication characteristic of Sylvis: "We must show them that when a just monetary system has been established there will no longer exist a necessity for Trades Unions."

In addition to the local support, strikers can also obtain a weekly benefit of $4 from the central union under the following conditions. If the strike involves less than twenty-five people, the decision lies with the executive committee, although if it refuses, the decision can be referred to all the local branches on appeal. If the strike involves more than twenty-five people, the president must refer the matter to all the local branches. Calling a strike usually requires an absolute majority, but strikes over wage claims require a two-thirds majority. Votes are allocated to the local branches in relation to their size: those with 7–50 members have one vote, those with 50–100 two, and 100–200 three, with additional votes granted for every additional 100 members.

4. When the workers belonging to the Chicago *Journeymen Stonecutters' Association* decide to go on strike, the union president must be informed immediately. He will then call a general meeting. A two-thirds majority is required in case the action concerns a wage claim, while a simple majority suffices to back action over a proposed wage cut. "On the eve of a strike, a delegation should be named, which will seek a friendly settlement with the employers and report the outcome to the Association. The latter will approve no strike by all or some of its members, except when all honorable means to resolve the grievance or dispute have failed."[65]

5. The *dockers' unions in the cotton-exporting ports* often do not have explicit rules on the withdrawal of labor in order to conceal their tactics from the employers. An exception is the Workingmen's Benevolent Association in Savannah, Georgia, which runs a fund to dispense sickness and death benefits as well as strike benefits. Strikes are decided by majority vote in specially convened general meetings. There is also a general rule that "When a strike for wages or some other objective is considered necessary, no member of the union may work on board the ship during the strike. Anyone who violates this rule will either be expelled or punished as the monthly meeting sees fit."[66]

6. Article 1 of the *Amalgamated Association of Iron and Steel Workers of the United States* constitution states that "The objects of this Association shall be to obtain by conciliation, or by other means that are fair and legal, a fair remuneration to the members for their labor; and to afford mutual protection to members against broken contract, obnoxious rules, unlawful discharge or other systems of injustice or oppression."[67] There is a strike fund administered by the county executive committee. The local branches, known here as *lodges,* are divided by counties and their executives have the right to call strikes.

65. [Retranslated from German.]   66. [Retranslated from German.]
67. [*Constitution, By-Laws and Rules of Order of the National and Subordinate Lodges of the Amalgamated Association of Iron and Steel Workers of North America* (1880), Article I, Section 2.]

7. The statutes of the German American *Typographia* (Typographical Union) do not contain sufficient safeguards against abuse of the strike weapon. The constitution states that "When differences arise that may lead to a strike, the branches involved must place a motion before the Board (the President, Vice-President, Secretary, Treasurer, and three Trustees) and abide by the decision of the Board. In cases of exceptional urgency, where members are forced to strike, the latter should sustain the decision, and in the event of such a decision the general board must send the needed assistance funds to the union involved. In the instances specified here unmarried and married members can claim the same amount of support, namely $5 per week for the period of four weeks."

8. The *International Typographical Union,* on the other hand, is generally opposed to strike action, unless the rules and principles of the international or the affiliated unions have been violated in some way. The union has a strike fund into which all members pay $1 per year. The maximum benefit is $7 per week. Calling a strike generally needs a three-quarters majority at the local level. Once a decision in favor of a strike has been taken, the president takes responsibility for its conduct. In some cases (in Typographical Union No. 21 in San Francisco, for instance), only members of more than six months' standing are entitled to vote in the strike ballots.

9. No branch of the *Granite Cutters' International Union* is allowed to withdraw its labor without the permission of the union president and a five-member standing committee. The union's central executive has no say in the matter. When a strike or lockout happens because workers are union members or because they have abided by union rules, support is granted immediately. In other cases, such as disputes over pay or changes in working hours, the standing committee decides on the course of action. Generally speaking, the union prefers negotiations and compromise, as the following passage in the statutes shows: "It has been decided that the International Union of Granite Cutters should strive to eliminate even the slightest resentment against the employers, since it is completely clear that the welfare of the workers depends on that of the employer. Moreover, should we recognize in our rules something unfair or arbitrarily in our interests, we will remove the same and pledge to the best of our ability to put something better in its place."[68]

As mentioned above, many trade unions do not have any detailed rules concerning the calling and sanctioning of strikes. These include some major unions, such as those of the locomotive engineers, firemen, and

---

68. [Retranslated from German.]

hatmakers. Other unions have not been cited here because their strike rules broadly coincide with those outlined here.

III. Conciliation Efforts and Courts of Arbitration[69]

In the previous article we tried to show that unionized workers generally cannot achieve anything more by going on strike than they would have been granted otherwise. Under these circumstances, then, strikes have virtually no effect on the determination of wage levels and seem futile if they are called in support of pay claims. The withdrawal of labor or the lockout by employers is thus only a means by which both sides seek to highlight the other's dependence or their usefulness to the other at a particular time. This raises the question of whether it is not possible to find a means of laying bare the social balance of power that does not have the disadvantages associated with strikes. For there can be little doubt that the disadvantages are considerable not only for those involved but also for the economy as a whole once one accepts the proposition that labor organization can secure higher wages but strikes cannot.

But let us first examine, on the basis of American experiences, the key events and circumstances which are the inevitable consequences of nearly all work stoppages. In the previous article we showed how strikes time and again undermined the understanding between capital and labor and generated mutual suspicion. It should be added that every struggle with a clear outcome rankles with the vanquished and stirs a desire for revenge. One dispute gives rise to the next and also threatens industrial peace for the future. In these actions, above all, we see that the profit motive is not the only one which shapes economic and social life, but that, as with all human drives, emotions are also of profound significance. Some strikes are not undertaken primarily to improve the terms and conditions of work but out of revenge – to satisfy those who harbor such sentiments.

It is frequently argued that strike action has a beneficial moral impact on the working class. That may be the case in some instances but can hardly have been the rule and, where trade unions and other associations are sufficiently organized, can hardly be expected to be so in the

---

69. "Die Gewerkvereine in den Vereinigten Staaten von Amerika (III)," *Jahrbücher für Nationalökonomie und Statistik*, Neue Folge, Bd. 8 (1884), 431–56.

future. In the period before the working class was aware of its own political muscle, an energetically pursued strike, involving untold hardship, may have forced employers to accept that they had to negotiate with people who would no longer tolerate injustice, and may have made some wageworkers aware of their own value and thus boosted their self-esteem. But does that still apply today, now that we have become accustomed to millions of workers overestimating their own importance? We need to look no further than the socialist movement in the various countries to encounter the notion that labor is the sole creator of wealth and that capital and its profit motive are no more than parasites on the natural order of production.

We should steer away from such ethical considerations and instead look at the general economic consequences of a production stoppage (because of either a strike or a lockout). The labor movement offers two lines of argument in defense of the view that strikes do not damage the economy. Firstly, they are seen, in effect, as a means of preventing overproduction in that they put at least some check on it; and secondly, it is argued that employers in any case do not use all the available working time and that every branch of industry lies idle for at least some weeks of the year, to the detriment of the workers (who, of course, do not get paid when nothing is produced). Strikes are thus said to shift the idle periods in a way that benefits the workers' cause.

It must be pointed out that these two views are rather inconsistent. For on the one hand, it is claimed that the manufacturers produce too many goods, and on the other, there seems to be a desire for employment to be extended over the whole year. In order to clarify the first assertion, let us combine the two views and accept that for natural and social reasons many factories have to interrupt production for several weeks in the year but that overproduction still arises despite the reduced working period, and to that extent a strike can forestall an economic crisis. The industrial history of all countries shows that many strikes have occurred during economic upturns, but they have not prevented downturns due to overproduction. So there are no grounds for claiming that strikes prevent recessions. But do they perhaps postpone them? That too seems rather unlikely. For if a strike is called in protest at wage cuts, prices are usually already depressed, which in turn is usually indicative of overproduction. And if a strike is called to back a wage claim, then domestic or foreign competitors of the company in question will seize the opportunity to step up their production to fill the gaps created temporarily by the strike. It is, after all, a characteristic of the modern mode of production, with its mobility of capital, that companies can increase their output to unprecedented levels and at short notice, depending on the situation in the marketplace. A well-equipped factory can attract many workers by raising wages or step up production by introducing night shifts.

The second assertion – that production tails off for several weeks of the year anyway – seems more persuasive. There is no doubt that many industries cannot work the whole year round because of fluctuations in the market or individual companies' modes of operation. But on closer examination this argument does not hold water either. During an economic depression, such as the one of 1873–8, machines stand idle in most branches for as long as the time lost due to strikes and probably longer. But the situation is quite different once economic activity picks up again. The general assertion can thus apply only in specific circumstances. The information on strikes in the annual reports of the Ohio Bureau of Labor Statistics covering the years 1879 and 1880 provides statistical backing for this view (Table 2). This list shows that the duration of strikes exceeded the average idle time per year by around four and a half weeks.[70]

But the main objection to the assertion that strikes do not damage the economy, even on the assumption that the strike duration coincides with idle time, is that it is by no means irrelevant *when* production is interrupted. At times when sales are very slack and when factories are perhaps in operation only to prevent them from closing down altogether, it certainly does not matter when a strike is called. But the situation is different whenever the produced goods have a market. In those factories which lie idle for natural reasons (e.g., water shortages during the summer), every strike will mean a loss of production because it cannot be made up in the idle period. The same applies to factories making seasonal or fashion goods. And even when goods can be supplied continuously but are not sold throughout the year because of lack of demand, so that production has to be scaled down to prevent overproduction, one cannot argue that it is irrelevant when this happens and that a strike can close the works at the best time. Consumers are after all not dependent on a single factory; almost invariably it is the combined output of all competitors that determines the point when sales drop off. One replaces the work of the other. But in the interest of general prosperity, one must hope fervently that all factories contribute

70. [It is not entirely clear what is being calculated here.]

Table 2

Year	Industry	Strike duration (in weeks)	Average working time per year (in weeks)
1879	Tanning	3	50
	Stovemolding	16	45
	Stovemolding	15	45
	Stovemolding	13	45
	Tobacco and cigarmaking	6	46½
1880	Ironmolding	9	44⅔
	Cigarmaking	5	50³⁄₇
	Ironmolding	10	44⅔

to national output according to their capacities and resources. And it should not be forgotten that work stoppages are usually not announced in advance but are called at short notice to heighten their impact. This has a detrimental effect on production in yet another way in that the manufacturer is likely to suffer a loss of raw materials as well.

There are a number of other damaging effects of strike action. That the public is directly inconvenienced by them was shown in the previous article in the discussion of the disruption of railway traffic. The situation is not much different with regard to the disruption of coal production. As Andrew Roy, inspector of mines in Ohio, observes, after trying to quantify the loss in wages, in a report published in [1881]: "These are not the only losses sustained, for the coal trade, like the surcease of Majesty[71] in Shakespeare, 'to whose huge spokes ten thousand lesser things are mortised and adjoined,' extends to every industry, and the whole body politic suffers. The hardest sufferers, especially during strikes in winter, are the worthy poor of cities. Coal goes up beyond their ability to purchase, and their fires go out, while the wealthy can import coal from distant districts."[72] In one way or another, although perhaps not as strongly as in the examples cited here, consumers will suffer from any disruption of production. As we know, in the modern

71. See Adolph Wagner, "Ueber die Schwebenden deutschen Finanzfragen," *Zeitschrift für die gesammte Staatswissenschaft*, 35 (1879), 68–114, [82]: "steam is king" is the real watchword of our age.
72. Ohio BLS, *Fifth Report*, 196.

division of labor the success of a business depends on the well-being of the others. A national economy has rightly been called an organic whole. This analogy can be extended by saying that when a part of the social body is ill, the whole body feels the pain.

Strikes also have disadvantages of a different kind. As the Ohio Bureau of Labor Statistics points out in its fifth annual report: "One of the classes indirectly connected with them, who nevertheless, under the force of circumstances suffer to as great, and frequently a greater degree than those directly connected with the same, are day laborers (unskilled). This class of workmen, unfortunately for themselves and their families, have not been accorded, or did not grasp the opportunity and advantages of acquiring any special trade in their youth; whose earnings in consequence are the lowest at all times. They generally do not participate, or have any voice in the inauguration or settlements of wage disputes, and are, therefore, not directly considered in the struggle. Whether the strike is right or wrong, whether lost or won, they gain nothing; but on the other hand, they are reluctantly thrown out of employment, and have therefore everything to lose, no matter how the struggle may terminate."[73]

Let us recall the question we raised at the outset of this article, namely, whether it is possible to find a procedure for determining the social power of capital and labor which does not entail the damage associated with strikes. Under conditions where workers are organized, wages are linked to the market conditions for the goods they produce (allowing, of course, for variations in standards of living). So what matters is that both sides, capital and labor, consider the prices of the goods concerned and how they are determined and on this basis decide a wage level appropriate to the general situation. This can be achieved through mutual persuasion or by an impartial third party making a judgment or *award*. The purpose of conciliation and arbitration is thus to avoid both the usually predestined outcome of strikes by unionized workers and the damaging effects of strikes.

Now what is the situation in this regard in the United States? In general it can be said that there are few signs of permanent institutions, although in some parts of the country notable efforts in this direction have been made since the 1860s. The reason conciliation and arbitration efforts are rarely translated into viable institutions is due to the *colonial* instability – the adjective can still be applied to wide stretches

73. Ibid., 197–8.

of the country – that is typical of the U.S. economy. As was stressed in the first article, this has also hindered the development of trade unions. In Britain institutions of conciliation and arbitration have become common property of the working class owing to their successes, their approval by public opinion, and (in the case of arbitration) their recognition in law. While in the United States the press has occasionally examined the options, the consensus remains that for the moment at least the British experiences cannot be transplanted across the Atlantic. How little arbitration figures in the United States is shown by the fact that the word *arbitration* has even more shades of meaning than in Britain.[74] It is understood to mean what it does in Britain, namely, an assessment made by a commission of employers and workers whose authority derives from force of argument and moral commitment or an award made by an impartial arbiter called upon to break a deadlock between the two sides. The procedure leading to the award is itself also called *arbitration*. In the United States there are also *committees of arbitration*. Composed of trade union members, their purpose is to determine the approach of workers to wage and other disputes. They will also consider demands and complaints from employers and will visit factories to establish the facts.[75]

74. Massachusetts Bureau of Statistics of Labor, *Twelfth Annual Report of the Bureau of Statistics of Labor* (Boston, 1881) [hereafter cited as Massachusetts BSL, *Twelfth Report*], 6–8.

75. The cloth-, hat-, and capmakers of New York City, for instance, have agreed to the following principles among themselves:

"Article 1. Neither the members of a branch nor a whole shop organization are allowed to withdraw their labor before the disputes between labor and capital are investigated by the executive committee and the strike has been approved.

Article 2. In order to settle such disputes justly and quickly and to avoid unnecessary loss of time by both sides, a committee should be chosen from the Executive Committee, which shall immediately investigate and adjudicate all disputes, which have not been resolved by the contracting parties themselves.

Article 3. This committee (Arbitration Board) shall consist of one cutter, two operators, three finishers, two blockers, and one trimmer, and the committee shall make a full report of its activities at each regular meeting of the Executive Committee.

Article 4. The decisions of this committee shall be binding on both parties until the next sitting of the Executive Committee; only the Executive Committee is allowed to modify such decisions.

Article 5. This committee (Arbitration Board) shall also have the right to decide by majority rule on requests for extension of the hours of work during the season, and of course, with immediate disposal of such a request."

[Rules and Regulations of the Tuch-, Hut- und Kappenmacher, *Gewerkschafts-Zeitung*, June 20, 1880.]

In addition to *arbitration,* the term *industrial conciliation* is also used in the context of settling differences between capital and labor. This does not involve a judgment or decision of any kind and should not be confused with Mundella's boards of conciliation either.[76] These are formally constituted and act on the basis of specific statutes. The American conciliation committees usually meet only to consider specific cases. With no fixed composition, they mediate between the two sides, follow their patrons' instructions, and require their prior approval for any concessions. Although rather haphazard, this means of settling disputes has achieved some notable successes, especially in the coal-mining districts and in the country's great iron-rolling centers. There *conciliation* also means not the procedure but the material basis on which a settlement is sought. A detailed historical description of developments in the iron industry is contained in a report by Joseph D. Weeks, who has done much to promote the British arbitration procedures in the United States.[77]

The method by which wages were contractually agreed between employers and workers in the iron industry was based on the *sliding scale* commonly used in Britain and the *basis system.* The first scale which calculated wages from the prices of goods produced by the workers was introduced in Pittsburgh's iron mills in February 1865. It was to be binding on both sides but could be canceled by either side at ninety days' notice. It set wage rates for puddling iron on the basis of the Manufacturers' Card of Prices for iron bars as shown in Table 3. This scale did not apply for very long, since the iron price plummeted from seven and one-half cents in February to four cents in July.[78] Such a drop was provided for in the scale, but it was not really expected, and the workers canceled the contract. After several rounds of negotiations, lockouts, and strikes, a new wage scale was agreed to in July 1867 (Table 4). The sharp difference in wage levels between the two tables points to one of the key features of this kind of wage determination. How, one may wonder, can employers accept such steep

76. [Anthony John Mundella (1825–97), British hosiery manufacturer, Liberal Member of Parliament, and educational and industrial reformer, proposed "Boards of Conciliation" with equal representation of employers and employees.]

77. Joseph D. Weeks, *Industrial Conciliation and Arbitration in New York, Ohio, and Pennsylvania* (Boston, 1881). The essay was also published in Massachusetts BLS, *Twelfth Report* (1881), 5–75, under the title "Report of Joseph D. Weeks."

78. [The author erroneously listed the prices as $7.50 and $4.00 per pound. The actual prices can be found in Weeks, *Industrial Conciliation and Arbitration,* 11.]

Table 3

Iron price per pound (in cents)	Workers' wage per ton (in dollars)
8½	9.00
8¼	8.75
8	8.50
7¾	8.25
7½ to 7¼	8.00
7 to 6¾	7.50
6½ to 5¾	6.50
5½ to 5¼	6.00
5 to 4¾	5.75
4½ to 4¼	5.50
4 to 3¾	5.00
3½ to 3¼	4.75
3 to 2¾	4.50
2½	4.00

Table 4

Iron price per pound (in cents)	Workers' wage per ton (in dollars)
5	8.00
4¾	7.75
4½	7.50
4¼	7.25
4	7.00
3¾	6.75
3½	6.50
3¼	6.25
3	6.00

wage rises and not go broke? Under the first scale they paid $8.00 when the iron price was 7.25–7¢, but under the second scale they paid the same wage at a price of 5¢. This can make sense only when one bears in mind that prices are not determined solely by the relationship between supply and demand but are also significantly influenced by production costs.

To return to the example of the mining industry, it is clear that one way of cutting costs is by increasing output. In a situation where, for example, labor productivity is doubled, prices are halved, and all the goods are sold, the sliding scale works perfectly. With doubled output and halved prices the employers achieve the same return as in the past, and the workers produce twice as much with the same effort and have the same income, even though they receive only half the pay for the same quantity of coal. Now production costs can also fall when employers save on capital and other nonwage costs. Competition among the companies will thus tend to depress the price of coal, and in this case, under the existing agreement, wages are also cut. This boosts profits and leads to the nonsensical situation where improvements in technology or efficiency lead to lower wages.

A simple calculation illustrates this point. An employer has invested $400,000 in his business and makes a profit of 20%. Half of the $400,000 capital is used annually for waterworks, buildings, and machinery; the other half is used to pay 500 workers piece rates of $400 per year. So the firm has to generate a turnover of $280,000 per year. But, like his competitors, the employer is able to reduce his fixed capital input to $50,000 through multiple use of the waterworks, installing cheaper machinery, switching from horse transport to railways, etc. So to realize a 20% profit he now needs to generate only $250,000 from the same volume of goods. The pressures of competition can thus depress prices by a rate of 250,000/280,000.[79] Now he turns to his workforce, with whom he has agreed on a sliding wage scale, and explains that the competition has forced him to cut his prices, and so wages have to be cut as well, from $400 per year to $357.

If the workers have any insight into the business situation, they will, of course, not accept this proposition. But it also becomes clear that a new wage scale has to be negotiated, which appears at first glance to favor the workers but in fact secures the employer his previous or per-

---

79. [The German original gives "280,000/250,000."]

haps an even better return. The introduction of a new wage scale thus allows workers to benefit from economic advances as well, which a fixed scale would not. Against a background of steady improvements in technology and efficiency, the sliding-scale system proves useless as a permanent institution and will satisfy both parties for only certain periods.

So when a sliding-scale system is in use, the reasons for the price cuts should always be considered. As long as the balance between supply and demand determines whether prices go up or down, wage increases or cuts can be easily implemented through the scale, without either side having any grounds for complaint. But when the price of goods falls[80] because they have become cheaper to produce, or rise because production costs have gone up, then the existing wage scale is no longer serviceable and has to be replaced by another. Small wonder, then, that in the rapidly industrializing America there are many reports of such tables being abandoned almost as quickly as they are agreed on.

It must be said that it would be very much in the interest of social peace if there were some stable material reference point according to

80. The prices of many industrial goods have, of course, fallen over the last twenty-eight years, despite changes in the money economy. There is general agreement that this is due to technological advances. Some figures from the American experience may underline this. Thus, in Ohio the price of a 100-lb barrel of nails (in dollars) changed as follows between 1864 and 1880:

August 1864	9.12½	September 1872	6.00
September 1865	6.75	September 1873	4.50
September 1866	7.00	August 1874	4.12½
August 1867	6.00	July 1875	3.25
December 1868	5.00	May 1876	2.75
September 1869	4.50	March 1877	2.75
August 1870	4.25	September 1879	2.60
October 1871	4.25	December 1880	2.85

Prices show a clear downward trend throughout this period, with the exception of the speculative boom of 1872–3. The main reason for this is the slide in the price of iron resulting from more efficient mining methods. In Massachusetts the price of so-called dry goods (i.e., textile fabrics) fell by 3–30% between 1860 and 1878. According to the 1879 annual report of the state's Bureau of Labor Statistics, the price of shirting brown fell by 18%, shirting bleached by 13%, sheeting brown by 16%, sheeting bleached by 11%, cotton flannel by 7%, prints by 30%, and satinet by 3% (Massachusetts BSL, *Tenth Report,* 1879, 81). All calculations are in gold dollars. In Missouri average prices of clothing fabrics fell by around 32% between 1873 and 1881. Wages, viewed over a longer period, did not fall to the same extent, rose in some cases, and often held their own. See August Sartorius von Waltershausen, "Arbeitszeit und Normalarbeitstag in den Vereinigten Staaten von Amerika," *Jahrbuch für Nationalökonomie und Statistik,* New Series, 4 (1882), 461–73, here 471.

which business earnings could be distributed between labor and capital. Permanent, formally constituted conciliation or arbitration boards – along lines we will discuss below – would not present any insurmountable difficulties. Far more problematic is the calculation of wages on the basis of the market prices of the goods produced by the workers. The question is, can the workers ascertain at regular intervals why prices have fallen? It is not prices as such that should be looked at, but the factors that determine them. A company's overall income can only be assessed in this way, and only on the basis of at least an approximation of this income can it be distributed to the satisfaction of both sides.

Let us take the following example. A wage scale has been agreed on. Soon afterward goods prices fall owing to foreign competition. The workers are presented with current prices in several towns and on this basis are told that a wage cut is unavoidable. The proposal is examined by a conciliation or arbitration board. To stop the firm from going under, it is eventually accepted. But the reason prices were squeezed was that foreign competitors introduced certain technical innovations that allowed them to produce more efficiently. The manufacturer involved in the settlement finds this out and gradually introduces the innovations in his own company. He can now undercut his competitors because he benefits from the improvements in the production process, as well as from the wage cut agreed on earlier. But when the workers put in a new claim following the increase in productivity, they are told it cannot be justified because goods prices have not risen and the production changes are needed to meet the challenge of intensifying foreign competition.

Now how can people involved in ten- to twelve-hour days of physically demanding work assess production improvements at their workplace or grasp the impact of technological developments abroad? The answer is, of course, that they cannot. But the situation is different when the factory workers belong to a large union. In a trade union, people work for each other, they share experiences, and, most important, not all union members are engaged in manual labor: its full-time officials, paid out of members' contributions, can use their brainpower to improve their comrades' lot. They have time to read the stock market reports, they can find out about free-trade issues and protective tariffs, and they can keep track of technological advances in their industry. During the great New York pianomakers' strike in 1880, the [Steinway] company directors were taken aback when one of the workers' leaders calculated their operating costs down to the cent for them. One of the managers of the Steinway factory reportedly observed that they would not have let the dispute escalate into a strike if they had known the breadth of business expertise among their workforce.

This highlights yet another way in which unionization is of over-whelming importance to the working classes. It gives them not only power, but also understanding. A mindless, clumsy mass is turned into a disciplined, thinking community. This transformation benefits not only the wageworkers directly involved, but also their employers, in fact the country as a whole. For it is only under these circumstances that arbitration can promise lasting successes, and crudeness and vio-lence can be replaced by considered debate. If forms of conciliation and arbitration are to become permanent institutions, every workers' asso-ciation should give at least one member the opportunity to research the industry and also one employer. But even the cleverest union offi-cial will not be able to gain an understanding of the business situation comparable to the factory owner's, so there will be occasions when arbitration boards will remain in the dark on some aspects of a ques-tion. The employers represented on them are unlikely to help out here, since, with a wary eye on their competitors, they will, understand-ably enough, not want to reveal confidential business information. So in the process of agreeing on a wage scale, as in the process of arbitra-tion overall, there remains a gray area that one cannot get away from. This is a not uncommon feature of today's individualistic, free, com-petitive production economy. Where there is light, there is, of course, also shade.

That union leaders are perfectly capable of understanding changes and developments in factories and workshops is an observation fre-quently made in the United States. From this some American theorists of the labor question have made the false deduction that the workers' association of today may one day be transformed into a producers' cooperative. In the course of many wage disputes, individual workers would acquire the employers' knowledge and skills and thus the ability to lead a producers' cooperative, the argument runs. Moreover, in seek-ing to improve the workers' lot, unions instill in the comrades a degree of discipline comparable to that enforced in the factories by the threat of dismissal. The above conclusion based on these considerations can be explained by the admittedly correct observation that voluntary work-ers' associations are by no means the final link in the chain of socio-economic relations. But the urge to posit the new form tempts theorists into presuming a state of affairs which, if possible at all, can only be the outcome of a long period of historical and cultural development. For even when such predictions become reality, the producers' cooperative is still not a viable proposition. It has no capital, a particularly serious handicap in the modern mode of production; there is no agreed-on method of dividing the work among the members to everyone's satisfaction; and, above all, the leader, despite all his knowledge, still lacks the entrepreneurial capacities that are usually acquired through actually owning and running a business. The union leader can become a competent manager, but does that mean he will be as keenly committed to the firm's development and expansion as an owner, who will be the sole beneficiary of any improvements?[81]

It is probably fortunate that the arbitration boards can produce, broadly speaking, satisfactory results. Otherwise one would have to conclude, devastatingly, that today's mode of production will neither achieve a reconciliation of capital and labor nor, assuming their continued opposition, be assured of a prosperous future.

To avoid the difficulties associated with setting wages on the basis of prices but still protecting their livelihoods, the workers in the Pennsylvania coal-mining districts using the sliding scale have tried to introduce the above-mentioned basis system. This puts a floor under the sliding scale below which wages are not allowed to drop even when goods prices keep falling. That this cannot be a permanent solution is clear. After all, which company these days can boast such a strong position that it can sell all its goods or dominate the market to such an extent that it can set prices?

The first report of the basis system dates from 1869, when it was proposed by the St. Clair Workingmen's Benevolent Association in the anthracite coal fields of Pennsylvania. To make it easier for the mineowners to keep to the minimum wage, this large union tried to regulate coal prices at the same time. This was to be done by reducing working hours or stopping work altogether for certain periods. It was hoped that this practice would restrict the supply of coal and thus maintain a certain price level. The union also began to recruit members among workers involved in transporting the coal, so that in the case of overproduction the market price could be propped up by restricting the movement of coal. One can hardly be surprised by this monopolistic

81. On the producers' cooperatives in the United States, see August Sartorius von Waltershausen, "Erfahrungen mit Produktivgenossenschaften in Nordamerika," *Politische Wochenschrift*, 20 May 1882.

effort, since capital indulges in the same tendency by setting up business cartels and has been able to realize its ambitions in this area, albeit only intermittently, in the most diverse areas of production and distribution.

The history of the coal industry in the anthracite fields provides some instructive lessons on these consequences of free competition. The owners of the railways which carry the coal to the markets in some cases also own the mines. Thus two different businesses which would normally represent their interests separately are joined in a profit relationship. While coal producers normally want low freight charges, in this case they want to make money from high ones. In some areas the cartels operated successfully over certain periods, for instance from 1872 to 1876 and in 1878. This is nothing less than a convenient arrangement among producer interests aimed at maximizing prices and thus fleecing the consumers! I cannot understand how people can see these cartels as the basis for the future organization of the economy. Without public control of prices, the interests of consumers cannot be protected; and a competitive tariff structure removes the main reason for forming a cartel.

What interests us here is the way in which capital embraces the sliding-scale system. The attempts at establishing a capitalist monopoly bring another element into the price formation equation, which must be considered in addition to production costs and supply and demand when wages are being set on the basis of prices. We are confronted here with the remarkable phenomenon that in such a wage-determination method the interests of the workers coincide with those of the employers (seeking to establish a monopoly in the market). The more the consumer is exploited, the more the employers gain, and, thanks to the sliding scale, the more the workers earn as well. This could be seen as removing an objection rightly raised against a production system organized around cartels.[82]

It has been argued that a more planned production directed by an employers' coalition, which would strengthen the power of capital, could force excessive demands on the workers. The implementation of sliding scales would ensure that labor is not disadvantaged. But it is

---

82. See Gustav Schmoller's review of Friedrich Kleinwächter, *Die Kartelle* (Innsbruck, 1883), in *Jahrbuch für Gesetzgebung, Verwaltung und Volkswirthschaft im Deutschen Reich*, 7 (1883), no. 1, 333–7.

doubtful whether they will actually be implemented, so the above objection still stands. Monopoly-based power over consumers also means power over the workers. When there is no competition, it is in the gift of the monopoly capitalist to say when the workers can work and when not. He can exercise strong pressure on wages even in the face of a united workforce. He will either not allow a sliding scale or permit only one that is very favorable to him, in which wages are set very low in the first place or price rises translate into much smaller wage increases, so that it will only seem like an equitable mechanism.

The above-mentioned attempt by the union side to control coal prices did not suit the mineowners, of course. And it became unworkable as soon as coal from other regions entered the picture and not all miners were union members. Not surprisingly, then, the basis system was initially applied in certain cases, soon abandoned, reintroduced shortly afterward, again abandoned when a strike broke out, and again recommended after it ended. Throughout this period the two sides never completely broke off the negotiations because neither would give up the illusion that, despite all the setbacks, a basis acceptable to both sides could still be found.

The many negotiations also led to the first-ever attempt to have disputes settled by an impartial arbiter. In April 1871 one such arbiter in Mauch Chunk[83] set out his views on the relationship between the mineowners and workers. Although he did not deal with the wage question as such, some passages from this document are particularly revealing:[84]

1. The right of an owner or lessee and operator of a colliery to the entire and exclusive control and management of his works is guaranteed to him by the law of the land, and is of such unquestionable character that it ought not to be interfered with, either directly or indirectly.
2. It is the undoubted right of men to refuse to work except upon such terms as shall be agreeable to them; but a general understanding that no person of a particular association of laborers shall work for any operator who has in his employ a member of such association, who has not paid his dues to the association, or any person who does not belong to the association, is contrary to

83. [Mauch Chunk was the birthplace and original headquarters of the coalminers' union, The Workingmen's Benevolent Association.]
84. [The author has paraphrased at this point three of the nine articles in the decision of Judge William Elwell. The editors have reproduced the original text of these three articles as they appeared in Weeks, *Industrial Arbitration*, 35–6, articles 1, 3, and 6.]

the policy of the law, and subversive of the best interests of the miners and their employers. An association may inflict fines upon its members for breach of by-laws, and expel for non-payment, but it has no right, by combined action, to place the defaulter in the light of an outlaw in the transaction of business with others.

3. Operators ought not in any manner to combine against persons who belong to the Miners' and Laborers' Benevolent Association. Any operator who refuses to employ a person because he is so connected, or who shall discharge him for that reason, would thereby give good grounds for censure, and for other members to refuse to work for him.

This and other decisions paved the way for several settlements. Arbitration became an accepted way of resolving all disputes except wage disputes. Later in the year both sides agreed to submit these to arbitration as well, and a "basis" for the scale of wages was worked out. The mineowners had previously committed themselves to accepting the arbitration awards. Various elements of the agreement were implemented. But the industrial peace lasted only a few months, until renewed disagreements surfaced and the arbitration procedure was suspended. Even so, over the coming years the sliding scale and the minimum basis were retained in some form or other, although extensively modified, so that both methods came to be seen as the "unwritten law" of the Pennsylvania anthracite-mining districts. But the ultimate vulnerability of the minimum wage was shown clearly during the deep recession of 1873–9.[85] The iron rule market forces – in this case the lack of markets – defeated all attempts at putting some floor under wages. So an effective conciliation system with or without arbitration has not been found in the coal-mining districts either. Doubtless these efforts had many positive effects: they prevented many strikes and much violence, and improved relations between capital and labor, and helped them to see each other's point of view. But the inescapable conclusion is that the method of regulating wages on the basis of prices has until now not produced a satisfactory result. For a rational wage-determination system can only be based on a comparison between wages and profits, not on a comparison between wages and production prices without taking into account of how the latter are formed.

A more elaborate structure of formal arbitration was developed in the coal-mining districts around Pittsburgh. At the instigation of Joseph

85. [Coalminers marked the summer of 1879 as the end of the crisis. Andrew Roy, *A History of the Coal Miners of the United States* (Columbus, Ohio, n.d.), 190.]

D. Weeks, the mineowners and their employees adopted the following code:[86]

1. The object of the said board shall be, First, to settle all questions of wages. Second, to determine such other general matters affecting the interests of either party as may be submitted to it from time to time by operator or miner, and by conciliatory means to use its influence to prevent disputes and to put an end to any that may arise; local questions may be referred to the board by either the miner or operator for adjustment.

2. The board shall consist of eighteen members, four from the railroad miners, four from the river miners, four from the railroad operators, four from the river operators, and a miners' secretary and an operators' secretary at large.[87]

3. The operators and miners shall each select their own representatives in such a way as shall seem to them best; *provided* only, that, with the exception of the secretaries, the representatives so selected shall be actively engaged in mining or in operating mines.

4. The members of the board shall be chosen the second Tuesday in January, and shall hold office for one year and be eligible for re-election. [. . .]

5. If any representative die or resign, or cease to be qualified by terminating his active connection with coal mining, a successor shall be chosen within one month, in the same manner as is provided in the case of an annual election.

6. If any miner representative or operator representative shall become incapable of serving on this board, by reason of negligence or crime, the party whom he represents shall have power to censure, suspend, or expel him by a two-thirds vote of the party aggrieved.

7. Each representative shall be deemed fully authorized to act for the parties which have elected him.

8. [. . .] A conference committee shall be chosen, to consist of one representative each of the river and railroad operatives, and of the river and railroad miners, and the secretaries.[88] [. . .] All questions shall, in the first instance, be referred to the conference committee, who shall investigate and endeavor to settle the matters so referred to it, but shall have no power to make an award, unless by consent of the parties. In the event of the committee being unable to settle any question, it shall, as early as possible, be referred to the Board.

---

86. Published in *Gewerkschafts-Zeitung*, 15 November 1879. [This is an abbreviated version of the agreement. The full text can be found in Weeks, *Industrial Arbitration*, 49–52. The wording of this translation is that found in Weeks, but the sequence and numbering of articles are those of the *Gewerkschafts-Zeitung*.]

87. [The version in *Gewerkschafts-Zeitung* said simply, "nine operators and nine miners, a secretary of the operators and a secretary of the miners."]

88. [The *Gewerkschafts-Zeitung* says four representatives of each side are to be elected to the conference committee.]

9. [. . .] If at any meeting of the board the operator and miner representatives are unequal, all shall have a right to discuss any questions that may arise, but only an equal number of each shall vote, the representative of the same section as the absent member not being entitled to vote. The decision of the majority of the board shall be final and binding on both parties.

10. In case of a tie vote in the board, it shall appoint an independent referee, whose decision in the matter in question shall be final and binding; but said referee shall be the unanimous choice of the board, and his selection and decision shall not occupy more than five working days.

11. The board shall meet for the transaction of business twice a year, in January and July; but on a requisition of the president, signed by five members of the board, specifying the nature of the business to be transacted, and stating that it has been submitted to the conference committee, and left undecided by them, he shall, within five days, convene a meeting of the board [. . .].

12. Pending the discussion and decision of any difference or dispute, there shall be no lock-out on the part of the operators, or strike on the part of the miners.

13. Neither operators nor miners shall interfere with any man on account of his being a union or non-union man.

14. Any expenses incurred by this board shall be borne equally by both parties; the operators paying one-half and the miners paying one-half; and it shall be the duty of the conference committee to establish the most convenient arrangements for collecting what may be needed to meet such expenses.

15. Parties may at any time join this board by filing with the two secretaries an agreement to be bound by these rules.

Unfortunately, in this case the result was not the desired one either. For one thing, some employers refused to recognize the code and preferred to settle the wage issue individually. And the workers, perhaps suspicious of their representatives, refused to grant them full discretionary powers. Instead they mandated them on certain issues and thus deprived them of any freedom to make concessions to the other side. The workers could invoke article 6 of the code to call their representatives to account and thwart any agreements they saw as unfavorable [despite article 7]. The settlement on wage rates was only temporary, and the two sides could not even agree on a sliding scale for a few months.

The wage table proposed by the miners was unusual in that it was based not on coal prices but on wages paid in the iron-rolling mills. Because most of the cut coal was used in the iron mills, the price of coal was largely dependent on the price of iron. And because wages in the rolling mills were determined by the market price of iron, it was thought that this relationship could be used to devise a wage scale which accurately reflected the market situation. The miners did not want to use coal prices as the basis of the calculation because local variations and their general volatility meant that they could not be determined accurately. The iron workers' wages, on the other hand, were based on a transparent price structure. So the miners thought they had a good yardstick, which reflected the market for coal at any one time. But the other side refused to discuss this proposition, and the arbitration sessions were postponed indefinitely.

At the same time as the Pittsburgh efforts took place, the mineowners of the Shenango Valley in northwestern Pennsylvania sought to accommodate the workers' demands through an arbitration procedure with rules similar to those above. The following divergent provisions deserve mention:[89]

1. The object of this board shall be: First, to determine the basis price of mining coal, and all questions relating to the same as may be submitted to it from time to time. Second, by conciliatory means use its influence to prevent disputes, and determine any that may arise in reference to the aforesaid basis price of mining coal.
2. The board shall consist of one operator and one miner representative from each mine joining the board.
3. When two or more mines belong to the same proprietors, either wholly or in part, each mine shall have the right to be represented in the board; and one operator may represent two or more mines in which he is an owner, having one vote for each mine represented.
4. The 'basis price' to be paid for mining coal shall be based on the price of number one (1) coal at Sharpsville.

This attempt did not produce anything permanent either. As in Pittsburgh, the reasons for the failure lay in the insufficient powers delegated to the workers' representatives and in the difficulty of devising an acceptable scale. Another flaw appeared to be that by the time an arbiter was appointed, both sides' positions had already become so entrenched that neither was willing to give ground. Consequently both sides would be dissatisfied with the eventual award. It would have been better to involve the arbiter from the beginning, invite him to the meetings, and turn to him for a judgment at an earlier stage.

The most successful arbitration schemes are reported from the boot- and shoe-making industry in Cincinnati. Sparked by the state legislature's attempts to provide a statutory framework for arbitration, efforts

---

89. Massachusetts BLS, *Twelfth Report*, 55.

in this direction have been widely debated in Ohio for some years now. In 1878 a bill was introduced into the state legislature with the following basic provisions:[90]

1. That when employers and employés met and agreed upon a question of wages, etc., for a definite period, such agreement could be legally enforced.
2. That if they met and failed to agree, an arbitrator, mutually acceptable, might be called in, and the decision to be legally binding for a definite term.
3. If the parties could not agree upon an arbitrator, then the judge of a court of record would, upon notification, be required to act as arbitrator, and his decision to be a court record and legally binding upon the parties.

The proposal was not adopted, however. As Governor Richard Bishop commented in his 1880 state of the state address: "Legislation can only aid in bringing about this certainly desirable system of preventing 'strikes,' by making such settlements legally binding upon both parties when voluntarily entered into by both."[91]

Ohio's footwear industry has been booming in recent years, with existing firms expanding and new ones being established. An average of 1,069 workers were employed in the industry in 1881 and 1,284 in 1882. That year foremen earned an average of $3.09 [per day], bootmakers $2.25, cutters $2.34, finishers $2.47, vampers $2.49, lastworkers $2.26, heelers $2.37, polishers $2.15, fitters $1.26, stitchers $2.02, boys $0.64, and girls $0.71.[92] A board of arbitration and conciliation for Cincinnati's shoe industry was set up in spring 1882 primarily at the behest of Mister Stribley, a factory owner who had observed the industrial unrest in his branch for over two decades. The institution has lasted through the end of the year, and all disputes have been settled to the satisfaction of both sides. The Board's statutes are as follows:[93]

1. The title of the Board shall be "The Board of Arbitration and Conciliation for the Boot and Shoe Factories of Cincinnati, Ohio."
2. The object of this Board shall be to settle all questions of wages, to determine such other general matters affecting the interests of either party, as may be submitted from time to time by the representatives of employer or

90. [Ohio BLS, *Second Report*, 67.]
91. [Massachusetts BSL, *Twelfth Report* (1881), 56.]
92. *Sixth Annual Report of the Bureau of Labor Statistics to the General Assembly of Ohio, for the Year 1882* (Columbus, 1883), 258–60.
93. Ibid., 258–60.

employe, and by conciliatory means use its influence to prevent and put an end to any difficulties that may arise.

3. This Board shall consist of sixteen members, to be equally divided between the employers and employes.

4. The manufacturers and employes shall elect their representatives in such manner as shall seem to them best, and shall all be selected of men actually engaged, as employers or employes, in the manufacture of boots and shoes.

5. The members of the Board shall be chosen to serve for one year. Either of the parties so desiring may divide their representation so as to elect semi-annually, the first Tuesday of June and December. The Board so elected shall meet the third Tuesday of June and December for the election of officers and hearing any amendments to these rules that may be offered, and acting on them.

6. If any representative die or resign or cease to be qualified by terminating his active connection in the manufacture of boots and shoes, either as employer or employe, a successor shall be chosen within one week in accordance with Article 4.

7. Each representative shall be fully authorized to act for the parties that have elected him.

8. The officers of this Board shall be a President, Vice-President, Treasurer, and two Secretaries. The President, Vice-President and Treasurer shall be elected by the Board. The President and Vice-President shall be, one an employer, the other an employe; each party shall have the selection of one Secretary from their number. The officers so elected shall serve until the next semi-annual meeting (election), and be eligible for re-election; the Secretary of either party shall be, one an employer, the other an employe; each party shall have the selection of one Secretary from their number. The officers so elected shall serve until the next semi-annual meeting (election), and be eligible for re-election; the Secretary of either party shall be privileged, if he so desires, to employ a person to act as his clerk and perform his duties before the Board. The minutes kept by each Secretary at each meeting of the Board shall be approved by the President and Vice-President by attaching their signatures thereto before the meeting adjourn.

9. The President, Vice-President and Secretaries shall be ex-officio members of all committees appointed by this Board.

10. The President shall preside over the meetings of the Board, in his absence the Vice-President, and in the absence of both the meeting shall elect a Chairman.

11. All votes shall be taken by a show of hands, unless the yeas and nays be called for; each member shall vote on all questions, except at any meeting of the Board where the representatives of the employers and employes are unequal in number, or where a member of the Board is individually interested in the question before the Board, he shall be excluded from voting. The surplus of names on either side shall be withdrawn by ballot by the Secretaries, and the member or members of the Board whose names are so withdrawn are not entitled to a vote on that question, but they shall have the

same right to discuss the matter as other members. The decision of a majority shall be final.

12. In case the Board fail to agree, each side shall elect some suitable person of unimpeachable character to act as arbitrators. The two shall have such opportunities of examing into the evidence in the case as will enable them to use proper judgment in selecting a suitable person to act as umpire, and the three – viz., the arbitrators and umpire – shall hear all or as much evidence in the case as will enable them to reach a just decision, and the case under consideration shall remain in the same condition as before it was presented to them, until they render their decision, which shall be accepted as final and binding on all parties. In case the aforesaid arbitrators and umpire fail to reach a decision in a reasonable time, the Board, by a two-thirds vote, may withdraw the case from them, and in that event the Board shall select three other persons in the same manner as described above in this article, whose duties and privileges shall be precisely the same as provided for the arbitrators and umpire in the first case.

13. There shall be a meeting of the Board on the first Monday in May and November each year, for the purpose of considering and settling the question of wages for the coming seasons. In case the Board fail to agree, the matter shall be referred for arbitration and decision.

14. Each factory shall have a committee of three. One shall be the proprietor or a member of the firm, the other two to be selected by the employes immediately after the semi-annual election of the Board, and the employes named shall not be members of the Board, this committee to be known as the Shop Committee.

15. The duty of the Shop Committee shall be to hear and investigate any dispute that may arise in the factory, and have authority to settle the same, by all three agreeing to the terms of settlement within forty-eight hours after said dispute is referred to them, failing in which they shall notify the President of the Board and the Secretaries, who shall call the Board together and submit the case to them.

16. All questions requiring investigation shall be submitted to the shop's committee or the Board, as the case may be, in writing, and shall be supplemented by such verbal testimony or explanation as may be thought necessary.

17. The President shall call special meetings of the Board upon the written request of five members of the Board, said request specifying the nature of the business to be transacted, and no business shall be transacted except that mentioned in the call. The meeting shall convene within five days after the request is made.

18. Pending the discussion and decision of any difference or dispute there shall be no lockout on the part of the employer or strike on the part of the employes.

19. Neither employer or employes shall interfere with any man upon account of his being a Union or non-Union man. Any employer refusing to comply with the decisions of this Board in cases submitted to it, his shop or factory

shall be declared on "strike," and any employe who refuses to comply with the decision of this Board when their case is submitted to it, he shall be deprived of work in any factory whose proprietors are associated with this Board.

20. Any expense incurred by this Board shall be borne equally by both parties, the employers paying one-half and the employes one-half. It shall be the duty of the Secretaries to establish the most convenient arrangement for collecting what may be needed to meet such expenses.

21. No alterations shall be made in these rules except by a majority vote at the semi-annual meeting of the Board, nor then unless notice is given in writing of the proposed change to the Secretaries at least one month before such meeting. All amendments or alterations to be voted on in accordance with Article 11.

With this we end our discussion of the efforts aimed at conciliation and arbitration. Suffice it to add that other reports published by the bureaus of labor statistics broadly cover the same ground as the examples discussed above.

Channeling the confrontation between capital and labor along more peaceful lines is becoming more urgent in the United States by the year. For the country's manufacturing industry, where most of the strikes originate, is expanding at a staggering pace. The 1860 census recorded 140,433 factories, employing 1,311,000 workers producing goods worth $1,885 million. In 1870 there were 252,148 factories with 2,053,000 workers and an output valued at $4,232 million. And in 1880 there were 253,852 factories with 2,738,000 workers and output of $5,369 million. So the number of businesses has not increased much over the last decade, but the total workforce and output certainly have. This indicates the growth of large-scale industry. As a result the employers are now opposed by large groups of workers, and individual strikes involve much larger numbers of people. We would like to recall here a finding from our first article: technological change destroys the old craft unions, levels out training and skills, and unites thousands of workers under the banner of common interests. Any disruptions in production affect the general population more immediately, and mechanisms for settling disputes are becoming ever more imperative for the sake of public welfare. But without cooperation among the various players, the conciliation and arbitration efforts will not move beyond the embryonic stage they are still in in America. The law should give recognition to the arbitration awards. Workers' leaders should study the capitalist enterprise to find out how prices are formed. The employers should not deny their employees information on the state of the business. And public opinion – which can achieve so much in America – should devote close attention to the needs and wishes of the disputants, take an impartial view, and intervene supportively whenever it believes an injustice has been committed.

4

Boycotts: A New Trade Union Weapon in the United States[1]

AUGUST SARTORIUS VON WALTERSHAUSEN

The craft guilds and journeymen's associations, which for centuries had framed the socioeconomic organization of artisans and their wage-workers, were destroyed by technical innovations and the victory of free competition. But considering the extent of the transformation of economic structures since their heyday, more of the spirit that imbued them survives in modern manufacturing industry than might be expected. Extreme economic individualism, whose triumph was proclaimed enthusiastically at the dawn of the bourgeois epoch in economic life, has not become a reality. The intrinsic value of the principle of collectivism is too great for it to be overwhelmed by the economic revolution of the last century. Taking account of the new age, it has merely appeared in a new guise.

That we can recognize some characteristics of the guilds in today's employers' and workers' associations is only partly due to the nature of the association as a form of organization, which tends to become particularly rigid in the economic sphere. What also matters is that supply and demand influence the prices of goods and labor among privately owned modern businesses as much today as they did a century ago, that markets for a product sold at a certain price are finite, and that every economic combination of whatever kind is constrained by these facts. And finally, the force of tradition and custom, which is often more powerful and persistent than any law, will also play a role (although it must be said that many gradations can be distinguished here).

The guilds, which were dependent on a local market, restricted the supply of goods in their area and standardized their prices. Today's

1. "Boycotten, ein neues Kampfmittel der amerikanischen Gewerkvereine," *Jahrbücher für Nationalökonomie und Statistik,* Neue Folge, Band 11 (1885), 1–18.

employers' cartels work on the same principle, except that their markets are much larger and hence more difficult to control. And acceptance of the primacy of the association could not have been more forcefully demanded in the craft guilds than in today's trade unions. Anyone outside the association cannot expect to be treated as a human being by his colleagues, then or now. The journeymen's rebellion has been replaced by the modern strike. In the old days the name of a "dishonest" craftsman was written on the *black board;* the workers of the United States, the most modern country of our age, know the *blacklist,* in which employers identify those workers who have been particularly active in the social struggle and who they therefore want to exclude from employment if at all possible. The denunciation [*Schelten*] and ostracism [*Auftreiben*], practiced among masters and journeymen in medieval and early modern Germany has reemerged in the British and American labor movement as the *boycott. Exclusion* was aimed at those guild members who had forfeited their rights as a result of a real or imagined offense:

Anyone who committed an offence could offer to indemnify his colleagues through the guild chest. But if the issue was considered too serious to be settled in this way, the guild could sanction the "exclusion" of the member in question. If he was a master, he was not allowed to employ a journeyman, could not attend guild meetings, could only sell his wares at the marketplace at three steps removed from the other masters, and so on; if he was a journeyman, he was forced to leave his job, he could not work with any other journeyman, he would also be excluded, and if he tried to practice his trade elsewhere, he would be "ostracized," i.e. pursued by letters to places where he had traveled or sought to secure work.[2]

Not only did masters exclude other masters and journeymen, but journeymen also excluded their masters, their employers. This is clear, for instance, from a passage in an imperial edict of 1731:

In particular there is the wholly unreasonable abuse by which journeymen presumptuously decide among themselves to prescribe to their masters all manner of absurd regulations, and when these are not followed, to exclude and punish them and even to rebel against them.[3]

The boycott of today is the ostracism of an employer declared by workers' organizations, but the modern boycott of an employer by a

---

2. J. A. Orloff, *Das Recht der Handwerker* (Erlangen, 1818), 128.   3. Ibid.

workers' association differs from the exclusion of masters by journeymen in that, inevitably in our age, it is directed more against goods than against the person. The intention is to damage the outcast indirectly, to make his life impossible by excluding him from all economic relations, to destroy him economically so that he either leaves the country or ends up in the poorhouse. Exclusions and boycotts also differ in terms of the reasons they are invoked. Many ways in which a master could be unreasonable toward his journeymen no longer exist in these days. The modern workers' boycott occurs because the employer imposes more onerous working conditions or because he commits a legal and moral transgression against his workforce against which the courts do not offer sufficient protection.

The word *boycott* and the systematic refusal of social or commercial relations it signifies originated in Ireland, that unsettled country so inventive in devising weapons against oppression. In the late 1870s Charles Cunningham Boycott was a land agent managing the estates of the Earl of Erne on the shores of Lough Mask, Country Mayo. Responsible for ensuring that the tenants met their obligations to the landowner, he performed his task with such heartless rigidity, severity, and chicanery that he became the most hated man in the country. By the autumn of 1879 popular resentment was so strong that the national Land League decided to take action against him. Its representatives urged the local people not to resort to violence but instead to sever all communications with him. His tenants left just before the harvest (he had leased land himself), and his domestic servants resigned their posts. He tried to hire new workers and traveled all over the island to find them. To no avail. There were usually thousands of vagrants willing to work for any wage, but this time none offered their services. But the campaign went much further. Coach drivers refused to carry him, hotel owners refused him accommodation, and butchers, bakers, and grocers refused to sell him food. He could not sell his beef cattle destined for the British market because the railway company refused to transport them to the port. In the end the government came to the outcast's aid. In the northern province of Ulster, where the Land League had little influence, a number of workers were hired and taken to Lough Mask under military escort to harvest his crops. But it was already too late: the grain had rotted in the fields. The workers returned home. The military escort reportedly cost £25,000.

Boycott was a ruined man. He could not stay at Lough Mask. Several English landowners, keen to remove a source of persistent rural unrest, provided him with funds to emigrate. He is supposed to have landed in New York in spring 1881. He did not last very long in the United States, however, and by 1883 was back in the Emerald Isle. He appears to have undergone a conversion and has joined the camp of his erstwhile adversaries, and now seems to enjoy a certain popularity.

The success of the first boycott spurred others in Ireland to attempt the same. Many unpopular people were forced to give up their positions following boycotts. Those who refused to participate in the boycott were themselves ostracized. Several tradesmen who sold goods to boycotted people were ruined as a result. The biggest company in Ireland to become the object of a boycott was the Guinness brewery, owned by Lord Ardilaun. The struggle ended with a compromise, but one which the boycotters regarded as a moral victory.

But it was in the United States that the system of boycotting was applied more generally and given a certain theoretical underpinning. Americans' inherent tendency to exaggeration makes them particularly suited to try out social experiments of all kinds. Boycotting is no exception and is now enjoying a "boom." (This word has been adapted recently to mean a rush of business activity or a fashion craze.)

Until now the American boycotts have not been sparked by the land question, as in Ireland, but have only occurred in the industrial sector. Boycotts are seen as complementary to the strike weapon and are practiced by trade unions and general workers' organizations linked to them. Because of the rapidly expanding population and the detailed division of labor in manufacturing, the prospects of prosecuting a strike successfully have dimmed especially in the major East Coast cities, even at a time of rising demand for labor, while employers find it ever easier to replace strikers with other workers. No matter how hard the union centrals try to recruit all types of skilled and unskilled manual workers in order to cut off alternative sources of labor during a strike, they are unable to control the large numbers of immigrants looking for work in the eastern ports and cannot prevent them from taking strikers' jobs. The main purpose of a boycott is to force the employer to dismiss the replacement workers, the so-called scabs. His goods are boycotted until the union members are reinstated under the conditions demanded by them. A boycott can also be called in response to a sudden lockout. It is also used to reinforce a strike by reducing the incentive to find replacement workers. Piles of unsold stocks should then induce him to give in to the strikers. In this case boycotts are usually not very practical, however, since they take time to have an impact, and time is usually not on the strikers' side.

The method by which a boycott is conducted is always the same, but it can be applied more or less extensively, depending on the nature of the banned goods. For instance, when a hat factory is boycotted, all workers participating in the action refuse to buy hats from the firm in question, and they try to persuade those who have commercial relations with it, retailers in particular, not to buy hats from it by threatening to withdraw their patronage from the shop. The factory's brand names and designs are publicized in the labor press and disseminated in leaflets so that no one can claim ignorance.

A more comprehensive approach is possible when the object of the boycott is a newspaper. The aim is to stop sales of and advertising in the publication. The first is the more important: when circulation drops, advertising revenue will drop of its own accord, since a publication's ability to attract advertising depends on its circulation. All those who continue to advertise in the newspaper are also boycotted until they withdraw their custom. Even wholesalers and manufacturers can be induced to stop advertising in the paper when sufficient retailers, their customers, support the workers' cause. In this case the boycott can be extended furthest, since a company's relations with a newspaper are, of course, made public by the publication of adverts and can thus be easily monitored.

The struggle of the New York trade unions against the *New York Tribune* provides the most interesting example of a boycott of a major political daily paper. I would like to examine it in some detail.

The *New York Tribune* was founded by the well-known Horace Greeley, one of those remarkable personalities which America has been fortunate to produce more than once.[4] Intelligent, upright, energetic (but without the criminal ambition that often impels larger-than-life figures to resort to dubious means to gain public approval), progressive, his whole life was dedicated to the struggle against oppression and slavery. Under his editorship the *Tribune* became the most influential organ of America's liberal elite. It achieved a huge circulation, especially among the intelligent farmers of the North, and was one of the key players in the campaign to abolish slavery in the South. Following his principles, Greeley was also one of the first to place himself in the leadership of the trade union movement when it emerged. He became president of the Typographical Union No. 6 (which is currently waging the bitter struggle against the *Tribune*). During his tenure as editor the paper only employed typesetters who had joined the union.

4. See *The Boycotter*, 24 May and 14 June 1884.

Exhausted from the strains of an abortive presidential election campaign, Greeley was pushed out as editor in 1872. His successor, the entrepreneur Whitelaw Reid, soon revealed himself as a fierce opponent of the trade unions. September 1877 marked the start of the long dispute between the Typographical Union and the *Tribune*. Management, faced with financial problems owing to the prolonged recession and the consequent slump in circulation, slashed staff wage rates. A strike called by the Typographical Union failed because management found sufficient replacements willing to work for the lower wages. The new employees had to sign an undertaking that they would not join any labor organization. The union was nevertheless able to recruit many of the paper's setters over the years. And when wage rates in New York's printing industry started rising appreciably, from November 1883 on, the union was able to recruit the remaining nonunion setters as well. Most New York papers agreed to a wage increase; only the *Evening Post, Brooklyner Freie Presse,* and *Tribune* rejected the workers' demands. But a strike at the last persuaded the management to give in. Under the contract signed between the union and Reid's foreman, W. P. Thompson, the setters would be paid 46¢ for 1,000 letters and the paper also undertook to employ only Typographical Union members. The agreement was for a year but could be canceled by either side at thirty days' notice. In December, only a few weeks after its conclusion, the management did exactly that. It had succeeded in the meantime in recruiting new staff in several small New Jersey towns. Willing to work for less than the union members, these people were brought to the printing works under police protection, and the unionized setters had to get up from their workplaces and leave the premises on the spot.

Since the union members were unwilling, and perhaps also unable, to embark on what would doubtless have been protracted court action, they decided to boycott the *Tribune* until the injustice done to them was redressed. Since they could achieve little on their own, they sought support from all the other unions in New York and beyond. After several weeks no fewer than 7,400 unionists in the city had agreed to join the battle with the *Tribune*. The boycotters found a powerful ally in the Knights of Labor, which did not formally decide to back them, but many, and eventually all, district and local assemblies joined the boycott.

To have a mouthpiece, the New York Typographical Union set up a weekly newspaper, *The Boycotter*. By January 1885 its circulation was said to have reached around 30,000. Since this publication has been distributed free and in large numbers to all parts of the United States, the *Tribune*'s opponents must have substantial financial resources. Where these originate is not entirely clear. Direct support from the Knights of Labor and the union centrals cannot be ruled out. It has also been suggested more than once that the *New York Herald*, the *Tribune*'s main rival, has some involvement in the production of *The Boycotter*. The paper's extent was enlarged considerably in the summer of 1884. Since late May it also has a German section to influence the large number of German-speaking workers in the major cities. It is well edited and contains much interesting material on the labor movement nationwide. It not only reports on boycotts in other parts of the country, but also carries news and information on the activities of the union centrals, the Knights of Labor, the Socialists, etc. It does not espouse a particular political view. But during the last presidential campaign it vigorously opposed the Republican Party and its candidate, James G. Blaine, who had made the *Tribune* into his main organ.[5]

The unions' systematic campaign certainly lost the paper readers and advertisers, although the losses were not as significant as the boycotters would have hoped. This was not least because it did not have a sufficiently large working-class readership, so that the boycott could not achieve an early impact. The boycotters claim that shortly before the paper acquired its political cachet during the presidential campaign, its earnings had fallen by $8,000, and that management had been prepared to make concessions and had instructed a negotiator to establish contact with the union (which had put only a single demand to him: the restoration of the old contract).

At first, several workers' delegations tried to persuade the Republican Party to turn away from Reid and his newspaper. In return they promised to deliver the typesetters' votes for a Blaine presidency. But the negotiations came to nothing. A large section of the New York workers then turned against the Republican Party, and the Typographical Union issued the slogan "Boycott Blaine and the Republican Party."

On 11 October 1884 *The Boycotter* specified its position on the political situation as follows:

Whenever in the past the workers of this country have tried to build their own parties, these efforts have been a failure because of the indifference of the masses,

5. [The boycott campaigns against the *Tribune* have been extensively recounted in George A. Stevens, *New York Typographical Union No. 6: A Study of a Modern Trade Union and Its Predecessors* (Albany, N.Y., 1913), 384–96.]

dissatisfaction with their leaders, the vagueness of its principles, or personal jealousies. However, when workers have had an opportunity to express themselves about an issue, completely independent of individuals, as in the case of the vote on the proposed bill about the convict labor contract system, their strength was clearly visible. We know today that the workers' vote represents more than 100,000 ballots in the city of New York alone.

If such strength is brought to bear for or against any one of the Presidential candidates now in the field, it will be decisive in the state of New York. Under the present political circumstances the state of New York will decide whether the United States is to be governed for the next four years by the Republicans or the Democrats.

We have no special liking for Mr. Cleveland, nor has Mr. Blaine ever done us any harm, that could cause us to open a personal war against him. We have nothing to thank the Democratic Party for, and also no audacious, thorough-going measures for our benefit to expect from it, but we find ourselves compelled to form a decisive front against a party whose campaign funds pour out of the pockets of the railroad and telegraph owners, bankers, monopolists and other useless members of society.[6] 19 October the New York printers, meeting at the Clarendon Hall, endorsed Grover Cleveland's candidacy and adopted the following resolution:

The printers of New York in convention assembled resolve: that the election of James G. Blaine would mean the elevation of Whitelaw Reid and of his hireling Thompson. That the newspapers of New York which support the Republican candidate strive with all their might to reduce the wages of the printers and thereby, in a way, encourage all employers to follow their example; that we call upon all workers, to consider the welfare of themselves and their families and to vote against James G. Blaine in the coming election, because he is the candidate of the bosses, who constantly preach the theory of the protection of labor while pushing the earnings of their workers down to the verge of starvation wages, and who make every effort to obstruct and impede the organization and progress of the workers.

We further resolve that in order to secure our goals, we must combine our votes for any candidate whose eventual election secures the defeat of James G. Blaine; that, with all due respect to the views and opinions of those who favor other candidates, we further declare it to be a well known fact that their efforts and exertions on behalf of those candidates will turn out to be futile; and that everyone who desires the defeat of James G. Blaine, champion of the "rat" Republican newspapers[7] of New York, should concentrate their efforts on achieving the election of Cleveland, whose friends among the newspapers of New

---

6. [Retranslated from German.]
7. Workers who deprive union members of jobs by accepting lower wages are called *rats* as well as *scabs*. Thus Reid is denounced as the "rat king," the Republican Party as the "party of the rat kings," and the *Tribune* as the "rat paper."

York acknowledge and respect the demands of organized labor and pay the wages set by the various unions.[8]

As we know, the presidential election on 4 November brought victory for the Democrats, and the result turned on New York State. Cleveland beat Blaine, but by a mere 1,145 votes. The boycotters claimed that their campaign had inflicted the defeat on the Republican Party. Many labor publications shared this view, as did several papers which did not have an ax to grind in the *Tribune* dispute. Be that as it may, there is no doubt that the Democrats' victory helped the boycotters, who could now resume the struggle with renewed vigor. They could expect that the Republicans would no longer support the paper financially, and that Reid would have to rely on his own resources again.

The Boycotter still appears regularly. In recent issues it has expressed its confidence that the *Tribune* management will have to restore the broken contract in the near future. So at the time of writing (July 1885) the bitter eighteen-month dispute has still not been settled.

But in a number of other cases over the last few years boycotters have been successful. They can claim victories over the *Washington Post;* the *Daily Herald* in Halifax, Nova Scotia; the bakeries in that town; Franc Tousey, a publisher and printer of fiction in New York City; the Ehret brewery in New York City; and a hat-making company in South Norwalk, Connecticut. The extent to which boycotts are conducted against newspapers is shown by the list compiled by the Knights of Labor and published last fall. It names the *New York Tribune, Philadelphia Press, New York Mail and Express, New York Commercial Advertiser, Utica Herald, Troy Times, Buffalo Commercial, Albany Journal, Newark Advertiser, Chicago Times, St. Louis Republican, Buffalo Courier, New York Evening Post, Boston Post, Atlanta Constitution, New York Journal of Commerce, Kansas City Times, Pittsburgh Post, Detroit Free Press, Philadelphia Free Press,*[9] *Philadelphia Labor World, Pittsburgh Leader* and *Illinois Evening and Sunday State Journal.*[10]

---

8. [Retranslated from German.]
9. [Following Karl J. R. Arndt and May E. Olson, *German-American Newspapers and Periodicals, 1732–1955* (rev. ed., New York and London, 1965), this should probably be the *Philadelphia Freie Presse* (publ. 1848–87).]
10. [This should probably be the *Illinois Staats-Zeitung* (published 1848–1922), which had evening and Sunday editions. See Arndt and Olson, *German-American Newspapers and Periodicals,* 73–5.]

New York City is the focal point of all boycott campaigns. Here they have been directed at a very wide range of goods, companies, and organizations. Besides various newspapers, the following goods were boycotted in January of this year [1885]: beef processed in Chicago, hats from the South Norwalk factories, textiles from Garry Brothers, stoves, grates and pokers from the John S. Perryrand Company, Tousey's books, and cigars manufactured in tenement houses.

To restrict sales of the latter, as well as cigars made by Chinese workers and prisoners, the International Cigarmakers' Union has been using *labels* since before boycotting became common. Under this system cigars made by union members are marked with a printed label so that they can be distinguished from cigars made by "cheap" labor. Labeling, like boycotting, aims to prevent the sale of goods produced by those competing with union members. It differs from boycotting in that it works indirectly, i.e., it seeks to restrict the sales of other goods by recommending those produced by union members.

Article 9 of the union's constitution sets out the relevant provisions on labeling in greater detail:[11]

Sec. 1. – The President of the International Union shall have prepared printed and copyrighted a Trade Mark Label to be known as the Union Label suitable to be posted on the sides or any other conspicuous place on the box. If the funds of the International Union will permit these labels shall be furnished to all local unions free of charge, but in no event shall the price of these labels be to the local unions more than the actual cost paid for, from the general expense fund. The paper shall be kept as nearly uniform as possible.

COPY OF UNION LABEL

Sec. 2. – Issued by authority of the Cigarmakers International Union of America.

UNION MADE CIGARS

This certifies that the cigars contained in this box have been made by a first class workman, a member of the Cigarmakers International Union of America, an organization opposed to inferior rat shop, coolie, prison, or filthy tenement-house workmanship. Therefore we recommend these cigars to all smokers throughout the world. Copyrighted.

All infringements upon this label will be punished according to law.

President C. M. U. of America.

11. *Constitution of the Cigar Makers International Union of America* (New York, 1880), 18–20.

Sec. 3. – Each L.U. [local union] shall furnish through its shop committeeman to all shops employing union members free of all charges as many of these labels as may be required from week to week, for all cigars actually made by members of the union. In the event of an employer or union member handling cigars made at any other factory or employing non-union cigar makers, the union is positively forbidden to allow the employers to use the union label on any boxes which contains [sic] cigars purchased or made by any non-union cigar makers.

Sec. 4. – In the event an employer employes [sic] both union and non-union cigar makers and mixes and packs both grades of work in the same boxes, the union is positively forbidden to allow the use of the union label.

Sec. 5. – In shops employing only union members in which the employers or foreman work at the bench the union may allow the use of the union label on all cigars made.

Sec. 6. – Employers agreeing to the use of the union label and violating any of the conditions for use shall be refused the use of the label for the space of six months for first offense, for a second violation, all use of the label shall be refused, until the employer deposits the sum of fifty dollars with the union as a guarantee for a faithful compliance in the future.

Sec. 7. – Shop committees are especially enjoined to strictly demand a faithful compliance of all parts of this article, by employers in the use of the union label, report any breach of agreement to the President, or to the union forthwith for violating or neglecting the enforcement of the conditions of this article. The shop committee shall be fined not less than one dollar for first offense and not less than two dollars for second offense; unions violating any of the conditions of this article or neglecting its enforcement shall be fined not less than five dollars for first offense payable to the International Union, and refused the use of the label for the space of six months and fined not less than five dollars for second offense.

The Cigarmakers' Union also campaigns to persuade members of other workers' associations to smoke only label cigars. But since the cigars made by Chinese workers and others are usually cheaper, this is not an easy task. The union has to appeal to class solidarity, a rather unevenly developed notion among American workers. In the last three years, during which the labor movement has made such extraordinary strides in terms of organization, the label system has been more successful than ever, particularly since it has been linked to boycotts. In saloons and shops union members demand label cigars. If the owner or manager does not supply them, the establishment is boycotted. When he accepts the workers' demand, they make further demands, for instance that he stock *only* label cigars (i.e., for all smokers). If he does not accede, the workers will again boycott his goods. In the smaller cities, where unionization is strong, this approach has been successful on many occasions.

A successful label system works like a protective tariff. It protects the livelihoods of a group of relatively well-off workers against competition from an impoverished or oppressed proletariat. Protective tariffs are intended to even out the competitive imbalances between workers from different countries, the label system those between different social classes. The problem under discussion here is important at a practical level and also intriguing from a theoretical viewpoint. For analogous situations can be found in all the major industrial countries. In all cases the problem cannot be tackled by the state. This is one of the few cases where self-help is the only option. Whether the state can impose a minimum wage in the current economic conditions is, of course, a highly contentious issue. But surely none of its advocates can argue that it should be set at the level of the highest-paid workers.

One might describe the American label system as selfish because its intention is to deprive the needy, underpaid proletariat, the tenement workers, of their livelihoods. That would be incorrect, however, since the system has the simultaneous aim of improving their lot. The idea is to force them to join the union so that they can then demand a higher price for their labor.

We noted above that the boycott has been given a certain theoretical underpinning in the United States. This should not be understood to mean that its significance within the overall economy or its role in the so-called solution to the labor question have been analyzed. At issue, rather, are, firstly, a moral justification of the boycott (no one can deny its formal justification), and, secondly, the conditions under which it can lead to a positive result for those who want to exercise it. Most Americans view boycotting merely as an extension of the basic business principle that people are free to buy goods from whom they like and that they sell only to those who are willing to offer an appropriate equivalent in return. There is nothing wrong, then, with an employers' cartel deciding not to buy the labor of union members and, to this end, locking them out of the factories, or a group of workers deciding only to work at a particular wage rate and withdrawing their labor when this is not offered. Freedom of movement applies not only to individuals but, on the basis of the constitutional right of freedom of association, also to workers' associations.

Incidentally, the workers are behaving no differently than the church or whole nations have occasionally done. From the pulpit preachers have called for temperance, which is tantamount to a boycott of saloons. At the start of the War of Independence the grandfathers of today's Americans considered it a patriotic act to prevent the importation of British tea. And what is a trade ban but a boycott of another country?

Given the American worldview, it is inevitable that arguments from the Bible are adduced to justify boycotts. As *The Craftsman* puts it, for instance:

BOYCOTT

"Have I not a right to do as I please with my own?" – Bible.

The above sentence from the Bible gives us a very exact and truthful definition of that terrible little word which heads this article. For over eighteen hundred years that sentence has been thundered into our ears, but was never thoroughly understood until boiled down into that little word of seven letters – "boycott." The rich, who were condemned, have used it all adown the tide of time to grind and crush that very class whom Christ had died to save, but at last that very poor hear the clarion note from heaven's throne – boycott.[12]

Similarly, *John Swinton's Paper* contains the following passages:

The Apostle Paul as boycotter – The practice of boycotting, which is currently in fashion, appears to be approved by the Apostle Paul. One of the correspondents to our journal draws our attention to a statement by the Apostle in the Second Letter to the Thessalonians, chap. 3, v. 11–14, where the following is written: "For we hear that there are some which walk among you disorderly, working not at all, but are busybodies. . . . And if any man obey not our word by this epistle, note that man, and have no company with him, that he may be ashamed." – It must be confessed, that this seems very similar to boycotting.[13]

Boycotting is probably best legitimized in terms of the right of self-protection. It can be seen as a means of social self-defense. There are occasions when the state's laws and judicial system cannot or will not protect one social class from another. Who would then deny the hard-pressed the right to self-protection? This also draws the line between justified and unjustified boycotts. If self-defense is justified, it is only a question of deciding which practical social means should be employed to achieve the desired end.

12. [*Craftsman* quoted in *The Boycotter,* June 14, 1884, 13.]
13. [Retranslated from German.]

On the conditions for a successful boycott by unions, the previously quoted New York paper of the Typographical Union No. 6 states:

The boycott has become a not insignificant part of the labor movement. Where a strike does not succeed in bringing an advocate of the "businesslike" worker-starvation system to heel, then this last plague is applied, and it has a more salutary effect than a costly strike can achieve.

Naturally, boycotts must be undertaken systematically, just like strikes. The workers are compelled gradually to develop a kind of science for their tactics, and its invention requires truly as many brains as the invention of the tactics and strategy of the Prussian military system.

We are still in the early stages of this science, and for the labor movement to work it through will be the task of generations. Nevertheless, all observations and thoughts about this matter must be to the advantage of the labor movement. We wish to spell out today's state of affairs. The boycott is applied where a strike is either not possible or has proven to be futile.

A boycott is to be used only where the industry involved has not yet become a monopoly. Other means have to be found against the Western Union Telegraph Company or the Standard Oil Company. The breweries, however, are still completely within our reach.

A boycott is to be used against those who show themselves to be enemies of the trade union movement in some way, whether they be politicians, manufacturers, or something else. If the action is limited to only a few targets at a time, that is an elementary tactical precaution. Everyone should understand that from the standpoint of justice nobody can complain that he, the designated worst enemy of our aspirations, becomes the victim of the workers' wrath. Many have deserved it, and everyone will have his turn, when his time comes. A boycott must be undertaken with energy. This punishment is cheaper than a strike, to be sure, but not as cheap as many workers' organizations seem to think. It costs money and a lot of work.

It takes only a few minutes to decide on a boycott. But to carry it off effectively is at least as difficult, but also as honorable as to win a strike.

It is true that the organized labor movement is in a position to hunt down almost all of its adversaries under the present circumstances, but it requires the most extreme exercise of the strength of a single union to bring the innumerable masses of workers into action and to make their latent power effective.

Lack of faith in their own strength has been the inherited failing of the lower classes at all times and among all peoples. But wherever the members of our class make a special effort, that lack of faith will surely be overcome, and once they have been brought into motion the masses are irresistible and not to be pacified until they have attained their goal.

The heart of the matter lies in the proposition: a boycott must concentrate on a few targets and must be carried out with great energy and perseverance.

One should not expect any easy or quick battles on this front – such an effort is ineffective – but a war that goes on for years and eventually brings victory.[14]

---

14. [Retranslated from German.]

The conditions for a successful struggle outlined above – concentrating the attack on a few opponents, persevering once embarked on it, and not getting involved with a monopoly – are neither comprehensive nor have they been examined in detail. Let me therefore make some additional comments.

1. A boycott's chances of success are improved the more people participate in it, the more thoroughly it is carried through, and the more centralized its leadership. In short, the decisive factor in a workers' boycott is organization. The centralization of the trade unions or their incorporation into nontrade workers' associations like the Knights of Labor are therefore highly conducive to the effective prosecution of a boycott. Just as important as strong organization can be the motivation behind a boycott. If it is perceived as a just response to an outrage, then not only large numbers of working people but also the general public will participate in it. Constant campaigning is of the essence, however, since otherwise the issue will drop out of the public eye.

2. Since boycotts are more successful when they can close down a particular market, it follows that an employer who operates in a local market can be defeated more easily than one who also sells his goods further afield. A manufacturer who produces for the export market is virtually impossible to get at in this way. A local campaign is also that much easier to organize because a local workers' association usually already exists or can be set up without too much difficulty.

3. Concentrating a boycott on a few goods is important because one cannot expect the masses to focus on many issues at the same time. It can be particularly counterproductive to take up a boycott with several producers of the same article, since this could ease competition among the nonboycotted and thus result in price hikes.

4. This leads us to draw a distinction between an employer who enjoys a monopoly position in the market and one who faces competition from others. In the first case it is impossible to stop the sale of boycotted goods, since the public would then have to forego the goods in question altogether. If there are competitors, what matters is their number and type. If there is only one major competitor, a boycott of its rival can provide it with a sales monopoly that will allow it to raise prices and thus cut workers' real incomes. This undermines the boycott because the boycotted but cheaper goods become particularly attractive to workers who do not want to see their living standards eroded. In fact boycotted goods will generally not hold their previous price, especially

not if they are perishable. The price cut need not be direct and open; it can be hidden. In the above-mentioned dispute between the unions and the *New York Tribune,* for instance, the paper offered its subscribers discounts and distributed many issues for free. Price cuts are always dangerous for boycotters, since they test their spirit of solidarity and ability to resist the temptation of the cheaper goods.

The increasing monopolization of business in the United States in the form of cartels and single-company industries will make it increasingly difficult for working people to organize boycotts. I even consider it likely that the boycott, if it becomes a common institution, will strongly stimulate an increase in the number of employers' associations. The need for reform of today's U.S. economy, which is based not on harmony but on a conflict of interests, will become ever more apparent – it is inevitable given the monopolization of capital – as the weapons available to both sides become more effective, i.e., more dangerous. For every new weapon deployed in the social struggle by one side triggers the development of an improved defensive or attacking weapon by the other. The strike gave rise to the lockout, which in turn was mainly responsible for the boycott.

This system is powerless against monopoly. It is hardly surprising, then, that employers will resort to the cartel structure to eliminate competition.

5. The success of the modern form of ostracism is also determined by the type of goods involved. Goods which are not for immediate consumption, such as railway tracks, are not susceptible to workers' boycotts. Luxury goods which are bought only by the rich are also difficult to boycott. In these cases the best possible outcome is an indirect effect on those tradesmen who, as is often the case in smaller towns, sell goods to all sections of the population. But in a fragmented retail sector, the producers who produce for the "upper ten thousand" are almost impossible to attack through a boycott. The prospects are more promising for goods that are used by everyone.

6. A final key issue is the degree to which the boycott can be monitored effectively. The workers have to check each other to ensure that no one buys the boycotted goods, and they also have to check the retailers to ensure that they respect the boycott in their businesses. Both are that much easier when the market for the goods in question is small. It is easier to boycott a local newspaper than one with a nationwide distribution. The type of boycotted goods should also be borne in mind in this context. In the case of newspapers and books the publisher is

always known; with textiles, leather, wood and hardware, experts can usually tell the origin of the goods; but in the case of many foodstuffs and stimulants the products of different producers are so similar that they are very difficult to distinguish from one another. Thus, while it is possible to deprive a bookseller of all his customers through a boycott, it is very difficult to hurt a large slaughterhouse the same way.

In the discussion of these six conditions for a successful boycott we have already touched on the role which the institution plays within the national economy. Since it is by definition a negative institution, it has no more value for the solution of the labor question than the strike, a weapon which merely intensifies the opposition between labor and capital. Strikes will disrupt production suddenly, can hamper the increase in national wealth, and may inconvenience the public. Strikers usually suffer great hardship, since they forfeit their wages. And their reduced spending power affects those who supply them, so that every strike acts as a drag on economic activity to some extent.

A successful boycott, however, merely shifts production around. The reduced demand for boycotted goods is compensated for by increased demand for similar goods from other sources. And boycotts may wipe out a factory or company altogether, but their production will then fall to other companies. If the former employed nonunion workers, they will lose their jobs, while the union members they replaced will gradually find new jobs. If the boycotted employer goes bust, his capital invested in tools, machinery, and materials is depreciated and lost to the national economy if it cannot be deployed elsewhere. The workers who conduct the boycott suffer only when prices go up as a result of it, as mentioned above.

Just as it would be sensible to replace strikes with conciliation and arbitration procedures, it would also make sense to rely on these to prevent boycotts. Unfortunately conciliation and arbitration are proving difficult to introduce, and their efficacy cannot be counted on.[15] In any case successful conciliation and arbitration cannot guarantee social peace, since they do not overcome the antagonism between labor and capital. This is often so strong that a settlement or *award*, the only thing arbitration can offer, cannot be implemented.

As said, the boycott is not a means of social reform, but a powerful weapon in the social struggle. This should not imply that it would be

15. See the author's earlier article, "The Trade Unions in the United States of America: Conciliation Efforts and Courts of Arbitration" [Essay 3, this volume].

wise to outlaw the practice. Quite apart from the fact that a secret instruction among workers not to buy goods from someone cannot be rescinded by the state, such a proscription would only replace one evil by an even greater one. For in addition to their antipathy toward capital the workers would then harbor an antipathy toward the state order, and the banned weapon would be replaced by an even more dangerous one.

5

Relief Funds in the United States[1]

AUGUST SARTORIUS VON WALTERSHAUSEN

At the start of the article on trade unions I pointed out that the United States has a large number of welfare associations based on mutuality.[2] I attributed their prominent position, and that of private associations in general, essentially to the country's circumstances. These organizations provide help to individuals confronted with overwhelming natural forces and are also involved in many aspects of social life which in densely populated countries have rightly been taken on by the state and local authorities. A distinction should be made here between the settled and the recently developed areas. For the more one moves to the latter, the more the above applies. In the West even criminal justice is often exercised through a private agreement among the settlers, who, it must be said, are greatly troubled by robbers and tramps.[3] In the East assistance to the poor is also largely dispensed by private charities, but public welfare provision, in particular schemes organized by local councils, is spreading gradually.

American people make quite a different moral judgment of poverty than we Europeans. It is no exaggeration to say that the average educated American cannot stand the poor as such. That is not to say that heartlessness is an inherent part of the American national character. Rather, this loathing is explained by the fact that the concept of work is held in higher regard than in Europe, something which I have highlighted on several occasions as a particularly appealing trait of this vigorous nation. The poor and the idle are thus often seen as one and the

1. "Das Hilfskassenwesen in Nordamerika," *Jahrbücher für Nationalökonomie und Statistik,* Neue Folge, Bd. 10 (1885), 97–154.
2. See Essay 3, this volume.
3. For a detailed description of a recent case of lynch law, see the *Kölner Zeitung* of 12 April 1884.

same, on the assumption that anyone who wants to can work and can earn a living. The general belief is that most of the poor have only themselves to blame, and that only those few who have been plunged into misery through force of circumstance deserve compassion. We Europeans would not accept the presumption that poverty is the result of a personal failing. In due course the Americans will also come to perceive the social dimension of poverty. For the prospects of wage workers have deteriorated to such an extent in the last decade that impoverishment due to external circumstances will become a common phenomenon there as well. The fact that public poor relief is becoming more prominent already suggests as much.[4]

The extensive network of private welfare activities is by no means inconsistent with the general contempt for the poor. What the latter has led to is a frequent rejection of a state role because of the reluctance to use public funds to support indolence. The appalling treatment meted out to tramps in the United States, who are often without work through no fault of their own, can only be understood from this perception of poverty. To a hard-working American, treating tramps with a degree of compassion is tantamount to desecrating the concept of work.

As we know, all things American are characterized by a touch of eccentricity. Here too. A typical example of abhorrent brutality toward tramps will suffice to confirm the above. Newspapers in Trenton, N.J., recently commended the measures taken by the city's "freeholders" against the tramps as "highly effective." These involved arresting them, putting them in chains, and forcing them to break stones. The papers reported gleefully that tramps were now avoiding Trenton and that those who had served their sentences immediately left the area. One of the supervisors would soon have to be made redundant because there were not enough tramps to supervise. This measure against the tramps was only an experiment, but it has proved so successful that it is likely to be adopted elsewhere. Trenton's way of dealing with tramps meets with the wholehearted approval of the American press. "This experiment," one newspaper opined, "should be introduced in every New Jersey county and in every other state which has no better alternative. Broken stones are always needed. Someone has to break them up. Put the

---

4. The Michigan Bureau of Labor Statistics, which published its first report recently, notes that while the state's population increased from 1,184,059 in 1870 to 1,636,937 in 1880, local poorhouses supported 3,156 people in 1871 and 6,547 in 1880 and gave temporary assistance to 11,600 and 33,302 people, respectively. Michigan, *Bureau of Labor and Industrial Statistics, First Annual Report* (Lansing, 1883), 187.

tramps to this necessary and honorable work wherever they appear, and the result will be satisfactory all round."

Private charity has nothing to do with the political attitude to the poor question. It is an axiom on the other side of the Atlantic that politics and the state should be kept strictly separate from religion and the church. And it is above all the latter which have been the driving forces behind the establishment of the many welfare institutions. During debates in the federal and state legislatures, members stress what they see as the usefulness of the particular measure under consideration. But none is likely to intervene in the debate with religious arguments for or against. In the American worldview church and state have quite distinct spheres of activity, and their separation is considered the height of political wisdom.

But in people's private lives religion and the church play an overwhelming role. Here the Americans happily follow their commandments. Most men's faith admittedly does not go very deep, but it would also be wrong to say that all activities carried out in the name of religion are hypocritical. Only someone who does not know history, who does not recognize that all truly effective actions, no matter how deleterious for humanity, arise from some kind of moral impulse would explain the foundation of the thousands of welfare institutions as acts of hypocrisy.[5] Anything created in bad faith carries the seeds of its own negation within it and thus cannot have a lasting and general effect. Most charities were set up by people who sought to obey the commands of their church, although they were not necessarily moved by a sincere concern or deep emotional commitment. Americans tend to be rather superficial in religious matters, men more so than women. Men do not have enough time to think about religion. For six days a week their mental powers are concentrated on work, and on the seventh day they are too tired to do anything but relax. This also explains why until now philosophy has not been able to dislodge religion. This would require people to take a critical view of the latter and then think through the former. This takes time, something not available to those who spend most of their waking hours in some kind of economic activity. Middle- and upper-class women, thanks to their specific education, have a wider knowledge than the men, who have to and want to devote themselves to gainful employment from as young an age as possible. That is why

---

5. See Heinrich Thomas Buckle, *Geschichte der Civilisation in England,* trans. by Arnold Ruge (Leipzig and Heidelberg, 1860), vol. 1, 160.

American women have a more profound faith and are thus able to persuade their men to take actions which Christianity considers their exalted duties. That philosophy is not spread by women is understandable, since this activity has always been a male preserve. Critical and rational thought is what matters here, and there is no doubt that men have an advantage over women in this regard. If the majority of Americans would only put the slightest effort into developing a philosophical worldview, they would become aware of the incompatibility of private charity and public contempt for poverty, and of the contradiction between widespread immorality in the economic sphere and the acceptance of Christian values as soon as one has left the office behind.

It would be unjust, however, to posit the above as a generalization applying to all Americans. As in so many other respects, there is a difference between East and West. Where the legacy of the English Puritans is strongest, in New England, the above applies most strongly. But where much of the population has German roots the situation is quite different. The Germans, above all those from the northern regions, are the most implacable opponents not only of puritanical hypocrisy but also of puritanical moral superficiality. Many, particularly in the working and middle classes, have broken with positive religion. They do not go to church and do not baptize or confirm their children or send them to Sunday school. That does not mean that German Americans are somehow morally inferior to the Yankees. But they are not as actively involved in welfare work because they do not submit to religion-imposed traditions, i.e., the overwhelming power of the conventional, and instead they do right because their heart tells them to.[6]

I would like to illustrate the extraordinary extent of private charity activity in the United States with a summary of the situation in the city of Philadelphia, on which I have reliable information dating from 1880. The *City Mission Directory of the Benevolent, Charitable and Humane Institutions of the City of Philadelphia* lists 171 private institutions devoted to providing assistance to the poor and sick, to widows and orphans, and for the education of Negroes and the reform of the morally corrupted. Generally granted legal personality by the state, they are not relief funds based on mutuality, but either associations set up by rich citizens which help the needy on the basis of voluntary contributions or foundations whose assets are used to carry out charitable work in a par-

---

6. On the power of the conventional, see Arthur Schopenhauer, *On the Basis of Morality* [Providence, R.I., 1995], section 13.

ticular field. Administratively some are closely linked to a particular church or sect or to a particular race or nationality. But in dispensing assistance virtually none distinguishes on grounds of religion, color, or language.

The Philadelphia directory lists the following organizations:

1. Albion Society
2. Almwell School Association
3. Apprentices' Library
4. Associated Institute for Soldiers and Sailors
5. Association for the Care of Colored Orphans
6. Association of Friends for the Free Instruction of Adult Colored Persons
7. Association of Friends for the Free Instruction of Poor Children
8. Baptist Home of Philadelphia
9. Baptists' Orphans' Home
10. Bedford Street Mission
11. Beneficent Building Association
12. Bethany Mission for Colored People
13. Bethesda Children's Christian Home
14. Bishop Potter Memorial House for Deaconesses
15. Blockley Almshouse
16. Board of Trustees of the Howard Building
17. Boarding Home for Young Women
18. Boarding House for Young Women
19. Burd Orphan Asylum of St. Stephen's Church
20. Caledonian Club
21. Cambrian Society and Welsh Benevolent Institute
22. Catholic Home for Destitute Children
23. Central Employment Association for Seamen of the Port of Philadelphia
24. Central Soup and Bath House
25. Christmas Fund for Disabled Clergymen (Protestant Episcopal)
26. Christ Church Hospital Home for Women
27. Children's Asylum
28. Children's Seashore House
29. Children's Week in the Country
30. Church Home for Children
31. Clay Mission for Colored People
32. Clergy Daughters' Fund (Protestant Episcopal)
33. Clinton Street Boarding Home for Young Women
34. Corporation for the Relief of the Widows and Children of Clergymen in the Communion of the Protestant Episcopal Church in the Commonwealth of Pennsylvania

35. Day Nursery established in the City of Philadelphia in 1863 and incorporated in 1873
36. Deaf Mute Mission
37. Educational Home for Boys
38. Emlen Institution, Manual Labor Free School
39. Female Association for Relief of Sick and Infirm Poor (Friends)
40. Female Association of Philadelphia for the Relief of Females in Reduced Circumstances
41. Female Episcopal Benevolent Society
42. Female Hebrew Benevolent Society
43. Female Society of Philadelphia for the Relief and Employment of the Poor (Friends)
44. Flower Mission
45. Forrest Home for Aged and Infirm Actors
46. Foster Home Association
47. Franklin Reformatory Home for Inebriates
48. Franklin Reformatory Home for Women
49. French Benevolent Society
50. Friends' Association for the Aid and Elevation of the Freedmen
51. Friends' Association for the Free Instruction of Poor Children
52. Friends' Association for the Relief of Colored Freedmen
53. Friends' Boarding House Association
54. Friends' Charitable Fuel Association
55. Fuel Savings Society of the City and Liberties of Philadelphia
56. German Society
57. Germantown Flower Mission
58. Germantown Relief Society
59. Girard College
60. Grandom Institution to Aid Young Men in Business and to Assist the Poor in Procuring Fuel
61. Hibernian Society
62. Hildise Bund
63. Home for Aged and Infirm Colored People
64. Home for Aged Couples
65. Home for Consumptives (City Mission, Protestant Episcopal Church)
66. Home for Destitute Colored Children
67. Home for Incurables
68. Home for Infants
69. Home for the Homeless
70. Home Missionary Society
71. House of Correction, Employment and Reformation
72. House of Employment
73. House of Industry
74. "House of Mercy" of the Protestant Episcopal Church in Philadelphia

75. House of Refuge
76. House of the Good Shepherd (Roman Catholic)
77. Howard Institution, under the Care of an Association of Woman Friends of Philadelphia
78. Humane Society for the Recovery of Drowned Persons
79. Indian Aid Association (Friends)
80. Indians' Hope Association of Pennsylvania (Protestant Episcopal)
81. Indigent Widow's and Single Women's Society
82. Industrial Home for Girls
83. Italian Society
84. Jewish Foster Home Society
85. Kensington Soup House
86. Kosciuszko Association
87. Ladies' Depository Association
88. Ladies' United Aid Society of the Methodist Church
89. Lincoln Institution
90. Little Sisters of the Poor (Roman Catholic)
91. Locust Street Mission Association
92. Lombard Street Day Nursery
93. Lutheran Orphans' Home
94. Lutheran Orphans' Home and Asylum for Aged and Infirm
95. Magdalen Society
96. Merchants' Fund Association
97. Methodist Home for the Aged of the Church
98. Midnight Mission
99. Mission for Colored People (Church of the Crucifixion)
100. Model Lodging House and Christian Home for Young Men
101. Moyamensing Soup House
102. Newsboys' Home
103. Northern Association of the City and County of Philadelphia for the Relief and Employment of Poor Women (Friends)
104. Northern Day Nursery
105. Northern Home for Friendless Children
106. Northern Soup Society
107. Northeastern Soup Society and Relief Association of the 19th Ward
108. Northwestern Soup House
109. Old Ladies' Home
110. Old Man's Home
111. Orphan Education Society
112. Orphans' Home of the Shepherd of the Lambs
113. Orphans' Society of Philadelphia
114. Penn Asylum for Indigent Widows and Single Women in the City of Philadelphia
115. Pennsylvania Colonization Society

116. Pennsylvania Industrial Home for Blind Women
117. Pennsylvania Institution for the Deaf and Dumb
118. Pennsylvania Institution for the Instruction of the Blind
119. Pennsylvania Seamen's Friend Society
120. Pennsylvania Society for Improving the Condition of the African Race
121. Pennsylvania Society to Protect Children from Cruelty
122. Pennsylvania Training School for Feeble-Minded Children
123. Pennsylvania Working Home for Blind Men
124. Philadelphia Society for the Employment and Instruction of the Poor
125. Philadelphia Soup House
126. Preachers' Aid Society (Methodist)
127. Presbyterian Board of Relief for Disabled Ministers, and the Widows and Orphans of Deceased Ministers
128. Presbyterian Home for Widows and Single Women in the State of Pennsylvania
129. Presbyterian Orphanage
130. Provident Society for Employing the Poor
131. Richmond Soup Society
132. Rosine Association
133. Sailors' Home
134. St. Anne's Widows' Asylum (Roman Catholic)
135. St. James' Industrial School and Mission
136. St. John's Orphan Asylum
137. St. Joseph's Orphan Asylum (Roman Catholic)
138. St. Luke's Home for Aged Women
139. St. Peter's House (Protestant Episcopal)
140. St. Vincent's Home for Destitute Infants
141. St. Vincent's Orphan Asylum
142. Sanitarium for Sick Children
143. Scandinavian Society
144. Scots Thistle Society
145. Seaside Boarding House, Asbury Park (Women's Christian Association)
146. Seaside Home for Invalid Women
147. Sick-Diet Kitchens: First City Mission (Protestant Episcopal Church) Central, Northeastern, Southern, Southwestern, Home for the Homeless
148. Society for Alleviating the Miseries of Public Prisons
149. Society for Organizing Charitable Relief
150. Society of the United Hebrew Charities
151. Soldiers' and Sailors' Home
152. Soldiers' and Sailors' Home (Children's Department)
153. Soldiers' Home (Children's Department)
154. Southern Home for Destitute Children
155. Southwark Soup House

156. Spring Garden Soup House
157. Spring Lawn Boarding House for Convalescents and Persons of Limited Means
158. Swiss Benevolent Society
159. Temporary Home Association
160. The Pennsylvania Seamen's Friend Society
161. Twentieth Ward Soup Society
162. Union Benevolent Society
163. Union Home for Old Ladies
164. Union Temporary Home for Children
165. Welsh Society
166. Western Association of Ladies of Philadelphia for the Relief and Employment of the Poor
167. Western Home for Poor Children
168. Western Soup House
169. Western Temporary Home
170. Women's Christian Association
171. Young Women's Home

These 171 organizations by no means exhaust the list of private charities active in Philadelphia. For instance, there are a number of German institutions which in addition to providing assistance also have educational aims. Thus the Sunday school of the Free German Congregation promotes the use of the German language and provides free education to many neglected children. The city's many hospitals and dispensaries, almost all of which have been established by private initiatives, also provide extensive assistance and charity by offering cheap or, under certain conditions, free admission. The *City Mission Directory* lists seventy-one such organizations in Philadelphia in 1880. There are also a large number of mutual associations linked to lodges, factories, or trade unions or acting independently. (I will discuss these in greater detail below.)

The *City Mission Directory* gives a detailed description of the aims and objectives of the individual organizations. It also includes forms for making bequests to most of them. Leaving money to charitable institutions is very common. Among the rich it is actually good form, just as it was the custom among Roman emperors or senior public servants to leave legacies.[7] Educational institutions also frequently benefit from

---

7. Two examples:
   a. Samuel Willetts, an industrialist who died in New York City recently, left most of his

large bequests. The Johns Hopkins University in Baltimore and Girard College in Philadelphia are two which spring to mind here, having been endowed with several million dollars. This confirms the observation – true not just in America – that great private wealth entails public obligations. Since current legislation concentrates on the *rights* of the property owner, it is left to tradition to stress the social *duties* of wealth. If the custom of making bequests to charitable and educational institutions were to become even more widespread, the effect would be the same as that of a high progressive inheritance tax, which can, of course, be advocated on social policy grounds. The tax burdens of the eastern states and their major cities would be rather heavier if revenues equivalent to what private benefactors now donate for educational and relief work had to be raised from all citizens. It is worth remembering in this context, however, that since these taxes would probably be levied primarily as a proportion of people's liquid and immovable assets, they would impinge rather less on the rich and would thus be less effective than voluntary bequests.

At this point I would like to say a few words about the American savings banks. These play a role similar to that of the welfare institutions and are also based exclusively on private initiative. Unfortunately their record is not as commendable as that of the above-mentioned institutions. The American savings banks have been hampered by shady prac-

---

fortune to his children and grandchildren but also bequeathed $500,000 to charitable institutions. This comprised $100,000 to Swarthmore College, of which he was president; $100,000 for the education of children without means; $50,000 to the Society for the Support of Cripples; $25,000 to the Orphanage for Colored Children; $25,000 to the Association for Improving the Condition of the Poor; $50,000 to the Infirmary for Women and Children, of which he was president; $25,000 each to the New York Juvenile Asylum and the Children's Aid Society; $10,000 each to the Five Points House of Industry and the Women's Prison Association; $5,000 each to the New York Dispensary, the De Milt Dispensary, the Northern Dispensary, the Northeastern Dispensary, the Williamsburg Dispensary, the Prison Association, the American Female Guardian Society, the Institution for the Blind, the Institution for the Deaf and Dumb, the New York Diet Kitchen, and the Hahnemann Hospital; $50,000 to the New York Hospital; and $25,000 to the Working Women's Protective Union. He also authorized his executor to allocate another $100,000 to other charitable institutions as he saw fit. Reported in the *Illinois Staats-Zeitung*, 19 February 1883.

b. "Once again an American millionaire has donated millions to charitable and other public-welfare causes, and this time it is a female millionaire, namely Mrs. Valeria G. Stone, the widow of one of the great Boston merchants, Daniel P. Stone, who died some days ago in Malden, Mass. In the spirit of her husband, who died five years ago, she has bequeathed nearly $2 million for the above-mentioned causes." Quoted from the *Illinois Staats-Zeitung*, 28 January 1884.

tices and speculation. Often they were founded not to give the middle and working classes an opportunity to invest their small savings easily and securely, but merely to allow the bankers to make a quick profit from the interest rate differential. Several states have passed laws aimed at giving depositors a measure of protection, but these efforts have not silenced the critics who claim that savings banks are often financially unsound.

The federal tax commissioner's 1882 annual report shows that on 31 May of that year 700 savings institutions were in operation. Of these 38 issued shares and 662 were based on mutuality. The former held deposits of $38 million, the latter $942 million. Among the share-based banks all capital losses affecting the investors have been assessed, while among the mutual banks all losses are restricted to a twelfth of the annual interest payments on the total deposits. The savings banks' total deposits seem, in absolute terms, high, but they are by no means exceptional given the national income and wealth creation of the United States during recent years. For instance, the people of Saxony, which has a population of about 2.75 million, had invested 318,289,085 marks in the region's banks in 1879. Allowing for the fact that the average money wage in Saxony is not even half that in the United States, a commensurate level of deposits for the 50 million Americans would be 11.6 billion marks, i.e., around three times as much as they had actually invested in 1879.

This is clear evidence, then, that the Americans do not have a strong saving instinct, as expressed in countless small deposits. The country's private enterprise is based on efficient production and inefficient consumption. Making and then spending a lot of money seems to be the guiding principle of individual households. American businessmen seem to be committed to making money by whatever means possible and are then happy to spread it around their families and dispense great hospitality toward outsiders. Relatively the most expensive factor of production is labor power, and its cost is kept to a minimum. There is a constant drive to replace wageworkers by machines, labor power by capital power. And one husbands one's own labor as carefully as possible, which is called *saving time*. Wasteful consumption is as apparent in private life as in public life. Rich Americans tend to refurbish their homes every couple of years, the amounts of money spent on clothes and household items are staggering, the waste generated by the large hotels can feed many thousands of poor people, and the terrible habit of *treating* in the bars means people spend three times more than if they just bought their own drinks. I will not bore the reader with more such examples. Suffice it to say that the states and cities are so deeply indebted because they show no self-restraint in putting up public buildings and schools and because public parks and promenades cost millions. There seems little doubt, then, that the Americans consume a larger proportion of their (admittedly huge) national income than the Europeans. But in absolute terms, per head of population, capital accumulation is still extraordinarily high. The falling interest rate, a symptom of growing wealth, is evidence of this.

Yet people's horizons, in terms of needs and desires, are also broadening. This applies quite specifically to the affluent classes. It is undeniable that under the current conditions national productivity benefits the rich above all. This is the key reason why comforts and luxuries are much more expensive in America than in Europe. This cannot be due to the protective tariffs, since these apply across the board and so do not single out luxury goods. Nor is it because they are expensive to produce or because inflation is higher. The real reason for the discrepancy is that, owing to the booming wealth on the other side of the Atlantic, demand for these goods always outstrips supply. This does not necessarily mean that luxury goods' prices invariably tend upward, only that they have remained high despite increasing supplies and intense competition.

Small savings account for only a small part of capital accumulation. Most capital is generated from investing the surplus of large incomes productively. In this way wealth becomes highly concentrated, a trend already evident in the expansion of big business.

While the above shows that American savings banks have not achieved anything outstanding, their weak performance becomes even clearer when deposit levels are analyzed by state. The above-mentioned sum of $981 million divides as follows:[8]

New York	$376,637,163
Massachusetts	$252,030,519
Connecticut	$ 80,981,859
California	$ 46,132,843
Pennsylvania	$ 42,706,793
Rhode Island	$ 40,915,759
New Hampshire	$ 35,580,031
Maine	$ 25,729,790

8. [U.S. Commissioner of Internal Revenue, *Report of the Commissioner of Internal Revenue for the Fiscal Year Ending June 20, 1882* (Washington, D.C., 1882), CXXXI.]

Maryland	$ 24,958,901
New Jersey	$ 23,859,302
Ohio	$ 12,661,399
Vermont	$ 8,391,159
Remaining 26 states and 8 territories	$ 10,795,278

The 9 million people of the New England states and New York, whose overall economic structures most closely correspond to European conditions and whose propensity to save is hence most strongly developed, account for around $820 million of the deposits. The remaining thirty-one states and territories, with a total population of around 41 million, account for a mere $160 million. And the thirty-four unidentified states and territories, with a population of around 30 million, account for only just over 1 percent of total deposits. This distribution provides a specific instance of an assertion made earlier, namely, that when people earn relatively large amounts they forget to restrain their consumption, so the easier people can make money, the less they are interested in saving. Wages and profits are lowest in the eastern states, such as New York, Massachusetts, and Rhode Island, and highest in the newly settled territories, such as Arizona, Idaho, and Montana. In the latter savings are virtually nothing per head of population, while in the former they amount to $95 per head.

However, it would be one-sided to claim that the above distribution of savings deposits is based purely on psychological motives. These may be the main factor, but the state of the savings-bank system cannot be ignored. There is, of course, a link here with perceptions of the local population, so that, for example, no one will set up a bank where it is unlikely to succeed. But there are clear differences in regions of similar development that must be attributed to the reputation and practical organization of the banks. This explains, for instance, why, at $1.2 million, deposits are relatively low in Illinois. Until recently the state's authorities had not addressed the issue of the savings banks. Only in the spring of 1883 was a bill introduced providing detailed regulations about how deposits could be invested. The relevant issues are more difficult to deal with in the United States than in Europe because the number of truly safe securities is very limited owing to the volatility of economic life on the other side of the Atlantic. Bonds issued by small towns are often of dubious value, since it is by no means assured that the settlements will be permanent. And debentures issued by the railroad companies are often anything but reliable, not least because they often are not backed by real share capital, while the intense competition among companies (often conducted by questionable means) can make a railway line worthless overnight. Bonds of the federal government have only a low yield at the moment, and many are held by the authorities to cover the circulation of notes. All that remains as potential low-risk investments are sound mortgages on property and certain state and county bonds. But even then it is often quite difficult to determine the quality of these securities.[9] Investors have often had bad experiences with state bonds. States have been known to default on interest payments, and in some cases repayment of the principal has also been in doubt.

The U.S. Congress has been considering plans to set up postal savings offices for years, but until now they have not secured majority support. The argument against such a measure is cast essentially in financial terms, while at the same time there is little sympathy for its sociopolitical impact. Thus it is said that running a bank for the benefit of savers is not the role of government. Accepting small deposits makes sense only when the government has to borrow money at interest. This might happen in Europe but not in the United States, where there is a surplus rather than a shortage of capital, with overall more than enough money available to redeem debts. When the government can borrow all the money it needs in large sums at 3 percent interest, why should it bother to accept hundreds of million of dollars in small savings and perhaps even pay a higher rate of interest? Neither governments nor individuals borrow and pay interest for the fun of it. It is thus

9. The Illinois draft law allows savings to be invested in the following securities: (a) U.S. Treasury bonds; (b) Illinois state bonds; (c) bonds from other states of the Union which have not defaulted on interest payments or capital repayments in the previous three years; (d) bonds issued by any city, county, or town in the state of Illinois; (e) bonds issued by cities or counties in the neighboring states of Ohio, Indiana, Michigan, Iowa, Missouri, Kansas, Nebraska, Wisconsin, Minnesota, or Dakota, provided that the total debt of the city or county in question does not exceed 5% of the estimated value of taxable assets; (f) dividend-paying shares of banks incorporated in the state of Illinois; (g) first mortgage bonds of railroad companies incorporated in the state and which have paid dividends in the last two years; and (h) mortgage loans on unencumbered real estate valued at at least twice the loan. In this context the *Illinois Staats-Zeitung* of 24 April 1883 comments that only those listed under (a), (b), and (h) can be considered "reliable" investments, that those under (d) are "dubious," and that those under (c), (e), (f), and (g) should be treated "with great caution." It goes on to say that "the draft bill will have to be subjected to the closest scrutiny to ensure that the harm which our failed savings banks have caused is not repeated, even if only in a milder form."

alien to the essence and function of the federal government to operate a savings bank when it does not need the money and, on top of that, has to pay interest. So, the critics argue, even on the most far-reaching interpretation of its powers it is not within the ambit of government to relieve, paternalistically, individual citizens from the responsibility of making their own savings work for them.[10]

That this line of argument is incorrect should be clear to anyone who acknowledges the overriding importance of confidence in the banking system as a precondition for fostering thrift. In the case of the United States, there is the added factor that setting up a postal savings network does not carry any great financial risk because there are unlikely to be any sudden massive withdrawals. Since the end of the Civil War, the United States has not been exposed to external aggression on the continent which could trigger a run on the banks and shake the financial system. For neither Canada nor Mexico has the political power to threaten the United States and its 50 million people. In the sparsely populated West, where few people are able to organize a savings bank, the thousands of post offices could take on the business. Farmers and miners tend to visit the post office from time to time, so it is already a convenient, almost unique, meeting place for the widely dispersed local population. Even if the venture had little success initially because of the poorly developed savings impulse, well-run banks would surely gradually exert an educative influence. The tens of thousands of migrant workers who annually traverse the continent in accordance with the sowing and harvesting seasons would benefit greatly from postal savings banks. They would be able to pay in and withdraw money at every post office and thus would have full and easy access to their financial resources without obstructing their freedom of movement.

Turning now to mutual assistance funds, we may note that they are used not only by the working class in America, but also by people with capital. In Europe the latter are protected against accidents and illness by their wealth; affluent Americans cannot feel so secure owing to the above-mentioned fluctuations in the value of property, shares, and other financial assets. But since the number of workers far outweighs the number of capital owners, one can justifiably categorize the mutual assistance associations on the basis of the relationship the workers have to them. Five types can be distinguished: (a) funds linked to lodges, (b) funds linked to the trade unions, (c) funds linked to large factories, (d)

---

10. See the *Illinois Staats-Zeitung*, 26 March 1883.

workers' welfare associations which are not linked to specific employ-
ments, and (e) mixed associations, i.e., ones composed primarily of
workers but also open to the self-employed, farmers, and public servants.

The main aims of all these organizations are to provide assistance for
the sick and to pay out a death benefit or cover funeral expenses. Accident insurance, old-age pensions, and disability payments are rare. Life
insurance is more common. The five types of associations tend to com-
pete against each other, which often compromises their administrative
procedures, and complaints about delays in promised payments are
often heard. It is also worth noting that economies of scale matter here
as elsewhere. The larger funds enjoy more generous borrowing facilities
with the banks, they get better terms when buying securities on the capital market, and their overhead expenses are relatively lower. And the
larger an association's membership, the less it can be shaken by deviations from the general risk probabilities. In short, the large associations
are exposed to fewer risks and can operate more cheaply. The upshot is
that the large associations have become stronger over the years, while
small associations are becoming rarer. In principle their passing should
not be lamented, since one wishes everyone to enjoy the cheapest possible insurance. But this trend does have the consequence – worrying in
the eyes of some people – that trade unions are losing a valuable cohesive element and are becoming mere strike organizations. Yet only those
who believe that craft-based unions will be with us forever can deplore
this. In the article on the U.S. trade unions I tried to show that technological advances and the increasing division of labor are squeezing
craft-based unions and that they are being replaced successively by
more broadly based labor organizations.[11] These general social coali-
tions correspond to the general welfare associations. These two types of
organizations have not yet formed any direct links, but they are likely
to do so in the future.

There is no demand for a system of compulsory public insurance in
the United States. This is largely because American workers can earn
much more than European workers, so they are less dissatisfied than
their European counterparts. Many unskilled workers can look forward
to setting up their own businesses as farmers, manufacturers, or traders.
Others can look forward to an income from investments. A compulsory
insurance scheme would therefore prove highly inequitable. In any case

11. See Essay 3, this volume.

it would be very difficult to implement given the geographically highly mobile labor force.

What would be desirable for the protection of investors would be a uniform body of relief-fund legislation across the country. At the moment the only government control over this sector consists of the states' right to confer or withdraw an association's legal status. Apart from that, the sector is not supervised in any way.

Below I will examine the statutes and activities of the five types of welfare associations identified above.

I. Assistance Provided by Lodges

Lodges and orders can be found throughout the United States. Their members are overwhelmingly recruited from the working class, but not entirely so, for membership extends to all social classes. There are various types of orders, distinguishable on the basis of their exclusivity, the race of their members, or the goals they espouse. They have moral, social, and economic aims. They try to achieve the moral aims by setting standards but also through punishments. The social activities are very expensive, but along with the fatuous mystery mongering (which appeals greatly to Anglo-American members, very little to German-Americans), they form a key cohesive element. The economic activities center on providing insurance and, to a lesser extent, on offering loans from the common fund under appropriate guarantees. Many people belong to two, three, or even four lodges and devote a not inconsiderable part of their earnings to them and their activities. Their financial contributions are by no means restricted to insurance premiums. In fact it is no exaggeration to say that the larger share of contributions goes toward realizing the orders' other goals. All orders reject political activities and affiliations on principle, but all are dominated by professional politicians pursuing political ends. Such people, who see their involvement in public affairs as nothing more than a source of income and who gear their political activity purely to the expected financial gains, belong to a dozen or more lodges. The lodge members are their constituents or supporters. Influence gained in this way is for sale at election time to the highest bidder, of course. That this business can be a lucrative one is evident from the orders' numerical strength. No reliable figures are available, but people familiar with the situation assure me that in Pennsylvania alone there are over 80,000 members and that the Independent Order of Odd Fellows, which is also prominent in Britain and even has some branches in Germany, has over 500,000 members in the United States.

Without claiming to be comprehensive, I can offer the following list of major lodges:[12]

1. Independent Order of Odd Fellows
2. Colored Odd Fellows
3. Rebecka Degree of Odd Fellows
4. Ancient Free and Accepted Masons
5. Ancient York Masons
6. Order of Masonic Ladies
7. Knights of Pythias
8. Legion of Honor
9. Knights of Honor
10. Temple of Honor and Temperance
11. Cadets of Temperance
12. Independent Order of Cadets of Honor and Temperance
13. Sons of Temperance, both sexes
14. Temperance Beneficial Association
15. True Temple of Honor
16. Royal Templars of Temperance
17. United Order of Sacred Temple of Liberty, both sexes
18. Improved Order of Free Sons of Israel
19. Beneficial Knights of Helcium Arma
20. Knights of Friendship
21. Knights of Maccabees
22. Order of Scottish Clans
23. Ancient Order of Foresters
24. Independent Order of Foresters
25. Druids
26. Order of Female Druids
27. Sons of Hermann
28. Treubund
29. Knights Templar
30. Seven Wise Men
31. Red Men
32. Independent Order of Red Men

---

12. This list has been compiled on the basis of information from the St. Louis address book and two labor papers, the *St. Louis Union* and *Progressive Age,* complemented by information in Arthur von Studnitz, *Nordamerikanische Arbeiterverhältnisse* (Leipzig, 1879), [193–200].

33. Improved Order of Red Men
34. Independent Order of Good Templars
35. Ancient Order of the Good Fellows
36. Sons and Daughters of Arcanum Ark
37. Sons and Daughters of America
38. Daughters of Temperance
39. Daughters of Samaria
40. Independent Order of Good Samaritans, both sexes and colors
41. Order of Progress, both sexes
42. Brotherhood of the Union
43. The Mystic Band of Brothers
44. Patriotic Order of Liberty
45. Knights of the Golden Rule
46. Band of Hope
47. Good Ladies
48. Plattdeutsche
49. Knights of Father Matthew
50. Ancient Order of Hibernians
51. Knights of St. Patrick
52. Patrons of Husbandry
53. Phoenix Lodge

Apart from the formalities during the meetings and in the greetings, the constitutions and administrations of these organizations are the same everywhere. So knowledge of one order's arrangements gives one a sufficient insight into all of them. For this reason I will restrict myself to a detailed examination of the statutes and ordinances of the Independent Order of Red Men and one of its affiliates, the Tecumseh Lodge No. 109. So as not to give a one-sided description of the lodge, I will also report on the rituals and practices which many members find so enjoyable and many consider the main point of the association.

The motto of the lodge is "Freedom – Generosity – Brotherly Love!" To set up a new lodge of the Independent Order of Red Men, six "respectable citizens" make a written request for a charter from the Grand Lodge of the United States, enclosing a sum of $16 with the application. Once the charter has been approved, the applicants are informed, the grand supreme chief Powhatan and/or the grand secretary or another nominated qualified former chief visits the new lodge, hands over the charter and the accompanying books of rituals, formally opens the new lodge, and installs its officers. The new lodge adopts a name and a constitution, which must conform with the federal constitution.

Meetings are held weekly, during which lodge affairs are discussed according to strict rules. The lodge is required to prepare a report and make a contribution to the grand lodge every six months. If a lodge fails to submit two consecutive reports to the Grand Lodge, its charter and book of rituals are withdrawn. A lodge can also be dissolved for violating the constitution of the United States or deliberately acting contrary to the spirit of the Order.

Each lodge has the following officers: a supreme chief, deputy chief, secretary, and treasurer. The outgoing supreme chief holds the honorary office of priest for a six-month period. Since most orders are not allowed to deal with religious matters, this "priest" is not involved in worship or faith but merely plays a specific role in the secret rituals and at most exercises a general moral authority on the lodge members. In addition to the above officers, a number of junior ones may also be appointed, including the assistant chief, marshal, herald, brave, interpreter, forester, and sentry. The duties of these officers are set out in the statutes. The marshal is the supreme chief's right-hand man and assists him in all the lodge's affairs. The herald is the supreme chief's left-hand man and assists him in the same way. The brave sits in front of the grand chair, checks the current password with the brothers, and collects dues. The interpreter looks after the lodge regalia, is responsible for the cleanliness of the meeting hall and the proper opening and closing of the doors, and also has certain duties in the rituals. The forester's role is to check that brothers who arrive late for the meeting perform the proper formalities before entering. The sentry guards the outside door and turns away all outsiders and brothers who have broken the rules of the association.

Applicants for membership in the Independent Order of Red Men should be between twenty-one and fifty years of age. Within these limits the individual lodges can introduce some modifications. This condition has been imposed in the interests of the security and simplicity of the insurance system. Membership in the Order is restricted to "white friends" of good character who have a doctor's certificate vouching for their good health. Once a vote has been taken to admit the applicant, he is inducted in an elaborate ceremony with all kinds of mumbo-jumbo, which all lodges must strictly adhere to.

All decked out, the lodge brothers await the candidate. They wear various *regalia* according to their office and degree of membership. Novices wear red collars and red aprons, brothers of the first degree wear red collars and red aprons with black stripes, those of the second degree have additional royal-blue borders on the aprons, those of the third degree have grass-green borders trimmed with black and royal-blue stripes. The officers are identified with additional silver trimmings. Other insignia on the collars also indicate their special status: the priest's is decorated with two crossed tomahawks and a bow and arrow, the assistant chief's with a bow and two arrows, the secretary's with two crossed feathers, the treasurer's with a silver tassel, the marshal's and the herald's with a spear on the right side, the brave's and the interpreter's with a tomahawk on the same side, the forester's and the sentry's with a bow and arrow. The former chiefs have red velvet collars, with two crossed tomahawks and two gold tassels on the edges, and aprons with gold borders, gold embroidered laurels, and black, royal-blue, and grass-green stripes. The collars of all the officers and brothers are held together with heart-shaped ties colored and trimmed for the appropriate degree. This quite extraordinarily adorned assembly receives the candidate with the cry "Enemy in the camp!" This is followed by a conciliatory song, a prayer and address by the priest, and the ceremonial administration of the Order's oath.[13] It is hardly surprising that these "red men" are often jokingly called "white Indians."

In public processions, usually funerals accompanied by music, a strict hierarchy is observed:

a. At the head of the procession the brave with a tomahawk,
b. the standard bearer and two companions,
c. the novices,
d. the sentries and foresters, each carrying a bow and arrow,
e. the brothers of the first degree,
f. the brothers of the second degree,
g. the brothers of the third degree,
h. the secretary and the treasurer,
i. the deputy chief and the assistant chief,
j. the priest wearing a white sash,
k. the supreme chief, led by the marshal and herald, each carrying a spear,
l. the former supreme chiefs.
m. The procession is closed by the interpreter holding a tomahawk.
n. A master of ceremonies wearing a white sash and holding a staff organizes the whole event.

13. This description of the ceremony and the regalia is based on an oral communication from a person familiar with these matters.

Advancement through the *degrees* or ranks, which requires substantial financial contributions and is based on seniority, plays a major role in the brothers' imagination. This vain attempt to use externals to represent something supposedly exceptional is particularly shocking in a democratic country like the United States. It cruelly caricatures the efforts to achieve political equality. The many Americans who arrogantly ridicule the bestowing of orders and titles in Europe would do well to reflect on their home-grown humbug, in which external recognition of merit is not even relevant.

Once the candidate has been accepted as a member, he is entitled to all the benefits granted by the lodge, provided, of course, that he pays his dues on time. The minimum contribution is 6.25 cents per week. The following provision is made regarding sickness benefits: "Every brother who is, according to the by-law regulations, entitled to the tribe's benefits will in case of sickness receive a weekly benefit of at least $3. A brother who is absent and ill is entitled to the same support, provided he is not in arrears and sends in a doctor's certificate authenticated by a justice of the peace." The regulations further provide that "When a brother in good standing dies, his widow or family receives a grant of at least $30 to cover the funeral costs. If the dead member has no relatives, the supreme chief uses the money to pay for the funeral and returns any balance to the lodge. When the wife of a brother in good standing dies, he receives a grant of at least $15 from the lodge."

The above are general principles that apply in all lodges of the Independent Order of Red Men. The individual lodges supplement them with a number of implementing regulations. Two adopted by the Tecumseh Lodge are worth mentioning:

1. Each member is required to pay a quarterly contribution of $1.25, 25¢ of which is allocated to the widows' and orphans' fund. All arrears must be paid to the lodge in cash and may not be set against forthcoming support or likely sickness benefit.
2. Each brother becomes eligible to receive all the lodge's benefits six months after his induction. Each brother who has been a tribe member for six months and is not in arrears will, if he is unable to work through no fault of his own, receive a weekly benefit of $4 for novices and $5 for the three degrees from the day [he is] reported sick. No benefit is paid out if the period of sickness lasts less than a week.
[The numbers were added by Sartorius; they are not part of the original text.]

Since the sickness benefit is not restricted to a certain period, these regulations show that the intention is to provide support for the disabled as well as the sick. A member of another lodge has informed me that this is enshrined in the statutes of many lodges. If the money runs out, specific levies may be imposed to meet the shortfall. But he also admitted that the Order commonly uses the reprehensible expedient of expelling the disabled member. Alleged noncompliance with the strict formalities required at every possible occasion – which, as we have seen, are set out at length in the statutes – and violation of the Order's general moral principles can provide convenient excuses for proceeding against a member. This illustrates vividly that for some lodges charity is not the main purpose of the association.

Of the many other welfare provisions, I would like to highlight the following:

The sickness committee consists of the lodge's supreme chief, the deputy chief, the assistant chief and four members. It is charged with visiting every sick brother at least once a week. The supreme chief, as chairman of the committee, is required to visit a brother who is reported sick within 24 hours and apprise himself of his condition. He should also ensure that brothers entitled to support receive it at the right time. The secretary prepares a list of sick members for the sickness committee. When a committee member has visited a sick brother, he is supposed to hand the list to the next member on the committee roster.

When a brother who has been a lodge member for more than six months and who is no more than $3 in arrears with his contributions, fines, etc. dies, the following happens. Every brother must make a donation to the widow and family of the deceased, 75¢ if the lodge has less than 200 members and 50¢ if it has more than 200 members. If (owing to a small membership) less than $40 is collected, the difference should be made up with a contribution from the lodge fund. If its resources do not allow this either, it can turn to the Grand Lodge for assistance. The death benefit is advanced by the fund on the day of the brother's death, with the other members' contributions subsequently collected by the secretary.

I should add that the tribe can turn to the Grand Lodge for assistance if its members and its treasury cannot raise the sum of $40.

In addition to paying out sickness and death benefits, the lodges may also, at their own discretion, offer donations or loans to members in need. "When a brother of the Tecumseh Lodge finds himself in straitened circumstances and asks for help, a three-member committee is appointed to examine his situation and report to the lodge. If he is deemed worthy of assistance, he will receive whatever the lodge decides and resources allow, but no more than $5, unless a larger amount is agreed unanimously or collected through voluntary contributions."

The lodge's capital should be deposited at a reputable savings bank or similar institution. Once the capital reaches $300, excluding cash held by the treasurer, the lodge can extend loans to lodge members against promissory notes and two or more guarantees. The maximum loan is $100 and the maximum repayment period is six months. Larger amounts can only be lent against unencumbered property. When the promissory note expires, a quarter of the original loan and interest must be repaid immediately, while the outstanding amount can be reloaned on request.

The lodges allow for a degree of mobility among their members. To this end they issue withdrawal cards. When a member moves away but wants to join another lodge in his new home, he can apply for a withdrawal card, which will serve as a means of identification for a certain period and will ease his introduction to a new lodge. His membership still has to be approved by a vote, but if accepted, he need only pay half the initiation fee. A lodge may also issue travel cards to members who spend long periods away from home on business. Such cards expire after a year and are granted only to those who have paid their contributions in advance to cover the period of absence.

To conclude the discussion of this lodge, I would like to highlight some general provisions which relate to the moral behavior of the members:

Any member who uses secret machinations to secure votes for himself in lodge elections and is found guilty is punished as the lodge sees fit.

Any member who through his actions violates the laws of the Union or of the State of Illinois (for the Tecumseh tribe) is to be expelled.

Any member who defames, badmouths, cheats or deceives another is to be suspended or expelled, as the lodge sees fit.

Any member who follows an immoral lifestyle and brings shame on himself or the Order is to be suspended or expelled, as the lodge sees fit.

Any member who uses profane or foul language towards an officer or other members at a meeting is to be punished as the lodge sees fit.

Any member who arrives drunk at a meeting or disrupts the affairs of the lodge is fined $1 for the first offense and $2 for the second; further offenses lead to suspension or expulsion, as the lodge sees fit.

Any member who refuses to abide by the principles, rules and traditions of the Independent Order of Red Men or who refuses to pay the fines imposed on him is to be suspended or expelled, as the lodge sees fit.

It hardly needs to be said that these regulations can be interpreted arbitrarily, and they can easily be bent to sanction the above-mentioned expulsion of disabled members. Any accusations of impropriety are examined in a quasi-judicial process. A member is allowed to appeal against a conviction to the Grand Lodge.

To anyone who assumes that North Americans have the same moral conscience as Europeans, it must seem odd that the lodge constitutions contain general moral prescriptions that one would have thought were properly within the realm of religion and as such would already be sufficiently impressed on the members. The prescriptions mentioned here would therefore seem superfluous. Given the Americans' practical bent, this would be unusual. Certainly the lodge system contains nothing that could be called impractical. Even the secrecy and the formalities at meetings and ceremonies doubtless make sense in terms of the Order's aims, its preservation, and its expansion. Today's Americans just love all these externals. To a large extent this is due to the hierarchical organization of the lodges, which appeals to a nation which has constitutionally renounced an honors system, and to a lesser extent to the rather shallow religious views among the people, who prefer to gloss over the inexplicable and mystical and instead lose themselves in pomp and circumstance, in the lodges as in other contexts.

The lodges aim at large memberships. For this reason they do not shy away from recruiting members in ways that many of their leaders may view with some distaste. Of course, one cannot condone this sort of behavior simply because it is practical. And as we will see below, some Americans who think about these things have made clear their criticism of the lodges by setting up other welfare associations.

The moral prescriptions enshrined in the lodge constitutions are also intended to achieve a practical aim, though despite appearances they largely fail, in my view. Because of the uniformity evident in American life, observers are prone to postulating an "American national character." But although some of its outlines are already emerging, it does not exist as yet. Of course, the conditions of the North American continent, the abundance of its natural resources, the variety of its geographical regions, its climate, and its geopolitical position determine the dynamism of economic activity in particular. These dominating factors mold all immigrants equally, whether they come from Britain, Germany, Ireland, or France. They arouse or accentuate their entrepreneurial spirit, their zest for work, and their self-confidence. But they do not affect moral convictions and their manifestations, selfishness and malevolence on the one hand and compassion, a sense of justice, and human kindness on the other. Although the American national character will eventually combine these features in some way or other, it will not be determined by the above-mentioned external aspects but solely by the mixture of races and nationalities.[14] The national character will certainly owe much to that of today's Yankees. Compared to Europeans, they tend to be rather relaxed about matters of conscience. They accept certain business practices, for instance, which Germans would not condone. This may be excused to some extent by the Yankees' conviction that the economic development of their continent is a patriotic duty, and that consequently the means to achieve this are selected more on economic and technical grounds than on the basis of a moral perspective. Germans, on the other hand, following their conscience, pursue more cosmopolitan aims and are more respectful of human needs, and hence also value the existence and well-being of individuals in the economic sphere and assess economic activities on the basis of their innate morality.

The Anglo-Americans' uninhibited entrepreneurial drive and their ruthless exploitation of others are part of their innermost being. That this carries a danger for the nation's future has been recognized by many people, including the founders of the lodges and similar associations.

The lodges have taken on the task of educating the Yankee conscience. That is why their constitutions often contain moral prescriptions. And given their strong representation across the country, they are well placed to achieve their ambition. Individual teaching will have little impact on the national conscience. But social organizations, which embrace the whole person, can often have a deep and lasting effect on the way people think. These bodies gain strength from force of habit and have power for good and evil. The lodges may thus influence their members' behavior. Through threats and rewards they may well be able to counteract the selfishness of the individual. But they are hugely mistaken if they believe they can change a person's innate morality.

I mentioned earlier that religion is generally excluded from the lodge activities. The main reason for this is the prevalence of religious sects, which would hinder the expansion of the lodges if they were acknowledged. Among the main groups, devout Catholics usually stay clear of the lodges because their secrets and oaths cannot be reconciled with confession.

14. I have developed this argument in greater detail in my articles "Die Ursachen der wirthschaftlichen Eigenschaften des nordamerikanischen Volkes [I–V]," *Allgemeine Zeitung*, 1881, no. 358 (24 December), 5265–7; no. 360 (26 December), 5297–8; no. 363 (29 December), 5329–31; 1882, no. 4 (4 January), 42–4; no. 9 (9 January), 122–3; and also in an essay, *Die Zukunft der Deutschthums in den Vereinigten Staaten von Amerika* (Berlin, 1885).

II. Benefit Funds Linked to Trade Unions

The collapse of so many trade unions during the depression of 1873–9 is rightly attributed to the fact that they were not linked to any support funds. In the late 1860s and early 1870s geographically widespread and numerically strong trade unions like those representing the coachmakers, millers, machinists, bricklayers, coopers, stonecutters, miners, and shoemakers had been able to negotiate high wages through joint action of their members. But when the economy turned, they were unable to keep members in line to consider and take joint action. They lacked the *material bond,* the money to assist and protect the sick, the disabled, and the unemployed. They lacked the financial resources which have given the British unions such a solid base and such power that despite soaring food prices and the long depression of the 1870s they have not been forced to accept reductions in real wage levels. Since 1880 American labor leaders have striven to give support funds their rightful place. They have not had great success so far, however, for a range of counterforces within the economy have proved stronger than all exhortations and all enthusiastically backed practical efforts.

The labor press has not tired of reminding its readers of the need to set up trade-based mutual insurance associations. It uses a line of reasoning that does it great credit. Thus the *New-Yorker Gewerkschafts-Zeitung* (which is no longer published) set out the case for linking trade unions to relief funds as follows:

The support funds offer us protection in cases of emergencies or help to alleviate them. They are the means by which we can shield our families against distress and privation and the effects of unemployment, sickness and so on. They generate interest for the organization concerned, even among our women, who because they are usually less idealistic and more egotistical than the men, consider participation in associations that offer no material benefits as pointless and a waste of time and money.

The support funds ensure that contributions are made regularly, since non-payment will lead to material losses, which is the only way to get through to the lax working masses. The funds impose a highly necessary discipline on the members. The notion of one for all and all for one engendered by participation in a support fund generates feelings of solidarity and fraternity, which ennoble the human spirit and curb selfishness.

Assistance in emergencies allows us to maintain our physical and mental well-being, to maintain our manliness. This effect is particularly beneficial in the case of unemployment. Workers who have lost their jobs, who are worried and distressed, and for whom the privations imposed on their families are like a dark shadow tend to accept work at lower wages. In other words, the lack of assistance depresses wages, while a support system tends to drive them up.

If we bear in mind that the wage level depends on the needs, habits, and expectations of a country's workers,[15] we have to conclude that the payments into support funds increase our needs, heighten expectations, and hence must result in higher wages. This is not fantasy, but reality, fact, as the higher wages in Britain and those of the engineering workers and members of the Amalgamated Carpenters and Joiners and others in this country illustrate. So it is already in our power to make the employers financially liable for the care of their victims.

The so-called principled workers' associations and trade unions, which do not offer assistance to their members, are always in danger of being decimated, if not destroyed altogether, whenever a labor dispute erupts. In these organizations the interest of members has to be rekindled time and again by novel and imaginative means, such as festivities. And when, as frequently happens, workers are opposed to appropriate measures and institutions such as support funds, they are actually inflicting great damage on the labor movement.[16]

The many and varied direct reasons why a union-sponsored insurance system has not thrived in the United States can be traced back primarily to the colonial volatility of the country's economy and secondarily to competition from the large welfare associations, whose goals in many ways overlap with those of the union funds. The nonunion funds have an advantage over the union funds owing to their size and resultant economies of scale (as mentioned earlier) and owing to their wide geographical distribution, which means that members' mobility is not or is hardly constrained. Unionization, on the other hand, is patchy and is extensive only within the industrial regions, so that individuals who move away or move into a different trade cannot remain within their previous insurance system.

The unions are, of course, trade-based, and since changes of occupation are very common in America, many workers are reluctant to join insurance schemes that presuppose stability of occupation. Some try to set up businesses in their trade and then turn against trade unions. Others move into politics or count on being employed by the state or the locality. And yet others head west to buy a farm or settle on homestead land. It is not unusual for factory workers to become farmers. The transition is not as difficult as one might think on the basis of conditions in Europe. Farming is not as varied an occupation in America as in Europe. Growing only wheat, raising cattle, or cultivating fruit in America is not

15. [The original article contained a parenthesis attributing this idea to Karl Marx, *Capital*, which Sartorius von Waltershausen omitted.]
16. *New-Yorker Gewerkschafts-Zeitung*, 15 March 1880.

as difficult to learn as the extensive knowledge which the European farmer has to acquire through study and practical experience.

Those workers who are well paid or who have a particular commitment to their trade or who cannot or do not wish to accumulate capital will be happy to join the union insurance fund because they are quite likely to benefit from it at some point. The others, however, show no inclination to pay into a fund whose benefits they may not be able to enjoy. These are the two extremes, and the extent to which they apply differs, depending on the type of insurance. The gap will be widest in old-age insurance, since the time lag between making contributions and enjoying the benefits is often many years. Protection against disability due to injury and sickness is more likely to be entrusted to union funds, since disability of this kind may occur at any time. But even then many workers prefer to join the general relief funds, since it may still be many years before they have to make a claim. Material support during periods of unemployment and during strikes is the exclusive preserve of the unions. Unemployment insurance has a number of big technical problems and remains in its infancy. Strike *insurance* is universal and provided under the general fund, but often its resources are not sufficient, and on its own it cannot be considered a lasting bond holding union members together.[17]

The above-mentioned reasons American unions have found it so difficult to achieve anything remotely satisfactory on the basis of mutual insurance explain the two almost universal organizational principles of union insurance funds, namely, voluntary participation by union members and the strict separation of the various funds. Only contributions to the strike fund, to which assistance for the unemployed is often linked, are compulsory for every union member. Without this stipulation the union would, of course, have no legal weapons to deploy. If joining and contributing to a range of insurance funds had been the precondition for union membership, the unions would never have achieved anything of note. The early activists were very familiar with British examples, but they refrained from seeking to regulate workers' spending, which an insurance system inevitably entails to some extent, and instead preferred to concentrate their efforts on securing better wages and working conditions. The constitutions of today's unions also set out a range of demands on workers' earnings. But on the issue of insurance they are either silent or hint at it in a very general phrase whose

17. On the strike funds, see Essay 3, this volume.

intention is to conceal the union's strike-happy character.[18] Only a few constitutions diverge from this pattern, including the German and American typographers and some local unions, such as that of the cotton classers.[19] The provisions on the insurance funds are usually

18. The statutory aims of some trade unions are set out as follows: Furniture Makers' Union: "The union aims to improve the material and spiritual welfare of all those workers active in the furniture trade in North America, primarily through the introduction of an appropriate normal working day." [translated from the German original]; United Brotherhood of Carpenters and Joiners: "We propose: to cultivate a feeling of friendship among the craft, and to elevate the moral, intellectual and social condition of all journeymen carpenters, to abolish Piece Work and the Subcontracting System and establish every Saturday as a regular payday." [retranslated from the German]; International Cigarmakers' Union: "To rescue our trade from the condition into which it has fallen, and raise ourselves to that condition in society to which we, as mechanics, are justly entitled, and to place ourselves on a foundation sufficiently strong to secure us from further encroachments, and to elevate the moral, social and intellectual condition of every cigar maker in the country, is the object of our International Union." [*Constitution of the Cigar Makers International Union of America* (New York, 1880), 5.] Very similar are the statutes of the Amalgamated Association of Iron, Steel and Tin Workers: "The objects of this Association shall be to obtain by conciliation, or by other means that are fair and legal a fair remuneration to the members for their labor; and to afford mutual protection to members against broken contract, obnoxious rules, unlawful discharge or other systems of injustice or oppression." [*Constitution, By-Laws and Rules of Order of the National and Subordinate Lodges of the Amalgamated Association of Iron and Steel Workers of the United States* (Pittsburgh, 1880), 1]; the Brotherhood of Locomotive Engineers: "The object [. . .] is to represent the interests of the locomotive engineers, to increase their standard of living and to cultivate their character" [retranslated from the German]; the Workingmen's Benevolent Association of Savannah: "We, the members of this association, have adopted a constitution to establish a mutual bond between us, so that we can defend our rights against attack by others, without violating their rights, to promote the general welfare of the members, and to strengthen the spirit of harmony among them" [retranslated from the German]; the Hod Carriers' and Laborers' Union of Chicago: "The object of the association is to promote the honor and material welfare of the members. This includes providing assistance to those members afflicted by hardship or misfortune" [retranslated from the German]; and the Weighers and Reweighers of Galveston, Tex.: "It seems appropriate to organize an association for mutual help and support" [retranslated from the German].

19. Article 3 of the German-American Typographia lays down the following principles for the realization of the union's aims, which are the material and spiritual improvement of the members: "[. . .] establishment and organization of sickness, death, benevolent and reserve funds, as well as support funds for unemployed members, the development of all funds set up under the union's auspices on the basis of full mutuality and voluntary participation, and promotion and establishment of union printing works" [translated from the German original]; the Typographia defines its objects as the following: "Sec. 1. To elevate the position and maintain and protect the interests of the craft in general; Sec. 2. To establish and uphold a fair and equitable rate of wages [. . .]; Sec. 3. To influence the apprenticeship system in the direction of intelligence, competency, and skill in the interest alike of employers and employes; Sec. 4. To endeavor to replace strikes and their attendant bitterness and pecuniary loss by arbitration and conciliation

appended to the constitution. This subsidiary treatment is also indicative of the general perception that they are a rather minor matter.

Below I will offer a survey of the various insurance types.

Unemployment Insurance. This is a problem which has been no more than touched on in any country. But the lack of success so far should not lead one to abandon the goal of providing greater protection against unemployment. For as long as the current unplanned and unfettered market-based method of production persists, overspeculation and overproduction, and hence temporary unemployment, will not disappear.

It would be a practical advance for the insurance system if a distinction were made between types of unemployment, since not all job losses are the result of speculative crises, and if insurance funds were organized and administered to take account of this.

For instance, there is the annual cyclical downturn in some branches, i.e., where factories operate for part of the year and lie idle for the remainder. These include establishments which are in some way dependent on the seasons, whether it be sowing and harvesting on the land, summer and winter fashions, or fluctuations in the availability of water as a power source. Since this type of closedown is largely predictable in terms of both its commencement and its duration, it is not that difficult to take precautionary measures. Most workers will probably be able to find other work in the off-season, so they will not need any insurance. But some will not, and it is with them that we are concerned here. In the United States they include, for instance, the workers involved in the loading and transport of cotton, who during the summer have no access to other work in the relatively underdeveloped economies of the South. The unmarried often travel north to look for jobs, but those men who have families have no choice but to stay behind and wait for the new harvest. Of course, wages paid during the period of employment should be high enough to cover expenses during the idle period. And one would not have to consider relief funds at all if workers were sensible enough to put sufficient funds aside to maintain themselves and their families during the idle period. Experience shows that this is rare, however. Quite the opposite, in fact, since high wages seem to encourage high living;

[. . .]; Sec. 5. To relieve the deserving needy, and provide for the proper burial of deceased members." [retranslated from the German based on the vocabulary used in *Constitution, By-Laws, and Scale of Prices of Chicago Typographical Union, No. 16* (Chicago, 1886), 1]; and the Cotton Classers and Employees' constitution states: "The aim of the association is to support the members in cases of sickness and on other occasions" [retranslated from the German].

money goes out as quickly as it comes in, so none is left when the work dries up. Unemployment insurance can thus be recommended not least as a kind of educational tool to promote thrift. It should be remembered that this insurance is not similar to sickness, accident, or old-age insurance. For the individual, losing one's job is not something that might happen at some distant point in the future; it will happen at a specific time. In that sense there is no risk, nor is it possible that one's contributions will benefit someone else. All that might happen before a person loses his job is that some of the other contributors have died; but since the family of the deceased person inherits his entitlements, as is only proper, this factor of uncertainty is eliminated as well. So this form of protection can be called an insurance only in the sense that the individual, by voluntarily joining an insurance fund, carries out an act of self-education by insuring himself against his own recklessness.

A second type of unemployment occurs frequently but not quite regularly in a large part of American industry during the *fat years* of an economic upturn. In some branches the rapid technological advances have created a situation where a year's supply for the domestic market can be produced by less than a year's worth of work. (Most factories do not produce for export.) These factories, therefore, have to be closed down for certain periods. If workers and consumers were identical, i.e., if all the former had all their earnings at their disposal, such a sales slump could not happen that easily, although there would still be the possibility that the national labor force was not correctly distributed over the various branches.

Insurance against this second type of unemployment is already rather more difficult to organize than the first. This is because the contributions cannot be calculated on something definite, but can only be abstracted from average experiences over several years, so mistakes and miscalculations cannot be ruled out. But this does not mean that nothing should be done. For even a rather inadequate insurance system is still far better than none at all.[20]

The third type of unemployment which is usually considered in the context of insurance is that which occurs during the *lean years,* the economic downturns and crisis periods, like the 1873–9 depression. But calculating the required levels of contributions is even more difficult in

20. The state bureaus of labor statistics have collected extensive information on factories' annual operating times. See, e.g., Missouri Bureau of Labor Statitics. *Third Annual Report, . . . 1881* (St. Louis, 1882), 20–30; Ohio BLS, *Fourth Report,* 8–11; Massachusetts BLS, *Tenth Report,* 1–13.

this case than in the second case. While there is clearly an element of periodicity in economic recessions over, say, a century, it is impossible to predict the exact year when an economy will slide into decline and, above all, how deep the recession will be. It is, therefore, virtually impossible to predict the number of months a worker will be out of a job. Yet here too the introduction of some sort of assistance would be an improvement on the current situation, in which nothing is provided.

In any case only the workers' associations themselves can provide this kind of insurance. Neither the state nor the employers nor a capitalist society can get involved in this. For the concept of unemployment is by no means an absolute one for the workers. They will understand it to mean, essentially, that they cannot find a job under any circumstances; but they will also apply it to situations where they can only get very low wages or can only get work they are not used to. When a skilled machinist, for instance, only has the prospect of breaking stones along a highway at a fraction of his previous wages, he will consider his plight tantamount to being unemployed.

But no one can prescribe to the trade unions the conditions under which their members can work or not. They would be signing their own death warrant if they let anyone do so. Their task is to protect the livelihoods of their members, so they alone can make judgments on the amount of remuneration. A commercial insurance company, on the other hand, would pay out benefits only once the worker in question had provided proof that he could not find any gainful employment at all.

The American trade unions stress the need for insurance against unemployment during recessions, particularly on the grounds that it offers the only security against excessive downward pressure on wages and that it is the only way of countering competitive undercutting among workers.

However, most unions do not have support funds for their unemployed members. To my knowledge, only the cigarmakers and the German printers refer to them in their statutes. Detailed provisions are left to the local branches. According to the Cigarmakers' Union No. 15, based in Pittsburgh, every member who has paid his contributions on time for one year is entitled to *out-of-work assistance* for three weeks, starting from the second week of unemployment. If at the end of the three weeks the worker has not found another job, further assistance can be provided only after six weeks, again for a three-week period. If someone has found a job before the end of the first three weeks, he is entitled to assistance for the remaining days if he loses his job again within six weeks. The union fund pays out $1 per day and 50¢ per half day. The union makes efforts to find work for the unemployed, and all who receive out-of-work assistance are obliged to take up jobs found for them by the union executive. If they refuse, they forfeit all assistance for the next eight weeks. However, workers are not expected to work for less than the minimum wage set by the union, and they need not accept a job they are not physically capable of performing.

In every factory the union has a *shop director*, who represents the interests of the workers. Every worker who loses his job receives a certificate confirming his status from the shop director. This is used to substantiate his claim on the union fund. If in a certain factory no shop director has been elected, then out-of-work assistance is provided only from four weeks after a worker has lost his job. If the unemployed worker is known to have made cigars after 8 o'clock in the evening and before 5 o'clock in the morning of the day he was laid off, assistance is provided only after eight weeks. This particular provision is rooted in the view, widely held among American workers, that overworking is a primary cause of economic crises because it contributes to overproduction. On these grounds it would be illogical to support someone who had lost his job in part as a result of his own thoughtless behavior.

The money for the benefits is raised from a weekly contribution of 10¢, payable by each member except the sick and those receiving out-of-work assistance. The International Cigarmakers' Union also stipulates that unemployed members who have been with the union for more than six months are entitled to advances from the local branches for the purpose of looking for work elsewhere. (For further details, see below under "Travel Funds.")

The German-American Typographical Union No. 7 has the following provisions:

a. A member who loses his job is entitled to assistance of $5 per week; no member can draw more than $60 in any one year.
b. A member is entitled to assistance two weeks from the day he reports being out of work; he is paid a benefit at the end of the week he becomes eligible.
c. An unemployed member who accepts casual work loses $1.50 in benefit per day, 75¢ per half day.
d. An unemployed member who refuses a job forfeits assistance for a four-week period; a member who refuses a day's casual work forfeits a week's benefit.

e. An unemployed member who claims assistance must report every day to the administrator or shop steward at a time set by the latter; a member who does not report in is deemed to be working that day.
f. A member who leaves his employment voluntarily is entitled to assistance only if the union executive approves of his action.
g. An unemployed member who has drawn benefits of $20 continuously is entitled to further assistance only after a gap of three weeks.[21]

Every member pays weekly dues of 25¢. This also covers sickness benefits, which are paid out of the same fund. Unemployment and sickness benefits are still administered separately, however. Participation in both insurance funds is a condition of union membership. (As noted above, this is rare among American trade unions.) If union assets drop below $3 per member, an additional 5¢ per week is levied until this level has been restored.

That the benefits offered by these two unions are not adequate is evident from the above. No assistance is provided for long-term unemployment. Nor is there a guarantee that the unemployed will receive assistance throughout the period stipulated in the statutes. For the sums required are raised through regular contributions, which can be paid only as long as the members are in a job and have an income. Only a reserve fund accumulated when members are earning would be able to provide adequate support during a recession.[22]

As mentioned, only a few American trade unions offer the type of assistance outlined above. Most do try to find jobs for their unemployed members and thus serve as labor exchanges. In trying to prevent unemployment in this way, they at least recognize their obligation to offer unemployment insurance at some time in the future.

Sickness and Death Insurance. This form of insurance is the most widespread among the American trade unions, but it offers little that is unusual, so it can be dealt with briefly here. In accordance with the

---

21. [Translated from the German original.]
22. Following on from the above categorization of forms of unemployment, it would seem appropriate to set up three separate reserve funds if a branch has all three types of unemployment. The money required to provide for the off season can be calculated with some accuracy. The second and especially the third funds should be organized on the principle that they are as large as possible. Any surplus from the second fund could be transferred to the third. This accumulation would become wasteful only if it became too large, i.e., if there was still money left over once the recession was over. This is impossible at the current high level of wages, however.

American workers' need for mobility, the union locals, with which the sickness funds are usually linked, are based on the principles of free movement and mutuality.[23] The statutes of the German-American Typographia, for instance, state that

[. . .] a member with a travel card should hand this over to the responsible local executive member. He is entitled to all the branch's benefits from the day he hands over the card. However, no local is obliged to support a sick member from another locality when it can be shown that he was already ill when he left it. A member who wants to obtain sickness benefit during his time of travel must pay the appropriate contributions in advance, and he is entitled to support for the period covered by the contributions.[24]

Contributions are paid only by those union members who have agreed to join the sickness and burial funds, which are completely separate from the main union fund. The employers are, of course, not involved in any way. Nor is there any form of supervision by the authorities. One does not need official permission to set up a welfare association. It must be formally constituted, however, but in most states legal personality cannot be refused if the application meets the formal conditions for acceptance.

I will highlight the main provisions of the sickness and burial fund set out in the constitution of the Furniture Workers' Union No. 6, based in Baltimore, with which I am familiar and which seems the most elaborate of all the union arrangements.[25]

The initial contribution is $3, regardless of the applicant's age. One dollar is paid at the time of admission and the remainder within three months.[26] The monthly contribution is 45¢. Members are also obliged to pay a $1 death benefit to the family of a deceased member.[27]

23. In some unions, such as those of the cigarmakers and the coopers, the sickness and burial funds are not linked to the local branch but to the central organization. In those of the ironmolders and locomotive firemen they exist at both levels, so that a sick person receives benefit from two sources. Checks on the sick person are always carried out by the local.

24. [Translated from the German original.]

25. Of the unions mentioned earlier, the following have no support funds: the hatmakers, the carpenters and joiners, the iron, steel and tin workers, the Galveston weighers and reweighers, and the Chicago hod carriers and laborers.

26. The granite cutters have a gradation, depending on age.

27. The granite cutters only have an initial contribution for setting up a specific large fund. If its interest income and surpluses cannot cover the benefit payments, further resources are raised by an additional levy.

Anyone can make claims on the fund after having been a member for three months. The sickness benefit amounts to $4 per week. When a member falls ill, he should inform the secretary by word of mouth or in writing immediately. He is then eligible for a benefit until his recovery or death.[28] If the sickness committee requests it, the sick person must agree to an examination by the union doctor. The committee is charged with visiting the sick person at least once a week and to satisfy itself of his inability to work. When a member dies, his wife and rightful heirs are paid $1 for every fund member.[29] When a member's wife dies, he receives 50¢ for every member.

Not entitled to assistance are: (a) those members who are three months in arrears with their contributions to the sickness fund and with their general union dues; (b) members who are a month in arrears with death payments ordered by the secretary or with fines imposed on them; (c) members who live outside the city of Baltimore and have not applied for membership in another local within three months are without benefit until they have conformed to this requirement. [. . .] With respect to the first two situations, unemployment or other exceptional grounds may be taken into consideration as mitigating circumstances.[30]

Members forfeit their membership when they are more than six months in arrears with their contributions. (Periods when members do not receive an income are not counted, however.) Members who have knowingly harmed the fund in some way or who have been expelled from the union are also expelled from the sickness fund. Automatic expulsion on the latter ground is one of the two ways in which the union and the fund are linked, the other being that fund members who owe the union money are not eligible for a sickness benefit. Normally the links between unions and their funds are even looser than in the case of the furniture makers, who have a particularly impressive record of militant struggle.

28. The cigarmakers provide eight weeks' full sickness pay and a further eight weeks at half pay, but no more than sixteen weeks in total in one year. The longshoremen of Savannah pay $6 per week, starting from the second week, for a maximum of eight weeks (for one period of sickness). The cotton classers pay $5 per week.
29. The cigarmakers pay $25 and the longshoremen $50, the molders 50¢ for every fund member.
30. The cigarmakers have a rule that if the assistance committee is not allowed into the house of the sick person, the union is not obliged to pay any benefit. (Committee members do not have to visit people with an infectious or contagious disease.) And pregnant women who are members of a local are not entitled to a sickness benefit from three prior to five weeks after giving birth. [All quotations from the constitution of the Furniture Workers' Union No. 6 are translated from the German original.]

The [furniture workers'] sickness fund is administered by the following officers: (a) a president, (b) a vice president, (c) a secretary, (d) a treasurer, and (e) a three-member central committee. The last can also function as an arbitration tribunal. Among the duties of the officers the following are noteworthy: "On taking office the treasurer is expected to post a $200 bond or provide a written security signed by two known guarantors. He must write receipts for all funds received, pay out all checks that are sealed and signed by the president and secretary, and present quarterly accounts to the central committee, which are then audited and approved. As soon as he holds $75 in cash, he should deposit $25 at a bank designated by the sickness fund (in an account in its name)." "The arbitration tribunal is charged with investigating and settling all complaints and grievances brought by sickness fund members."

Accident Insurance.   Accident insurance on a mutuality basis is not very common in the United States. Neither the lodges, nor other voluntary welfare associations (see below under Sections 4 and 5), nor the trade unions have achieved anything satisfactory in this regard. Occasionally unions have set up accident funds, out of which victims of industrial accidents receive compensation. In cases of minor accidents, which damage a worker's health only temporarily, the sickness funds usually provide assistance.

Why is this type of insurance so underdeveloped? The first reason that springs to mind is that the need is met by commercial insurance companies. These certainly operate in this field, but only a small proportion of the working class has signed up with them, mainly manual workers whose trades are prone to accidents resulting from clumsiness.

Most American workers are not insured against accidents at all, even though the hustle and bustle of economic activity and the selfishness of employers in business matters would lead one to expect otherwise. After all, the greater the risk of accidents, the greater the need to reduce it. The press is certainly littered with reports of accidents of all kinds, including industrial ones. It must be said, however, that these reports do not offer a very accurate guide to their frequency. The newspapers love to exaggerate and titillate readers with sensational details. They seek out stories across the continent so that, albeit with several days' delay, readers in New York, New Orleans, and San Francisco are presented with the same lurid reports. Bearing in mind the size of the United States, the daily toll of accidents does not seem that excessive. Even so, there is no doubt that in some branches rates are far higher than in Europe.

Let us take boiler explosions, for instance. According to a report by the Hartford Steam Boiler Inspection and Insurance Company, published in its magazine *Locomotive,* there were 132 such explosions in the United States in 1880 and 159 in 1881. The number of people who died as a result was 208 and 251, respectively, the number of injured 213 and 313, respectively. Since U.S. Treasury statistics show that the number of movable and fixed boilers was 61,708 in 1881,[31] the rate of explosions that year was 2.6 per thousand.[32] British statistics kept over an eighteen-year period show an incidence of only 0.5 per thousand, while in Germany the incidence for 1879 was less than 0.3 per thousand.[33]

Or another example, railroad accidents. The latest census showed that 418,957 officials and workers were employed on the railroads in 1880. No specific statistics are available on how many were involved in accidents, but several related figures suggest that around 7,000 is a good estimate, which yields an accident rate of around 16.7 per thousand.[34] In Prussia 81,470 people were employed on the railroads in

31. According to the *Western Machinist.*
32. Ohio, *Sixth Annual Report of the Bureau of Labor Statistics [. . .] for the Year 1882* (Columbus, 1882), 319–25. Referring to the high number of explosions, the commissioner of the Ohio Bureau of Labor Statistics observed in 1882: "One of the first duties of the State is to afford every possible protection to the lives and property of its citizens. A large number of persons comprising a part of our most important population – the working people – who, because of their limited circumstances financially, are necessarily compelled to labor in factories, foundries, mills, and other workshops. In order to relieve these people of all such unnecessary dangers as are caused by the employment of inefficient steam engineers, the Commissioner would suggest that the General Assembly give this matter some attention, and enact such laws as will require the inspection of steam boilers used in manufactories of all kinds regularly at least once in every twelve months, and that no persons be permitted to take charge of steam boilers in any manufactory until they shall have passed a satisfactory examination before a board of examiners or inspectors, which board should be composed of such men as are possessed of a practical knowledge of steam engineering." Ibid., 325.
33. According to the *Statistik des Deutschen Reiches* [*Statistical Series of the German Empire*], XLIII, iv, 1, there were 70,815 boilers in Germany in 1879. The number of registered explosions was twenty in 1877, eighteen in 1878, eighteen in 1879, twenty in 1880, eleven in 1881, and eleven in 1882. Over this six-year period 292 people were involved in accidents, of whom 104 died and 188 were injured.
34. Heinrich Semler observes in his new book *Das Reisen nach und in Nordamerika* [(Wismar, 1884)] (p. 94): "North America no longer takes a special place in the statistics of railway accidents. According to recently published statistics the North American rail-

1875, of whom 3.7 per thousand were killed in accidents and 13.3 per thousand injured that year. This gives a total of 17.0 per thousand, comparable to the U.S. figure. But the fact that the number of accidents on U.S. railroads is relatively no higher than in other countries cannot be used to refute the assertion that accident rates are generally higher in the Unites States. It should be borne in mind that the railroad network on the other side of the Atlantic is far less dense than in Britain, Germany, Belgium, or France, so that there are far fewer occasions for collisions at railroad stations, where most accidents occur. Hence if the same amount of care was taken on the U.S. railroads as in Europe, the number of lives lost in accidents should be appreciably smaller.

The incidence of industrial accidents is not the same across the country. It is generally higher in the West than in the East. Very important in this context is the amount of compensation an employer is obliged to pay when he is deemed liable for the accident. Employers who may be heavily fined for negligence – as is the case in a number of states – are more willing to provide a range of safety measures for their employees than those employers who are not exposed to such financial risks. And in states where the law is strictly enforced, workers have less need to insure themselves against accidents. In a case reported in December 1883, a factory owner in Philadelphia was ordered to pay $10,000 compensation to one of his female employees who, because no fire escapes had been installed in the factory (despite an order by the authorities), had been forced to jump out of a window during a fire and as a result had been crippled for life. If the court had decided to assess the compensation on the basis of lost wages, the amount would have been far less. But it also took into account the worker's loss of quality of life and awarded a considerable additional sum as compensation for pain and distress.

Practice is not the same everywhere, however. For this reason a number of states have passed laws to protect workers in factories and mines. Employers' liability bills have also been introduced in Georgia, Iowa,

roads convey 275 million passengers per year. 2,500 get injured and one third of them do so through their own fault. Furthermore, 7,000 railroad employees and nontravelers were injured." The census of 1880 showed that 418,957 officials and workers were employed on the railroads. U.S. Department of the Interior, Census Office, *Compendium of the Tenth Census* (Washington, D.C., 1883), 1266–7. The 7,000 injuries yield an accident rate of around 17 percent. In Prussia 81,470 people were employed on the railroads in 1875, of whom 3.7 percent were killed in accidents and 13.3 percent injured that year. This also gives a total of about 17.0 percent.

Kansas, Mississippi, Missouri, Rhode Island, Wisconsin, and the territories of Montana and Wyoming.[35]

Since workers are sometimes unable to take their employers to court because they do not have the financial resources to do so, many trade unions have set up funds to provide the necessary money. It is obvious that as the unions back more compensation claims, employers will take more measures to prevent accidents.

One consequence of employers' facing potentially high compensation bills is the practice, frequently observed in American factories, of disabled or injured workers remaining on full or partial pay until their recovery. This precludes the imposition of a court award, since by accepting continuation of pay the injured person in effect accepts a compromise with the employer. The Missouri Bureau of Labor Statistics has investigated this phenomenon and found many cases of it. In a questionnaire most factory owners indicated, however, that although they continued to pay wages, they did not consider themselves obliged to do so, and that they paid compensation at their own discretion.[36] Employers are likely to continue to pay wages when they are worried that they might lose a court case and for the same reason are also likely to pay a larger compensation sum when the injured worker turns out to be permanently disabled.

Leaving aside the cases where accidents are caused by negligence on the part of the factory owner, workers still need to insure themselves against accidents caused by unforseeable circumstances or by others' or their own carelessness. But the impetus to insure against such eventualities is considerably weakened by an extensive private charity network.[37] I must say here that although one does, of course, respect the

---

35. See W. Cave Tait, *Die Arbeiterschutzgesetzgebung in den Vereinigten Staaten* (Tübingen, 1884), 131ff.

36. Missouri Bureau of Labor Statistics, 1881 annual report, 166ff.

37. The *Illinois Staats-Zeitung* reported the following on 18 February 1884: "Regarding assistance for the families of the coalminers killed in the major accident in Braidwood, Ill., the following has emerged from a report by the secretary for labor statistics. A total of $42,228 was collected for the families. Some $27,469 was donated by individuals in Illinois, $4,759 by individuals in other states, and the state of Illinois contributed $10,000. The support fund was divided as follows: families of six or more people received $1.50 per head per week, five-person families $1.60, four-person families $1.70, three-person families $1.55, two-person families $1.50, and widows without children and old women $4.00. Families who wanted to leave the Braidwood area received the following compensation: widows with no children $300, with one child $500, with two children $600, with three children $700, with four children $800, with

American people's willingness to help those afflicted by misfortune, it is doubtful whether, particularly in the kinds of cases discussed here, the benefits for the victims outweigh the moral damage this goodwill inflicts on the working class as a whole. A dependence on handouts degrades the working class, while the demand for justice and legal rights preserves its autonomy.

In the previous paragraphs we touched on some of the main reasons for the modest interest in union-sponsored accident insurance. But it is by no means explained by these factors alone. In addition to the general factors militating against the emergence of union insurance funds, one should not underestimate the technical difficulties of organizing this type of insurance, which the volatility of the U.S. economy make considerably greater than in Europe.

Virtually the only reason unions are interested in industrial accidents is their relevance to the campaign for a shorter working week. They claim that most cases of negligence by workers occur during the final hours of the working day, when the physical and mental strain has inevitably taken its toll on their ability to concentrate. Hence they claim that the most effective way of reducing accidents is to restrict the number of working hours by law.[38] In speeches, declarations, and newspaper articles on the eight-hour working day, advocates regularly cite lower accident rates as evidence that workers and employers have a common interest in its introduction.

The few trade unions which help their members when they have an accident generally do so in one of three ways. There are those which take a vote on whether any assistance will be provided, so that the person in question is wholly dependent on the goodwill of his comrades or the liquidity of the union fund; those which have linked the accident fund to the burial fund; and those which have set up a separate insurance fund for accident victims.

The first system is used by the Brotherhood of Locomotive Engineers, for instance. Its constitution states: "When a Division decides to support a brother who is unable to work, the required funds can be taken

---

five children $900, with six or more children $1,000. More than $17,000 was dispensed in this way. The remainder will be used to buy simple homes for 20 families who want to stay in Braidwood and to care for them until the children have grown up."

38. Details in August Sartorius von Waltershausen, "Arbeitszeit und Normalarbeitstag in den Vereinigten Staaten von Amerika (II)," *Jahrbücher für Nationalökonomie und Stastik*, 39 (1882), 107–46.

from the general fund, raised by a special levy or through voluntary contributions, whichever the Division sees fit."[39]

The second system is used by the Ironmolders' International Union. Only members who are wholly incapacitated are considered for assistance. When they become unable to work, they can ask for their death benefit (the 50¢ from each member which would have gone to their wives, children, or heirs on their death) to be paid out. In doing so they waive all further claims on the union.

The third system is, to my knowledge, most developed among the National Union of Granite Cutters and may consequently be considered in more detail. Every union member who has met all his obligations to the organization may join the accident fund. The initial contribution is $2, half of which is paid into the general fund and half into a supplementary fund. The general fund, whose capital is invested in U.S. Treasury bonds, can only be used for interest payments and not for benefit payments or administrative costs. The latter are covered by the supplementary fund, which is also used to pay benefits if the membership dues dedicated for this purpose are not all collected. When an accident so disables an insurance fund member that he can no longer work as a granite cutter, he is paid an amount of dollars equivalent to half of the fund membership. This sum is raised by imposing a levy of 60¢ on every member after an accident, of which 10¢ is paid into the supplementary fund and 50¢ goes directly to the injured worker.

Assistance is provided only after a detailed medical examination and must be approved by the local and the central committee. Benefits are paid from three months after the accident unless the worker has lost a limb or an eye. In these cases the money should be released as quickly as possible. The same applies when a member dies as a result of an accident, in which case the money is paid to his family. No money is paid out when an injured worker returns to work as a granite cutter during the three-month deferment period unless he has lost a limb or an eye.

Life Insurance and Pensions. Life insurance is far more common among American workers than accident insurance. This is probably because American men from all social classes attach great importance to providing for their wives and children. The volatility of the economy is likely to be the main reason for this. Just as most people who can and want to work have the opportunity to make money, the chances of los-

---

39. [Retranslated from the German.]

ing it are also high. A man does not know how well off or otherwise he will leave his wife and children, so taking out life insurance seems a sensible precaution.

Several large trade unions have set up life insurance funds, such as those of the coppers, locomotive firemen, machinists, and granite cutters. These funds are administered broadly in the same way as the funds described in the previous section. Reserve funds have been set up to provide the necessary means to operate them, with benefit payments being raised from the members equally when one of them dies. The burial funds described earlier are very similar to these life insurance funds. But the former only contribute to the funeral and can thus be organized by the local, while the latter require larger payments, which can only be provided by a larger number of contributors and thus have to be organized by the union central.

The National Union of Granite Cutters' life insurance fund differs from the accident insurance fund mainly in that the initial contribution is not the same for all members but is graduated according to age. No one over the age of fifty-five is admitted. People under the age of thirty-five pay $2, those under forty $4, under forty-five $5 and under fifty $6; fifty-year-olds pay $7, and $1 is added for every year until fifty-five. The beneficiary is paid a sum in dollars equivalent to the number of fund members. Each of these is obliged to pay $1.10 at every death; the additional 10¢ is used to cover administrative costs.

The granting of pensions is very rare. I have found provisions to this effect only among the unions of the machinists and blacksmiths, steam engine makers, and carpenters and joiners. I do not know whether they have been put into practice. In the case of the machinists and blacksmiths, a proportion of the life insurance contributions is held back and put into a special fund. The interest payments are used to assist disabled members from the age of fifty on, provided they have been fund members for at least fifteen years.

Travel Funds. The travel funds are credit institutions linked to the trade unions. They provide loans to cover travel costs to members who are out of work and want to look for a job elsewhere. They are thus a means of extending mobility. Since the loans are fixed at modest levels, they are usually not sufficient for a working-class family. Traveling is very expensive in the United States because the major industrial centers are so far apart. Hence it is mainly the unmarried workers who benefit from the travel funds. These have proved extremely useful, not only because they often enable an unemployed person to get a job, but also because they help balance the supply of labor within a region and thus prevent wage-depressing competition.

The constitution of the International Cigarmakers' Union contains the following provisions on travel funds:

Sec. 1 – Any cigar maker being a member in good standing for six months in the International Union, and not being able to obtain employment, wishing to leave the jurisdiction of the union under which he has been working to seek employment, shall be entitled to a loan sufficient for transportation to the nearest union by the shortest and cheapest route, such loan or loans not to exceed in the aggregate $20.00. But in no case shall any member, working under the jurisdiction of any union one week, be entitled to such benefits from said union, and no member shall receive a second loan from the same union until the first loan be paid.

Sec. 2 – Any member quitting a job without a sufficient cause shall not be entitled to the traveling benefit for a term of three months.

Sec. 3 – Any member receiving loans on card[s] shall after obtaining employment, pay to the collector of the shop in which he is employed, 10 per cent of his earnings weekly.

Sec. 4 – Every shop shall elect a collector, and in every shop in which there is but one union man employed, he shall constitute the shop collector.

Sec. 5 – It shall be the duty of the collector to collect and pay to the Secretary of the union, all amounts that he may have received within 48 hours after receiving the same.

Sec. 6 – Any member refusing to comply with the provisions contained in this article, shall not be entitled to receive further loans, for the period of three months after he has paid his arrears in full.

Sec. 7 – All local unions shall be required to report, in connection with their monthly reports to the International President, all loans granted on cards, and collected on cards, together with the names and numbers of the borrowers and payees. The International President is charged with the duty to carefully keep a record of all loans granted and collected, [and to] publish monthly, [the names of] all persons delinquent ninety days in the payment of loans.[40]

The cigarmakers' travel fund has occasionally been abused, especially during the 1873–9 depression. Unemployed union members applied for a travel loan even though they had no plans to look for a job elsewhere (because they knew there were none to be found) and used the money to live for a couple of days without having to beg or tramp around. The travel fund's original purpose was thus distorted, and it became a support fund for the unemployed. It did not have the resources to provide this service, so it had to suspend its operations on several occasions.

40. *Constitution of the Cigar Makers' International Union of America* (New York, 1880), 11–12.

The German-American Typographia operates a *viaticum fund* on the following basis:

§1. The viaticum fund is a central fund, although the local branches must defray or advance the necessary expenses.

§2. Every member passing through or leaving the branch with a valid travel card is entitled to a $3 viaticum.

§3. Every traveling member may claim no more than one viaticum from a local branch over a six-month period.

§4. If a traveling member obtains work in a city, soon after he has claimed a viaticum there, he must repay the appropriate amount at the earliest opportunity.

§5. The local branches must submit to the presidency half-yearly accounts of the travel allowances paid out; the presidency settles the accounts on the basis of the federal union's total membership.

§6. The submitted receipts must be signed by both the recipient and the cashier.[41]

Tool Insurance.   Unlike their European counterparts, American factory workers commonly own their own tools. The system used on the other side of the Atlantic is certainly preferable, for, as Studnitz has noted, it means that American workers choose their tools according to their own needs, while European workers are forced to adapt to the tools they are provided with.[42] Tools often constitute a sizable proportion of a worker's wealth. It is therefore in his interest to protect these possessions against loss or damage.

The Missouri Bureau of Labor Statistics has used questionnaires to establish the monetary value of the tools belonging to the state's workers. The information is summarized in the table below:[43]

	Trade value of tools
1. Cigarmakers	$1–3
2. Bricklayers	$3–5
3. Stovemolders	$5–20

41. [Translated from the German. This version of the constitution could not be located by the editors. The earliest version found was the *Constitution der Deutsch-Amerikanischen Typographia [. . .] in Kraft seit 2. Juli 1888* (New York, 1891). Its description of travel insurance, 24–5, stressed the voluntary nature of participation and provided for travel expenses of two cents per mile, rather than the viaticum described by the author.]

42. See Studnitz, *Nordamerikanische Arbeiterverhältnisse*, 330.

43. Missouri Bureau of Labor Statistics [original unavailable.]

4. Saddle-tree makers	average $10
5. Painters	$ 8–15
6. Coopers	$10–30
7. Plasterers	$10–15
8. Saddlers	$10–50
9. Leadminers	$10–30
10. Stonecutters	$10–25
11. Millers	average $20
12. Engineering workers	$20–75
13. Marble cutters	average $20
14. Machinists	$20–100
15. Shoemakers	average $30
16. Furnituremakers	$35–100
17. Leatherworkers	average $50
18. Patternmakers	average $75
19. Tailors	average $87
20. Carpenters	average $97
21. Boilermakers	average $100
22. Cartwrights	average $100

As these figures show, different trades have different insurance needs. Workers whose tools are relatively cheap may not be very concerned to insure them, those with expensive tools more so. Insuring tools against the payment of a premium with the established commercial insurance companies has not proved a success because, firstly, it is too expensive and, secondly, this type of insurance is usually limited to fire damage, which is not sufficient for various trades. The policies are too expensive because the tools are insured at the same rate as household furniture, which often contains highly flammable materials and is thus at far greater risk than the tools, which usually contain a large amount of metal.

So it is understandable that the trade unions have set up separate tool insurance funds for their members. These policies also have the added advantage that the insured objects are similar. Since the fund will operate most effectively with the largest possible membership, most union statutes which provide for tool insurance insist on compulsory participation. There is a good reason for this. After a factory fire, for instance, a tool insurance fund may have to pay out large amounts of money, and it can do so only if it has a large membership base. Of all the types of insurance discussed in this article, these funds are most likely to face a sudden rush of claims and hence demands on their reserves. So in this case compulsory insurance seems justified.

The Furniture Workers' Union's tool insurance system is based on the principle that losses are replaced as quickly as possible out of an accumulated guarantee fund. This is replenished as required by levies on the members. The purpose of the fund is to insure all union members who use their own tools and who want to join against damage or loss "by fire, water, falling of building, explosion, etc. and to replace the losses at the tools' insured value."[44] The minimum insurance is set at $25, the maximum at $150. The guarantee fund must have assets equivalent to 7 percent of the total insured sum. There are no annual contributions, only an initial payment and additional levies in case of losses. Some 7 percent of the collected money is set aside for administrative purposes, 5 percent going to the local and 2 percent to the central organization. Any losses should be replaced by the local within four days, to keep the worker's loss of earnings to a minimum. If the local branch does not have sufficient funds, the central fund helps out. It also imposes the levies to refill the guarantee fund. This ensures that each loss is borne equally by all the members. Every local elects a standing investigating committee, which in conjunction with the treasurer decides "the amount of loss to which a member is entitled."[45]

If a member thinks he is entitled to a higher amount than the committee has decided upon, he must appeal before he is paid by the Treasurer. In this case, the investigators and the applicant shall each appoint an additional member to the Investigating Committee, and these two members shall appoint a third one. These three members, together with the standing Investigating Committee, shall then give a final decision.[46]

Among the general provisions, the following are worth mentioning. "If a Local Union is suspended" from the International Furniture Workers' Union of America for violating a section of the central constitution, it must return "all monies belonging to the Tool Insurance, Sick Benefit or Mortality Fund." The same applies to individuals. And "This fund compensates no losses incurred during work on Sundays or outside regular hours."[47]

---

44. *Constitution of the International Wood Workers' Union of North America, And Regulations for Local Unions* (New York, 1887), 14. [There are minor differences in wording and claims procedures between the 1887 constitution and the earlier version quoted in German by the author.]
45. Ibid., 29.
46. Ibid., 29.
47. Ibid., 6, 14.

III. Relief Funds Linked to Factories

Even less common than insurance funds linked to trade unions are funds linked to factories. The explanation for this lies, firstly, in the general mobility and frequent changes of trade among workers, factors which make it unlikely that links with a factory could ever prove stronger than those with a union, and, secondly, in the sharp division between capital and labor characteristic of American conditions.

It follows from the first reason that most workers are not employed in the same factory for a long time, which makes it impossible to organize an efficient factory-based insurance system. But this is no longer the case everywhere. Labor market conditions are more stable in the East than in the West to the extent that in some parts of the New England states, New York, and Pennsylvania, they are comparable to those in Western Europe. And even in some localities in states to the west the labor market is sometimes fairly stable.

That employers and workers see each other as no more than buyers and sellers of labor power and that both work on the basic principle of "help yourself" – the outcome of which is, of course, the "self-made man" of American life – is probably largely due to the fact that people whose sole resource is their own labor have so often been able to achieve a certain degree of prosperity. Hence the factory owners feel no moral obligation to provide their employees with anything more than the agreed-on wage, and the workers are too proud to accept gifts from their employer and too clever to tie themselves permanently to a factory by making support claims.

Since the deterioration of manual workers' prospects over the last decade, their relationship with capital has undergone some changes, again more so in the East than in the West. But broadly speaking, the workers still go their own way.

I have come across the following examples of factory-based insurance funds:

1. After a major strike by New York brewery workers in 1881 the local brewers' association set up a "benevolent association."[48] The preamble to its statutes states:

The constitution of the Association of United Lagerbeer Brewers, etc., set forth that benevolence is one of the objects of its organization, and provides for a

---

48. *Fourth Annual Report of the Bureau of Labor Statistics of the State of Missouri [...] 1882* (Jefferson City, 1883), 134–5.

standing Benevolence Committee. The association provides assistance to workers when they fall ill or are unable to work as a result of a work-related accident (provided it is not caused deliberately). The assistance amounts to a benefit of $1 for every day of sickness, free medical treatment by a doctor, and a life annuity of $10–25, depending on circumstances, in case of permanent disability. (The benefit can be paid in a lump sum as well.) The association is administered by the employers, who top up the relief fund by the equivalent of half the workers' contributions. The workers contribute $1 as an initial payment and then 80¢ per month. Every three months the workers of each brewery elect one of their number to discuss the state of the fund and possible amendments to the statutes with the employers. Disputes are adjudicated by an arbitration committee composed of three workers and two owners nominated by the member with a grievance.

While this institution at first glance seems to be in the workers' interest, two articles in the statutes reveal the undisguised selfishness of the powerful employers. Thus, a) "An employee is not eligible to the benefits unless his employer certifies to his good character." In effect, then, assistance is not provided on the basis of rights and entitlements but arbitrary dispensations, and the fund can be used as a means of entrenching the workers' subjugation. And, b) "If a member of the Benevolent Bureau should be employed by a brewer not a member of the association, he shall not be entitled to any assistance." This provision also helps to consolidate the cartel in that it restricts rival breweries' access to the labor supply. In this way the efforts to monopolize the business coincide with downward pressure on workers' wages.[49]

2. The relief society of the New York City firm Straiton & Storm, a cigar factory, is composed of all male and female employees and the owners.[50] The latter pay $25 per month into the fund, while the workers pay 5¢ out of their weekly wages. The initial payment is $1. The fund is administered exclusively by the workers, who alone elect its officials. The assistance consists of a sickness benefit and a death benefit. The former amounts to $5 per week; the latter is a one-off $100. Women who are off work to give birth are not entitled to support.

When members lose their jobs without having received any assistance in the past, half of their contributions are reimbursed. If they leave their jobs voluntarily, they forfeit all rights unless the company approves their departure. There is also a special arrangement related to

49. Ibid., 134, 135.
50. Ibid., 135–6. [The plan is also described by company owner George Storm in a manner consistent with this account in U.S. Senate, *Report of the Committee of the Senate upon the Relations Between Labor and Capital* (3 vols., Washington, D.C., 1885), vol. 2, 820.]

strikes. When a wage dispute between the employer and employees escalates into a strike, the strikers remain within the fund for three months. If the dispute is not resolved within this period, the fund is divided up so that each striker receives half of the amount which a division of the whole fund by the total membership would have yielded. No benefits are paid during a strike.

The above provisions show that the relationship between the company and its employees is far more balanced and that the latter are far more independent than the New York City brewers, for instance. This is no doubt because their union is strong and well led.

3. A pension and disability fund was set up in A. Dolge's felt factory in Brocketts Bridge, N.Y., at the start of 1882.[51] Benefits are restricted to workers who have been with the company for at least ten years without interruption. They are made in cases of both permanent and temporary disability, the latter until the worker returns to work. It does not matter whether the disability is caused by illness, old age, or an accident. Pensions are calculated on the basis of a worker's average wage during the final year of work. They amount to 50 percent of wages after ten years' employment in the factory, 60 percent after thirteen years', 70 percent after sixteen years', 80 percent after nineteen years', 90 percent after twenty-two years' and 100 percent after twenty-five years'. Workers who are unable to work owing to an illness or an accident at work receive half of their previous wages, with the ten year qualification period waived.

The pension entitlements are personal, i.e., they cannot be transferred to others. If workers become only partially disabled, they receive payments as a proportion of the above scale. The company bears the full costs of the insurance scheme. It retains the right to dismiss workers, without any obligation to pay compensation in this case. It is solely responsible for the administration and can amend the fund statutes at any time without having to consult the workforce.

4. The workers at the Steinway & Sons piano factory in New York City have set up a sickness and burial fund.[52] It is administered and con-

---

51. Ibid., 133–4. [Wilhelm Bode, "Alfred Dolge, ein deutsch-amerikanischer Arbeiterfreund," *Arbeiterfreund*, 27 (1889), 329–37; Victor Böhmert, "Das Lohn- und Arbeitswesen von Alfred Dolge in Dolgeville (Staat New York)," *Arbeiterfreund*, 31 (1893), 353–63.]

52. Its constitution is reprinted in Studnitz, *Nordamerikanische Arbeiterverhältnisse*, [86–8: "Fabrikordnung des Pianoforte-Geschäfts von Steinway & Son in New York"].

trolled by the workers alone, and they alone pay contributions into it. It is organized on lines similar to those of the union-sponsored funds outlined above. I have not been able to establish whether the company makes an occasional donation to the fund.

A comparable scheme is the sickness and accident fund set up by the workforce of the Bradley Reis linen factory in New Castle, Pa., in the spring of 1881.[53] It pays out $6 per week to every sick or temporarily disabled worker. Fund members pay 50¢ into the relief fund every pay day (usually at two-week intervals). An unusual feature of this scheme is that at the year's end the fund's remaining assets are distributed equally among all the members. Because the contributions are very high in relation to the benefits granted, the fund seems sound enough to meet the claims on it and to cope with these end-of-year settlements, which are therefore quite acceptable. The employers are not involved in the scheme in any way. This type of factory fund is rare but should not be ignored.

5. The city of Lawrence has the most sophisticated company-linked relief funds in the industrial state of Massachusetts. They have been set up in nearly all of its spinning and weaving mills.[54] The Pacific Mills Society has the most members and is hence the most active. It dispensed $20,104 in benefits in the three years between 1878 and 1880, providing assistance to 300–400 sick and injured workers every year. The statutes of Lawrence's factory funds are broadly similar. Most of the money is put up by the spinners and weavers, with the factory owners contributing only minor amounts, in the case of the Pacific Mills around 5 percent of the total. The funds are usually administered by the workers themselves.

It is worth noting that the lowest-paid workers sometimes do not participate in the factory funds. These workers, who need the sickness benefits the most because they never put any money by for an emergency, are notoriously incapable of paying even the smallest contributions on a regular basis because they have no foresight and seem to live carefree for the day. As a result their lives are a misery and a desperate struggle for survival. American labor leaders have assured me on a number of occasions that workers' appreciation of relief funds and of the social duties of the working class as a whole increases in line with their incomes. The lowest-paid are manipulated by demagogues, and

53. See the labor paper *The Union*, 14 May 1881.
54. See Massachusetts *Report of the Bureau of the Statistics of Labor* (Boston, 1882). 331–7.

those who do use their brains see robbing and stealing as the only way of improving the quality of their lives. This proletariat is already numerous in the eastern industrial states. Mass immigration from half-starved Irish and easily satisfied Canadians, and lately the competition from the cotton mills of the South, which can produce at low costs because of the incredibly cheap Negro labor they employ,[55] have seriously eroded the living standards of the New England working class and thus cut off the option of migrating west. Some relief funds occasionally help out these poor workers, who are not actually members. But this is no more than a discretionary gift and thus is of minimal sociopolitical value.

6. Because of the still very fragmented state of the U.S. mining industry, institutions analogous to the German miners' insurance funds and pension schemes [*Knappschaftskassen*] are still very rare. I have come across only one case, in a Michigan copper-mining district. (This state has large reserves of copper, guaranteeing substantial production for years to come.) The coal-mining areas of Pennsylvania and Ohio apparently have only union-sponsored relief funds.

A correspondent for the *Illinois Staats-Zeitung*, a German-language paper, reports the following about Calumet, Mich.:

This famous copper mine, which is owned by a corporation, deserves special notice not merely because of its output but even more because of the liberal way in which the management seeks to create decent conditions for its workforce. All the accommodation in the Calumet district is owned by the mine and is rented out only to workers employed in it. These homes are nothing like tenement blocks, however. They are built for single families. Most have gardens, which yield vegetables and fruit whose value far exceeds the token rents. Of course the homes have different numbers of rooms, appropriate to the sizes of the families who live in them. If a home is vacated because a worker leaves, the family most in need has first claim to it. This means that no worker at the Calumet mine has reason to complain about expensive accommodation.

Every miner pays 50¢ per month into the sickness fund. In case of an accident this entitles him to admission to the fund hospital, where he will receive proper medical care and attention at a cost of $17 per month. The sickness fund – which has accumulated assets of $18,000 and is administered by the mining company – pays him $25 per month during his absence from work. When a fund member becomes permanently disabled or is killed in an accident, he or his family receives $500.[56]

55. [Contrary to the author's claim, virtually no black workers were employed on production machinery in southern textile mills. See Jacquelin Dowd Hall et al., *Like a Family: The Making of a Southern Cotton Mill World* (Chapel Hill, N.C., 1987), 44–112.]
56. *Illinois Staats-Zeitung*, weekly edition, 31 July 1882.

IV. Crosstrade Workers' Welfare Associations

The general labor funds, which workers from any trade can join, have several obvious advantages over the other types of welfare associations. They are an improvement on the lodges because they stick rigidly to their objectives and do not bother with irrelevant and costly formalities; on the union funds because they have larger memberships and so are cheaper and more efficient; and on the factory funds because they cannot make claims conditional on terms of employment and workers' compliant behavior.

Welfare associations of this kind are not trade based but geographically based. This allows them to branch out widely, which is the main reason for their success. They can recruit members wherever manual workers are employed. The only precondition is that members are adult, healthy, and solvent workers. Membership levels can mushroom once the people have realized the advantages of insuring themselves. And they all benefit, for the larger the association, the cheaper its administration and the smaller the individual contributions, since the likely demands on the fund can be calculated more accurately.

The objection to this kind of general mutual insurance is that it imposes an uneven burden on the various types of workers, for the health and accident risks to which they are exposed differ widely from trade to trade. This point is, of course, theoretically irrefutable, but practically it is of little consequence when the membership of a trade association can be small but is usually very large. This tends to be the rule in the United States, so that at a particular level of membership it becomes cheaper for less-at-risk workers to join a general scheme rather than set up their own mutual insurance fund. The savings in general costs and in covering the risk (when the costs are shared this, of course, becomes irrelevant) are then greater than the spread between the premiums paid by workers from different risk categories. In other words, the least-at-risk workers have to pay even less into the large funds than into their own union-sponsored funds. This also explains why, for instance, commercial life insurance companies, despite their dividend payments and high agency commissions, can sometimes offer individuals better terms than a small trade association based on mutuality.

A general workers' mutual insurance association made up of many local branches was set up in the state of Michigan at the start of 1870 and incorporated in 1872. The original constitution of the Workers' League of Michigan [*Arbeiterbund*] has been amended on several occasions, at congresses in Mount Clemens in 1876, Marshall in 1881, and Port Huron in 1882. Currently its main provisions are as follows. The central fund provides life insurance. Within thirty days of a fully qualified member's death, his family receives a fixed sum. At the moment (1884), with the total membership at around 3,900, this is $375; it will rise to $400 when the membership reaches 4,100. Every member pays 10¢ when another dies; this is collected by the local treasurer and passed on to the central treasurer. Leaving aside the above-mentioned advantages of a large membership, it is evident that when members share the costs equally, these will be far less heavy in a large association than in a small one. While some of the trade union–sponsored funds require members to put up $1 in case of a death (as we saw above), only 10¢ is demanded here, although payments will, of course, be more frequent than in the small funds. But even so, it is much easier for a worker to pay 10 times 10¢ in the year than $1 in one go, which may be as much as a day's wage. In this sense the large and small funds can be compared with indirect and direct taxes. The former are paid in small amounts on many occasions, while the latter have to be paid all at once.

The league currently has 42 fully incorporated local branches in several Michigan cities.[57] Local organizations which want to affiliate to the central league must submit their statutes to the president and ensure that they conform with the central statutes. A general meeting is held annually, at which each local branch sends a delegate, those with less than 100 members send two, and larger ones send additional delegates.

The local branches also look after sick members and after the families of deceased members. The sickness benefit for a fully qualified member usually amounts to $5 per week, payable for six months in one year. Nursing and other care is provided night and day on request and at no extra charge. Cases requiring support for more than six months are considered on their merits by the union's officials. Members who fall ill elsewhere in Michigan are entitled to the same level of care and assistance from their nearest branch as they would receive at their home branch. The latter reimburses the former for any costs incurred. The local branch pays for a member's funeral, whose costs are set at $30, and also pays his widow a grant of $50, so that together with the centrally disbursed death benefit of $375 she receives a total of $455, a major help for the family of the deceased. New members must be

57. See *Illinois Staats-Zeitung*, 31 December 1883.

younger than forty-five years, present a doctor's certificate vouching for their good health, and belong to the union for some time before they qualify for all benefits.

I do not think it is right for the local branches to pay out benefits on the death of a member, since the central fund is better placed to do so. It is right, though, that the sickness benefits are disbursed by the local branches, since malingering can be countered effectively only at the local level. One could imagine centrally administered sickness funds, on the basis of equal contributions, if settlements were carried out at regular intervals, yearly, say, so that the more depleted funds received money from those which had paid out less over the year. This system has been implemented by several trade unions for their strike funds, but the Michigan Workers' League does not operate it.

Because of the great diversity of peoples within the United States the welfare associations, like the trade unions, often have a national character. They are often the only bond holding immigrants together and thus help to maintain the language and customs of the old homeland. Restricting membership to a particular nationality has clear disadvantages, in that in small towns workers from other nationalities may not be strong enough numerically to set up insurance funds and will thus remain uninsured and in that they restrict the potential membership of the general association. But at the same time these associations have special pulling power, in that some people will join precisely because of their national roots and interests.

Most local branches of the Michigan Workers' League stipulate that their members must be able to speak German. As a correspondent of the *Illinois Staats-Zeitung* observes in this context:[58]

In a smaller city the German workers' association is the focal point for all those who still keep up the German language and German traditions, who love German culture but are also proud of their new fatherland. In the larger cities there are also choral societies, gymnastics clubs, scientific associations, and artistic groups of all kinds which have set themselves more ambitious tasks and also achieve great successes in their own terms. But they cannot surpass the workers' associations in their efforts to improve the conditions of working people.

The Workers' League of the state of Michigan is an undertaking which deserves close examination in the neighboring states of Ohio, Indiana, and Illinois. The cities of these states also have workers' associations which pursue the same goals as the Michigan league, but do they have links to each other? Their mem-

58. Ibid.

bers cannot count on assistance in cases of emergency outside their home town, as can those in Michigan. A workers' league in Illinois, Indiana, and Ohio as it exists in Michigan and a confederation of these bodies would be enormously beneficial for German workers and for German life in America overall.

Another example of a crosstrade relief fund, but one which has no local branches, is the General Workers' Sickness Relief Society [*Allgemeiner Arbeiter-Kranken-Unterstützungsverein*] in Baltimore. Founded in January 1851, its constitution was last amended in 1880. It had 800 members in 1881. At that time it paid out $4 a week in sickness benefit, $75 on the death of a member's wife, and $375 to his family on his own death. The contributions amounted to $8 per year. In the past members' widows and surviving children were also given long-term assistance: the former received $5 per month for life or until they married again and the latter received $1 until age seven and $2 until age fourteen. These benefits were abolished recently because the fund could no longer afford them. The administration has no special features, except that a domicile in Baltimore is not a requirement for membership. According to article 3 of the constitution, "A member may change his domicile within the United States without losing any rights, provided that he has met all his obligations under the constitution and the ordinances."[59] As article 20 of the ordinances elaborates:

A member living outside the city can only claim sickness benefit if he has reported his condition within a week and sent in a notarized doctor's certificate signed by two witnesses, which states the nature of his illness and the period of disablement. Such a certificate is only valid for four weeks, however, and the sick member must send in a new certificate every four weeks if he wishes to continue receiving benefit. In questionable cases the association reserves the right to postpone benefit payments until it has examined the situation and taken a decision in the light of its findings.

The implementation of this system is obviously fraught with difficulties. It cannot replace a wide network of local branches.

The Baltimore society is also used mainly by Germans. Knowledge of German is not a precondition of membership, but the proceedings are conducted in German. In addition to providing sickness and other ben-

59. Most recent statutes from the year 1880. [The editors have not been able to locate these statutes. The original 1851 statutes are reproduced in their entirety in Studnitz, *Nordamerikanische Arbeiterverhältnisse*, appendix, 43–72.]

efits, the society also organizes social and educational activities. It has a sizable library.

V. Mixed Associations

By *mixed associations* I mean welfare associations for which, unlike those discussed in the previous sections, being a worker is not a condition of membership, although most of their members nevertheless belong to the working class. There are many such organizations, almost invariably dedicated to wider goals than relief and assistance.[60] Sometimes employers also participate in these funds. The commissioner of the Missouri Bureau of Labor Statistics finds this solidarity particularly praiseworthy, arguing that "it distributes the supply of labor at least locally and ensures equal treatment of workers in different types of workshops and factories."[61] Unemployed members use the meetings to approach fellow members who are employers and so often get a job. The associations thus also serve as a labor exchange.

Mixed associations generally provide assistance in cases of sickness, accident, and death. Life insurance has become highly popular in recent years, doubtless largely because commercial companies have lost credibility among the public after several collapses.

Some objections have been raised against the "benevolent associations" offering life insurance.[62] These arguments are also used in part against the other insurance funds discussed above.

Firstly, there is their status within state law. Missouri, for instance, prohibits charities from engaging in any kind of profit-making business. This includes, according to a state supreme court ruling, offering life insurance.[63] That is why many people are worried that they will not be able to assert an eventual claim legally and so prefer not to take out insurance at all. This situation can only be clarified by an amendment to the law.

Secondly, the insurance funds impose regular contributions on their members, and those who fall into arrears lose their entitlement to ben-

---

60. For instance, the aims of the German Harmony Club in New Orleans are defined, in article 2 of its constitution, as "engaging in harmonious and fraternal cooperation for the promotion of art and science, as well as providing support to the families of members who have died, as set out in greater detail in the rules and regulations."
61. Missouri Bureau of Labor Statistics, 1882 annual report, 13ff.
62. See ibid., 13ff.
63. [See William C. Niblack, *The Law of Voluntary Societies and Mutual Benefit Insurance* (Chicago, 1888), 3.]

efits. (Many funds discussed in Sections 2 to 4 do not require contributions from members who are out of work. This is logical, since they are associations of workers, i.e., people in work.) But when the economy slows down or is thrown into recession, workers often lose their jobs and earnings, so that during the lean years they lose everything they have saved in the good years. To allow for this, the commercial life insurance companies accept irregular contributions, which are then treated as payment on account. If the benevolent associations had sufficiently large memberships, they could consider something on these lines. At the moment the situation is highly fragmented, with large numbers of generally small associations.

Thirdly, following on from the previous point, the associations' financial base is often shaky. This is due not only to their small memberships but also to the keen competition among them. The larger ones are cheaper to run than the smaller ones, which, to redress the balance, are often pressed into reckless business practices to attract potential members. Many associations have already gone under as a result, which is most unfortunate, as they often hold a worker's life savings.

To conclude this discussion of relief funds in the United States, I would like to say that I have tried to highlight the most important types out of a plethora of organizations. Unfortunately I was not able to provide comprehensive statistical material on the number, assets, and memberships of the insurance funds, since to my knowledge such information has never been collected. This essay should therefore be seen as no more than a first attempt to analyze the American relief funds, which have never been examined in sufficient detail. At this time, when the concept of workers' insurance is at the forefront of all economic and social debate, I hope it will be of some value.

6

Bibliography of Sartorius von Waltershausen's Writings

JAN GIELKENS

1879

"Der deutsche Weinbau-Congreß zu Coblenz [I–II]," *Allgemeine Zeitung* (Augsburg), 1879, no. 177 (19 September; commercial supplement), pp. 705–6; no. 178 (20 September; commercial supplement), pp. 709–10.

1880

Die wirthschaftlich-sociale Bedeutung des obligatorischen Zuschusses der Unternehmer zu den Arbeiterversicherungskassen. Ein Beitrag zur Kritik der Arbeiterfrage (Göttingen: Vandenhoeck & Ruprecht's Verlag, 1880). 34 pp. [Doctoral thesis.]

Die Stellung des Staates zu der Alters- und Invalidenversorgung für Lohnarbeiter (Berlin: Weidmann'sche Buchhandlung, 1880). 96 pp.

1881

"Die Ursachen der wirthschaftlichen Eigenschaften des nordamerikanischen Volkes [I–V]," *Allgemeine Zeitung* (Augsburg), 1881, no. 358 (24 December), pp. 5265–7; no. 360 (26 December), pp. 5297–8; no. 363 (29 December), pp. 5329–31; 1882, no. 4 (4 January), pp. 42–4; no. 9 (9 January), pp. 122–3.

1882

"Die Gewerkschaften der Cigarrenarbeiter in Habana," *Jahrbücher für Nationalökonomie und Statistik* (Jena), vol. 38 (1882), pp. 292–305.

"Arbeitszeit und Normalarbeitstag in den Vereinigten Staaten von Amerika," *Jahrbücher für Nationalökonomie und Statistik* (Jena), vol. 38 (1882), pp. 461–73; 39 (1882), pp. 107–46.

"Eine junge Stadt in dem Felsengebirge Colorado's," *Allgemeine Zeitung* (Augsburg), 1882, no. 106 (16 April; supplement), pp. 1554–6.

"Production und Verladung der Baumwolle in den Vereinigten Staaten [I–II]," *Allgemeine Zeitung* (Augsburg), 1882 no. 174 (23 June), pp. 2339–40; no. 175 (24 June), pp. 2554–5.

"Die Wechselbeziehungen von Reichthum, Bevölkerung und Geldmenge in den Vereinigten Staaten," *Allgemeine Zeitung* (Augsburg), 1882, no. 70 (13 April; commercial supplement), pp. 277–8.

"Die bedeutendste Arbeiterorganisation in den Vereinigten Staaten von Amerika [I–II]," *Politische Wochenschrift* (Berlin), 1882, no. 4, pp. 29–30; no. 5, pp. 37–8.

"Erfahrungen mit Produktivgenossenschaften in Nordamerika," *Politische Wochenschrift* (Berlin), 1882, no. 10, pp. 84–6.

"Das überseeische Transportgeschäft der Vereinigten Staaten," *Politische Wochenschrift* (Berlin), 1882, no. 17, pp. 141–2.

1883

"Die Gewerkvereine in den Vereinigten Staaten von Amerika [I–III]," *Jahrbücher für Nationalökonomie und Statistik* (Jena), vol. 40 (1883), pp. 517–60; 41 (1883), pp. 315–44; 42 (1884), pp. 431–56.

"Die Verteilung des ländlichen Grundeigentums in den Vereinigten Staaten von Amerika," *Jahrbücher für Nationalökonomie und Statistik* (Jena), vol. 40 (1883), pp. 469–74.

"Die Chinesen in den Vereinigten Staaten von Amerika," *Zeitschrift für die gesammte Staatswissenschaft* (Tübingen), vol. 39 (1883), no. 2, pp. 320–431.

[Review: P. F. Kupka: Die Verkehrsmittel in den Vereinigten Staaten von Nordamerika (Leipzig, 1883)], *Jahrbücher für Nationalökonomie und Statistik* (Jena), vol. 40 (1883), pp. 482–3.

[Review: R. Meyer: Ursachen der amerikanischen Konkurrenz. Ergebnisse einer Studienreise (. . .) (Berlin, 1883)], *Jahrbücher für Nationalökonomie und Statistik* (Jena), vol. 40 (1883), pp. 574–6.

[Review: Rudolf Meyer: Heimstätten- und andere Wirtschaftsgesetze der Vereinigten Staaten von Amerika, von Kanada, Rußland, China, Indien, Rumänien, Serbien und England (Berlin, 1883)], *Jahrbücher für Nationalökonomie und Statistik* (Jena), vol. 40 (1883), pp. 585–6.

1884

Das deutsche Einfuhrverbot amerikanischen Schweinefleisches (Jena: Verlag von Gustav Fischer, 1884). 84 pp.

"Die Eventualität eines Zollkrieges mit den Vereinigten Staaten," *Allgemeine Zeitung* (Munich), 1884 (27 February), pp. 842–3.

[Review: C. Herzog: Aus Amerika. Reisebriefe (. . .) (Berlin, n.d.)], *Jahrbücher für Nationalökonomie und Statistik* (Jena), vol. 40 (1883), p. 384.

[Review: Sozialistische Briefe aus Amerika (Munich, 1883)], *Jahrbücher für Nationalökonomie und Statistik* (Jena), vol. 42 (1884), p. 400.

1885

Die Zukunft des Deutschthums in den Vereinigten Staaten von Amerika (Berlin: Verlag von Carl Habel, 1885). 40 pp. (Deutsche Zeit- und Streit-Fragen, 212.)

"Städtegründung im nordamerikanischen Westen [I–V]," *Globus* (Braunschweig), vol. 47 (1885), pp. 102–3, 121–4, 135–8, 150–3.

"Boycotten, ein neues Kampfmittel der amerikanischen Gewerkvereine," *Jahrbücher für Nationalökonomie und Statistik* (Jena), vol. 45 (1885), pp. 1–18.

"Das Hilfskassenwesen in Nordamerika," *Jahrbücher für Nationalökonomie und Statistik* (Jena), vol. 45 (1885), pp. 97–154.

[Review: W. Cave-Tait: Die Arbeiter-Schutzgesetzgebung in den Vereinigten Staaten (Tübingen, 1884)], *Jahrbücher für Nationalökonomie und Statistik* (Jena), vol. 44 (1885), p. 86.

[Review: H. Vukassowitsch Neelmeyer: Die Vereinigten Staaten von Amerika (Leipzig, 1884)], *Jahrbücher für Nationalökonomie und Statistik* (Jena), vol. 44 (1885), pp. 276–7.

[Review: George Seelhorst: Die deutsche Ware auf dem Weltmarkt (Augsburg, 1883)], *Jahrbücher für Nationalökonomie und Statistik* (Jena), vol. 44 (1885), p. 283.

[Review: Albrecht Franzius: Deutschlands Kolonien. Ein Beitrag zur Kolonisationsfrage (Bremen, 1885)], *Jahrbücher für Nationalökonomie und Statistik* (Jena), vol. 44 (1885), p. 368.

[Review: B. Aba: Skizzen aus Amerika (Vienna, 1885)], *Jahrbücher für Nationalökonomie und Statistik* (Jena), vol. 44 (1885), pp. 368–9.

[Review: Heinrich Semler: Das Reisen nach und in Nordamerika, den Tropenländern und der Wildnis, sowie die Tour um die Welt (Wismar, 1884)], *Jahrbücher für Nationalökonomie und Statistik* (Jena), vol. 44 (1885), p. 369.

1886

Die nordamerikanischen Gewerkschaften unter dem Einfluß der fortschreitenden Productionstechnik (Berlin: Verlag von Hermann Bahr, 1886). XV, 352 pp.

"Die mexicanische Volkswirthschaft und deren Beziehungen zu den Vereinigten Staaten von Amerika [I–II]," *Unsere Zeit. Deutsche Revue der Gegenwart* (Leipzig), 1886, part 1, pp. 799–817; part 2, pp. 101–17.

1887

[Review: Marquis de Nadaillac: Affaiblissement de la natalité en France, ses causes et ses conséquences (Paris, 1886)], *Jahrbücher für Nationalökonomie und Statistik* (Jena), vol. 48 (1887), pp. 74–5.

[Review: Andrew Carnegie: Amerika, ein Triumph der Demokratie, oder die nordamerikanische Republik vor fünfzig Jahren und heute (Leipzig, 1886)], *Jahrbücher für Nationalökonomie und Statistik* (Jena), vol. 48 (1887), p. 91.

[Review: Albert Shaw: Ikaria. Ein Beitrag zur Geschichte des Kommunismus (Stuttgart, 1886)], *Jahrbücher für Nationalökonomie und Statistik* (Jena), vol. 48 (1887), pp. 193–4.

1888

[Review: Henry George: Schutz oder Freihandel (Berlin, 1887)], *Jahrbücher für Nationalökonomie und Statistik* (Jena), vol. 50 (1888), p. 304.

1890

Der moderne Socialismus in den Vereinigten Staaten von Amerika (Berlin: Verlag von Hermann Bahr, 1890). 422 pp.

1892

"Die Kolonisation und die Agrarverfassung der Insel Nantucket im 17. und 18. Jahrhundert," *Jahrbücher für Nationalökonomie und Statistik* (Jena), vol. 59 (1892), pp. 342–65.

"Die Gewerkvereine in den Vereinigten Staaten von Amerika," *Handwörterbuch der Staatswissenschaften*, vol. 4 (Jena: Verlag von Gustav Fischer, 1892), pp. 42–6.

1894

Die Arbeits-Verfassung der englischen Kolonien in Nordamerika (Straßburg: Verlag von K. J. Trübner, 1894). XI, 232 pp.

1895

"Ein Stück Sozialgeschichte in Zahlen," *Allgemeines Statistisches Archiv* (Tübingen), 4 (1895), pp. 595–603.

"Chinesenfrage," *Handwörterbuch der Staatswissenschaften. Erster Supplementband* (Jena: Verlag von Gustav Fischer, 1895), pp. 265–73.

"Einwanderung," *Handwörterbuch der Staatswissenschaften. Erster Supplementband* (Jena: Verlag von Gustav Fischer, 1895), pp. 300–6.

"Die Gewerkvereine in den Vereinigten Staaten von Amerika," *Handwörterbuch der Staatswissenschaften. Erster Supplementband* (Jena: Verlag von Gustav Fischer, 1895), pp. 413–21.

[Review: Carl Kindermann: Zur organischen Güterverteilung [. . .] (Leipzig, 1894)], *Jahrbücher für Nationalökonomie und Statistik* (Jena), vol. 65 (1895), pp. 139–40.

[Review: W. T. Stead: Der Krieg zwischen Arbeit und Kapital in den Vereinigten Staaten (Stuttgart, 1894)], *Jahrbücher für Nationalökonomie und Statistik* (Jena), vol. 64 (1894), pp. 932–3.

1896

"Die Entstehung des Tauschhandels in Polynesien," *Zeitschrift für Social- und Wirthschaftsgeschichte* (Freiburg and Leipzig), 4 (1896), pp. 1–66.

[Review: Bulletin of the Department of Labor (Washington, D.C., 1895)], *Jahrbücher für Nationalökonomie und Statistik* (Jena), vol. 66 (1896), pp. 621–2.

1897

[Review: Karl Marx: Revolution und Kontre-Revolution in Deutschland (Stuttgart, 1896)], *Jahrbücher für Nationalökonomie und Statistik* (Jena), vol. 69 (1897), pp. 299–300.

"Touren im Aetnagebiet [I–II]," *Allgemeine Zeitung* (Augsburg), 1897, no. 178 (11 August; supplement), pp. 1–4; no. 179 (12 August), pp. 3–6.

1898

Deutschland und die Handelspolitik der Vereinigten Staaten von Amerika (Berlin: Siemenroth & Troschel, 1898). XI, 84 pp. (Schriften der Centralstelle für Vorbereitung von Handelsverträgen, 2.)

[Review: George M. Fink: Die handelspolitischen und sonstigen völkerrechtlichen Beziehungen zwischen Deutschland und den Vereinigten Staaten von Amerika (Stuttgart, 1897)], *Jahrbücher für Nationalökonomie und Statistik* (Jena), vol. 70 (1898), pp. 397–9.

[Review: Ernst von Halle: Baumwollproduction und Pflanzungswirtschaft in den nordamerikanischen Südstaaten (Leipzig, 1897)], *Zeitschrift für Socialwissenschaft* (Berlin), vol. 1 (1898), pp. 238–40.

[Review: Alfred Zimmermann: Die Kolonialpolitik Großbrittanniens (. . .) (Berlin, 1898)], *Zeitschrift für Socialwissenschaft* (Berlin), vol. 1 (1898), pp. 766–7.

1899

[Review: Louis Vigouroux: La concentration des forces ouvrières dans l'Amérique du Nord (Paris, 1899)], *Jahrbücher für Nationalökonomie und Statistik* (Jena), vol. 73 (1899), pp. 689–90.

1900

Die Germanisierung der Rätoromanen in der Schweiz. Volkswirtschaftliche und nationalpolitische Studien (Stuttgart: Verlag von J. Engelhorn, 1900). 110 pp. (Forschungen zur deutschen Landes- und Volkskunde im Auftrage der Centralkommission für wissenschaftliche Landeskunde von Deutschland, vol. 12, no. 5.)

"Chinesenfrage," in *Handwörterbuch der Staatswissenschaften.* 2d rev. ed., vol. 3 (Jena: Verlag von Gustav Fischer, 1900), pp. 44–8.

"Einwanderung (in die Vereinigten Staaten von Amerika)," in *Handwörterbuch der Staatswissenschaften.* 2d rev. ed., vol. 3 (Jena: Verlag von Gustav Fischer, 1900), pp. 455–61.

"Die Gewerkvereine in den Vereinigten Staaten von Amerika," in *Handwörterbuch der Staatswissenschaften.* 2d rev. ed., vol. 4 (Jena: Verlag von Gustav Fischer, 1900), pp. 710–15.

"Knights of Labor," in *Handwörterbuch der Staatswissenschaften.* 2d rev. ed., vol. 5 (Jena: Verlag von Gustav Fischer, 1900), pp. 116–20.

"Kuli," in *Handwörterbuch der Staatswissenschaften.* 2d rev. ed., vol. 5 (Jena: Verlag von Gustav Fischer, 1900), pp. 436–8.

"Negerfrage," in *Handwörterbuch der Staatswissenschaften.* 2d rev. ed., vol. 5 (Jena: Verlag von Gustav Fischer, 1900), pp. 970–80.

"Ein deutsch-niederländischer Zollverein," *Zeitschrift für Socialwissenschaft* (Berlin), vol. 3 (1900), pp. 494–518.

[Review: Carl Simon: Der Export landwirtschaftlicher und landwirtschaftlich-industrieller Artikel aus den Vereinigten Staaten von Nordamerika und die deutsche Landwirtschaft (Leipzig, 1899)], *Zeitschrift für Socialwissenschaft* (Berlin), vol. 3 (1900), pp. 162–3.

[Review: Die Handelspolitik des Deutschen Reichs vom Frankfurter Frieden bis zur Gegenwart (Berlin, 1899)], *Zeitschrift für Socialwissenschaft* (Berlin), vol. 3 (1900), pp. 400–1.

[Review: Arthur Humann: Der Deutsch-Russische Handels- und Schiffahrtsvertrag vom 20. März 1884 (Leipzig, 1900)], *Zeitschrift für Socialwissenschaft* (Berlin), vol. 3 (1900), pp. 477–9.

[Review: R. van der Borght: Handel und Handelspolitik (Leipzig, 1900)], *Zeitschrift für Socialwissenschaft* (Berlin), vol. 3 (1900), pp. 753–4.

1901

Die Handelsbilanz der Vereinigten Staaten von Amerika (Berlin: J. Guttentag, 1901). VI, 71 pp. (Schriften der Centralstelle für Vorbereitung von Handelsverträgen, 17.)

"Der Verkauf der dänischen Besitzungen in Westindien," *Beiträge zur Kolonialpolitik und Kolonialwirtschaft* (Berlin), vol. 2 (1901–2), pp. 476–80.

[Review: Ernst Rausch: Französische Handelspolitik vom Frankfurter Frieden bis zur Tarifreform von 1882 (Leipzig, 1900)], *Zeitschrift für Socialwissenschaft* (Berlin), vol. 4 (1901), p. 341.

[Review: Statistical Abstract of the United States 1900 (Washington, D.C., 1901)], *Zeitschrift für Socialwissenschaft* (Berlin), vol. 4 (1901), p. 552.

[Review: Richard Calwer: Die Meistbegünstigung der Vereinigten Staaten von Nordamerika (Berlin and Bern, 1902) (!)], *Zeitschrift für Socialwissenschaft* (Berlin), vol. 4 (1901), pp. 846–7.

1902

"Beiträge zur Beurteilung einer wirtschaftlichen Foederation von Mitteleuropa," *Zeitschrift für Socialwissenschaft* (Berlin), vol. 5 (1902), pp. 557–70, 674–704, 765–86, 860–94.
[Review: G. K. Anton: Ein Zollbündnis mit den Niederlanden (. . .) (Dresden, 1902)], *Zeitschrift für Socialwissenschaft* (Berlin), vol. 5 (1902), pp. 552–3.

1903

Die italienischen Wanderarbeiter (Leipzig: C. L. Hirschfeld, 1903). 44 pp.

"Die italienischen Wanderarbeiter," in *Festschrift zu August Sigmund Schultze's 70. Geburtstag* (Leipzig: C. L. Hirschfeld, 1903), pp. 51–94.

"La réforme des impôts directs en Alsace-Lorraine," *Revue de science et de législation financières* (Paris), 1903, pp. 641–78.

[Review: Leo Berkholz: Die Wirkung der Handelsverträge auf Landwirtschaft, Weinbau und Gewerbe in Elsaß-Lothringen (Tübingen and Leipzig, 1902)], *Zeitschrift für Socialwissenschaft* (Berlin), vol. 6 (1903), pp. 205–7.

1905

"[no title]," in W. Borgius (ed.), *Imperialismus. Beiträge zur Analyse des wirtschaftlichen und politischen Lebens der Gegenwart* (Berlin: Liebheit & Thiesen, 1905), pp. 40–2.

"Die fortschreitende Verdeutschung der Rätoromanen in Graubünden nach der eidgenössischen Volkszählung vom 1. Dezember 1900," *Deutsche Erde* (Gotha), vol. 4 (1905), pp. 56–9.

1907

Das volkswirtschaftliche System der Kapitalanlage im Auslande (Berlin: Georg Reimer, 1907). IV, 442 pp.

1908

"Der englische Imperialismus und seine Rassenfrage," *Zeitschrift für Socialwissenschaft* (Leipzig), vol. 11 (1908), no. 12, pp. 742–7.

1909

"Die Selbstversicherung bei der Kapitalanlage," *Münchener Neueste Nachrichten* (Munich), 1909, nos. 52–3.

"Die belgische Volkswirtschaft und die vlämischen Wanderarbeiter in Deutschland," *Münchener Neueste Nachrichten* (Munich), 11 May 1909.

"Soziale Wandlungen in Mexico," *Münchener Neueste Nachrichten* (Munich), 2 July 1909.

"Zwischenstaatliche Wanderung und Ungleichheit der Menschenrassen [I–II]," *Zeitschrift für Socialwissenschaft* (Leipzig), vol. 12 (1909), no. 9, pp. 379–92, 520–31.

"Aus- und Einwanderung und die Lehre von der gesellschaftlichen Auslese," *Zeitschrift für Socialwissenschaft* (Leipzig), vol. 12 (1909), no. 11, pp. 637–56.

"Einwanderung," in J. Conrad [et al.] (eds.): *Handwörterbuch der Staatswissenschaften.* 3rd rev. ed., vol. 3 (Jena: Verlag von Gustav Fischer, 1909), pp. 765–76.

"Die Gewerkvereine in den Vereinigten Staaten von Amerika," in J. Conrad [et al.] (eds.): *Handwörterbuch der Staatswissenschaften.* 3rd rev. ed., vol. 4 (Jena: Verlag von Gustav Fischer, 1909), pp. 1217–23.

"Knights of Labor," in J. Conrad [et al.] (eds.): *Handwörterbuch der Staatswissenschaften.* 3rd rev. ed., vol. 5 (Jena: Verlag von Gustav Fischer, 1909), pp. 891–4.

1910

"Kuli," in J. Conrad [et al.] (eds.): *Handwörterbuch der Staatswissenschaften.* 3rd rev. ed., vol. 6 (Jena: Verlag von Gustav Fischer, 1910), pp. 285–8.

"Negerfrage," in J. Conrad [et al.] (eds.): *Handwörterbuch der Staatswissenschaften.* 3rd rev. ed., vol. 6 (Jena: Verlag von Gustav Fischer, 1910), pp. 902–13.

"Die Wanderung ins Ausland als nationales Problem," *Zeitschrift für Socialwissenschaft* (Leipzig), vol. 1 ["Neue Folge"] (1910), no. 3, pp. 133–47.

"Die Anthroposoziologie und die politische Oekonomie Smiths und Ricardos," *Politisch-anthropologische Revue* (Hildburghausen), vol. 9 (1910), no. 4, pp. 188–98.

"Anthroposoziologie und Malthusianismus," *Politisch-anthropologische Revue* (Hildburghausen), vol. 9 (1910), no. 10, pp. 514–27.

1911

"Die Wanderarbeit als weltwirtschaftliches Problem," *Zeitschrift für Socialwissenschaft* (Leipzig), vol. 2 ["Neue Folge"] (1911), no. 2, pp. 75–88.

"Die süditalienische Auswanderung und ihre volkswirtschaftlichen Folgen," *Jahrbücher für Nationalökonomie und Statistik* (Jena), vol. 96 (1911), pp. 1–27, 182–215.

[Review: Gerhard Hildebrand: Die Erschütterung der Industrieherrschaft und des Industriesozialismus (Jena, 1910)], *Zeitschrift für Socialwissenschaft* (Leipzig), vol. 2 ["Neue Folge"] (1911), no. 5, pp. 352–4.

1912

[Review: Wilhelm Mönckmeier: Die deutsche überseeische Auswanderung, ein Beitrag zur deutschen Wanderungsgeschichte (Jena, 1912)], *Zeitschrift für Socialwissenschaft* (Leipzig), vol. 3 ["Neue Folge"] (1912), no. 12, pp. 907–8.

1913

Die Sizilianische Agrarverfassung und ihre Wandlungen 1780–1912. Eine sozialpolitische und weltwirtschaftliche Untersuchung (Leipzig: A. Deichert'sche Verlagsbuchhandlung, 1913). XII, 385 pp.

Begriff und Entwicklungsmöglichkeit der heutigen Weltwirtschaft (Straßburg: Heitz, 1913). 24 pp. [Rektoratsrede, May 2, 1913.]

Rede bei der akademischen Feier des Regierungsjubiläums S.M. des Kaisers (Straßburg: Heitz und Mündel, 1913).

[Review: Bernhard Harms: Volkswirtschaft und Weltwirtschaft. Versuch der Begründung einer Weltwirtschaftslehre (Jena, 1912)], *Zeitschrift für Socialwissenschaft* (Leipzig), vol. 4 ["Neue Folge"] (1913), no. 2, pp. 145–9.

1914

"Die Weltwirtschaftslehre," *Zeitschrift für Socialwissenschaft* (Leipzig), vol. 5 ["Neue Folge"] (1914), no. 7/8, pp. 468–89.

"Deutschlands Zahlungsverkehr mit dem Auslande während des Krieges," *Straßburger Post* (Straßburg), 1914, no. 1054 (22 October; evening ed.), p. 2; no. 1058 (24 October; afternoon ed.), p. 2.

[Review: Robert Züblin: Die Handelsbeziehungen Italiens vornehmlich zu den Mittelmeerländern (Jena, 1913)], *Zeitschrift für Socialwissenschaft* (Leipzig), vol. 5 ["Neue Folge"] (1914), no. 2, pp. 128–31.

1915

Der Paragraph elf des Frankfurter Friedens (Jena: Verlag von Gustav Fischer, 1915). 46 pp.

Das Auslandskapital während des Weltkrieges (Stuttgart: Verlag von Ferdinand Enke, 1915). 53 pp. (Finanzwirtschaftliche Zeitfragen, 15.)

"Weltwirtschaft und Weltkrieg," *Weltwirtschaftliches Archiv* (Jena), vol. 5 (1915), pp. 292–316.

"Die Entwickelung der deutschen und der englischen Volkswirtschaft im neunzehnten Jahrhundert und der Weltkrieg," *Zeitschrift für Politik* (Berlin), vol. 8 (1915), pp. 43–87.

1916

Die Kriegsanleihen in der volkswirtschaftlichen Eigenart der einzelnen Länder (Stuttgart: Verlag von Ferdinand Enke, 1916). 49 pp. (Finanz- und Volkswirtschaftliche Zeitfragen, 26.)

"Das Geld bleibt im Lande. Ein Beitrag zur Kriegswirtschaftslehre," *Hansa-Bund. Offizielles Organ des Hansa-Bundes für Gewerbe, Handel und Industrie* (Berlin and Leipzig), vol. 7 (1916), no. 1, pp. 9–10.

"Deutschland und die Weltwirtschaft nach dem Kriege," *Zeitschrift für Sozialwissenschaft* (Leipzig), 1916, no. 6/7, pp. 349–73.

[Review: Josef Szterényi: Wirtschaftliche Verbindung mit Deutschland (Warnsdorf i.B., 1915)], *Weltwirtschaftliches Archiv* (Jena), vol. 8 (1916), pp. 204–6.

[Review: Carl Irresberger: Das Deutsch-Österreichisch-Ungarische Wirtschafts- und Zollbündnis (Berlin 1916)], *Zeitschrift für Sozialwissenschaft* (Leipzig), 1916, no. 6/7, pp. 467–8.

1917

[Review: Franz Eulenburg: Weltwirtschaftliche Möglichkeiten (Berlin, 1916)], *Weltwirtschaftliches Archiv* (Jena), vol. 10 (1917), pp. 385–6.

1920

Deutsche Wirtschaftsgeschichte 1815–1914 (Jena: Verlag von Gustav Fischer, 1920). X, 598 pp.

1921

Die Vereinigten Staaten als heutiges und künftiges Einwanderungsland (Stuttgart: Verlag von Ferdinand Enke, 1921). 70 pp. (Finanz- und Volkswirtschaftliche Zeitfragen, 75.)

1922

Einführung in die Volkswirtschaftslehre. Geschichte[,] Theorie und Politik (Leipzig and Berlin: B. G. Teubner, 1922). VIII, 283 pp.

1923

Einführung in das Studium der Weltwirtschaft. Repetitorium in Frage und Antwort. 253 Fragen (Kempten: Ferd. Oechelhäuser, and Füssen am Lech: Athenaeum, 1923). VIII, 163, 55, 20 pp. (Lehrschriften des Athenaeums über "Staat und Wirtschaft," 4.)

Deutsche Wirtschaftsgeschichte 1815–1914. 2d enl. ed. (Jena: Verlag von Gustav Fischer, 1923). X, 636 pp.

"Knights of Labor," *Handwörterbuch der Staatswissenschaften.* 4th rev. ed., vol. 5 (Jena: Verlag von Gustav Fischer, 1923), pp. 731–4.

[Review: Heinrich Sieveking: Grundzüge der neueren Wirtschaftsgeschichte vom 17. Jahrhundert bis zur Gegenwart (Leipzig and Berlin, 1921)], *Jahrbücher für Nationalökonomie und Statistik* (Jena), vol. 120 (1923), pp. 168–9.

[Review: H. Preller: Weltgeschichtliche Entwicklungslinien vom 19. zum 20. Jahrhundert in Kultur und Politik (Leipzig and Berlin, 1922)], *Jahrbücher für Nationalökonomie und Statistik* (Jena), vol. 120 (1923), pp. 361–2.

1924

Zeittafel zur Wirtschafts-Geschichte (Halberstadt: H. Meyer's Buchdruckerei, Abteilung Verlag, 1924). VII, 110 pp.

Zeittafel zur Wirtschafts-Geschichte. 2d ed. (Halberstadt: H. Meyer's Buchdruckerei, Abt. Verlag, 1924). VII, 110 pp.

"Die wirtschaftliche Entwicklung Deutschlands," in F. Lampe and G. H. Franke (eds.), *Staatsbürgerliche Erziehung* (Breslau: Ferdinand Hirt, 1924), pp. 272–83.

1925

"Kuli," *Handwörterbuch der Staatswissenschaften.* 4th rev. ed., vol. 6 (Jena: Verlag von Gustav Fischer, 1925), pp. 100–3.

"Auswanderung," *Handwörterbuch der Staatswissenschaften.* 4th rev. ed., vol. 2 (Jena: Verlag von Gustav Fischer, 1925), pp. 60–115.

1926

Die Weltwirtschaft und die staatlich geordneten Verkehrswirtschaften (Leipzig: G. A. Gloeckner, 1926). 416 pp. (Schriften des Weltwirtschafts-Instituts der Handels-Hochschule Leipzig, 2.)

"Einwanderung," *Handwörterbuch der Staatswissenchaften.* 4th rev. ed., vol. 3 (Jena: Verlag von Gustav Fischer, 1926), pp. 491–6.

"Englands Plan einer neuen Handelspolitik nach dem Kriege," *Norddeutsche Allgemeine Zeitung* (Berlin), vol. 57 (1918), no. 436 (27 August; morning ed.), pp. 1–2.

1927

Weltwirtschaft und Weltanschauung (Jena: Verlag von Gustav Fischer, 1927). 172 pp.

Zeittafel zur Wirtschafts-Geschichte. 3d ed. (Halberstadt: H. Meyer's Buchdruckerei, Abt. Verlag, 1927). VII, 138 pp.

[Review: Masao Kombe: Grundzüge des japanischen Steuersystems der Gegenwart (Jena 1926)], *Allgemeines Statistisches Archiv* (Jena), vol. 16 (1927), pp. 661–2.

[Review: Rudi Schlesinger: Die Zollpolitik der Vereinigten Staaten von Amerika (. . .) (Jena 1926)], *Allgemeines Statistisches Archiv* (Jena), vol. 16 (1927), pp. 662–3.

1928

"Die Einwanderungsquotengesetze in den Vereinigten Staaten von Amerika," *Allgemeines Statistisches Archiv* (Jena), vol. 17 (1927–8), pp. 247–57.

[Review: Richard Büchner: Die Finanzpolitik und das Bundessteuersystem der Vereinigten Staaten von Amerika von 1789–1926 (Jena 1926)], *Allgemeines Statistisches Archiv* (Jena), vol. 17 (1927–8), pp. 191–2.

1929

"Weltwirtschaft," *Handwörterbuch der Staatswissenschaften.* 4th ed., suppl. (Jena: Verlag von Gustav Fischer, 1929), pp. 892–934.

1931

Die Entstehung der Weltwirtschaft. Geschichte des zwischenstaatlichen Wirtschaftslebens vom letzten Viertel des achtzehnten Jahrhunderts bis 1914 (Jena: Verlag von Gustav Fischer, 1931). X, 676 pp.

1932

"Geburtenrückgang und Weltwirtschaft," in Siegfried von Kardorff [et al.] (eds.), *Der internationale Kapitalismus und die Krise. Festschrift für Julius Wolf zum 20 April 1932* (Stuttgart: Ferdinand Enke Verlag, 1932), pp. 97–114.

[Review: Imre Ferenzi: Kontinentale Wanderungen und Annäherungen der Völker. Kieler Vorträge (Jena, 1930)], *Vierteljahresschrift für Sozial- und Wirtschaftsgeschichte* (Stuttgart), vol. 25 (1932), pp. 77–9.

[Review: Walter F. Willcox (ed.): International Migrations, 2 vols. (New York, 1929–31)], *Vierteljahresschrift für Sozial- und Wirtschaftsgeschichte* (Stuttgart), vol. 25 (1932), pp. 382–4.

[Review: Ernst Schultze: Pfundsturz und Weltkrise (Leipzig 1932)], *Allgemeines Statistisches Archiv* (Jena), vol. 22 (1931–2), pp. 618–19.

1934

"Auslandsbetätigung der reichsdeutschen Banken," in: Carl Petersen/Otto Scheel (eds.), *Handwörterbuch des Grenz- und Auslands-Deutschtums,* Vol. 1 (Breslau: Ferd. Hirt, 1934), pp. 286–7.

1935

Die Umgestaltung der zwischenstaatlichen Wirtschaft. Ein geschichtlicher Rückblick 1914–1932 (Jena: Verlag von Gustav Fischer, 1935). 326 pp.

1936

Wirtschaft und Technik als Entwicklung und in der Geschichte (Jena: Verlag von Gustav Fischer, 1936). VIII, 174 pp.

1939

Gesellschaft und Wirtschaft vor- und frühgeschichtlicher Völker. Eine Darstellung in Typen (Jena: Verlag von Gustav Fischer, 1939). VIII, 156 pp.

Index

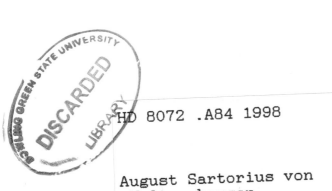